Turning Miniatures in Wood

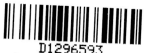

JOHN SAINSBURY

Published by Guild of Master Craftsman Publications Ltd

ISBN 0 946819 05 X

First published in 1986 by
Guild of Master Craftsman Publications Ltd
166 High Street, Lewes, Sussex BN7 1XU,
England

Reprinted 1989, 1992, 1995

Designed by
Ian Hunt of Guild Graphic Services Ltd

Typeset by
Eager Typesetting Company

Printed and bound in Great Britain by
Hillman Printers (Frome) Ltd

Contents

Acknowledgements

The author expresses his grateful thanks for use of equipment and photographs to:
Tony Walker and Robert Sorby Ltd.
Tyme Machines (Bristol) Ltd.
C. Z. Scientific Instruments Ltd.
Craft Supplies of Millersdale.
Multistar Machine and Tool Ltd.

And to the craftsmen who helped with know-how, photographs, etc:
Marsh Dawes
David Francis
David Wadsley
John Warner
Graham Spalding
Hugh Greenland
Del Stubbs
Mike Baker
Nick Perrin
Ken Smith

Also to:
My wife for putting up with me.
To Bernard Cooper, the most patient of men, and the staff at GMC Publications Ltd.
My stand-in daughter, Sheila Kew, for reading the proofs.
My many pupils for their forbearance and Alan Phillips for his faith.

Introduction

Readers may well ask how small is miniature?

Lathe manufacturers tend to think in terms of fairly large work and lathe accessories are designed with this type of work in mind. There is indeed very little provision made for the holding and turning of really small work on the majority of lathes. Certainly, we don't have to have a small lathe to turn small items, but certain it is we need some provision to be added so the holding of small pieces is simplified.

A really small lathe for the type of woodturning which I have in mind has yet to be designed, other than a small lathe called the Hobbymat Variant. There are one or two small metal lathes which can be adapted, but these often have problems of suitable fixtures and speeds. The Tyme Cub Machine comes closest to the requirement and even a shorter bed could be obtained, particularly if working and storage space is a problem.

To attempt to define miniature is difficult, but most people will think in terms of articles to fit the average size dolls' house. This will involve the designing and making of furniture, articles for the table and kitchen and a host of decorative articles presently found in the average home. Smaller versions for actual use in the kitchen and other rooms will also be considered.

The third group ought really to be classed as 'micro'. My good friend Del Stubbs in California turns boxes and goblets so small they are difficult to see, much less turn. Mere breathing is indeed a threat to their survival. He might be heard to say – if you can't see it, you can't turn it. Taking photographs of such work is a nightmare for air, heat and movement are all forbidden and you become maniacal after a brief spell. Micro work is certainly a challenge to the skill of the turner, to his eyes and to his perfection of approach to the spinning wood, both in tools and hold, and also to man's infinite capacity for attempting to achieve the impossible.

The book hopes to show most methods of holding work, the tools to make a start and also some of the work of contemporary workers in this field.

The Lathe

There are many lathes from which to make a choice, but if the work is to be mainly in the exceptionally small, the choice of suitable lathes is considerably reduced.

The Tyme Cub

My choice is the Tyme Cub and there are a number of bed length options. It is well made, mainly in grey iron, and the machining is good. All the components which are available for the larger machines are scaled to fit. The fastest speed will meet the needs of most mini-turners.

My lathe is fixed to a thick hardwood top, which in turn is bolted to a metal stand. It is a complete mini-turning centre, having its own storage cabinet, tool rack and flexible light. I would suggest also fitting a magnifying glass on a flexible arm. Such an aid is needed when working to such tiny sizes and the light is vital. I can take this unit out into my yard and turn wood happily in the Devon sun when the days are long and working inside impossible.

The lathe comes complete with lathe driving centre (¾″) and a dead centre (¾″) and a standard (8″) tool rest, but the following tools will be needed:

- Short tool rest.
- Mini four prong drive.
- Lace bobbin drive.
- Running centre if not a mini dead centre.
- Drill chuck with No. 1 morse taper arbor, ½″ capacity.
- Screw chuck – the combination set or the precision combination chuck with the addition of the ¼″ screw chuck.
- A shielded lamp on a flexible arm.

The Cub Lathe from Tyme Machines (Bristol) Ltd. Constructed from cast iron and aluminium castings with twin solid steel bed bars. A high speed motor is also available for very small turning

Typical Lathe Accessories

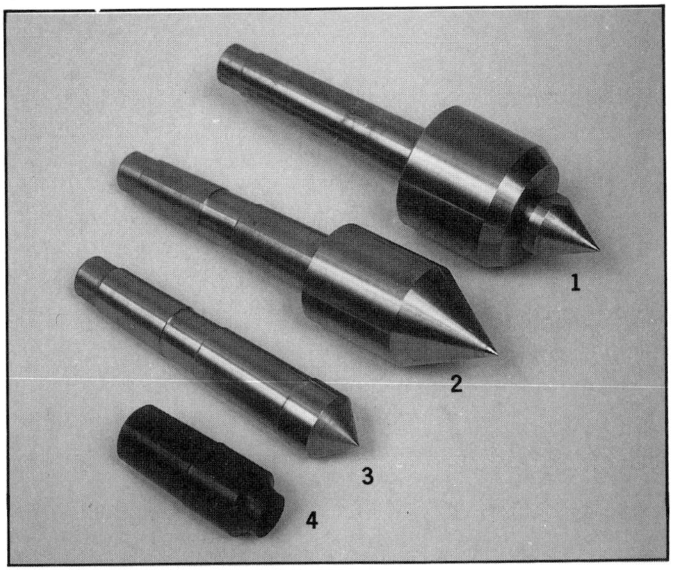

1. Heavy duty running centre 2. Standard running centre 3. Dead centre 4. Cup centre

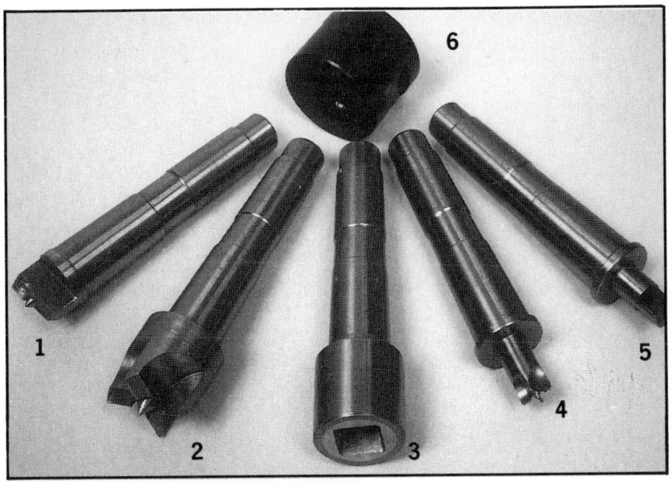

1. 2 prong drive centre 2. 4 prong drive centre 3. Lace bobbin drive 4. Mini 4 prong drive 5. Mini 2 prong drive 6. Centre ejector/thread protector

6″ faceplate (left) and 4″ faceplate

Woodscrew chuck set with interchangeable faceplates

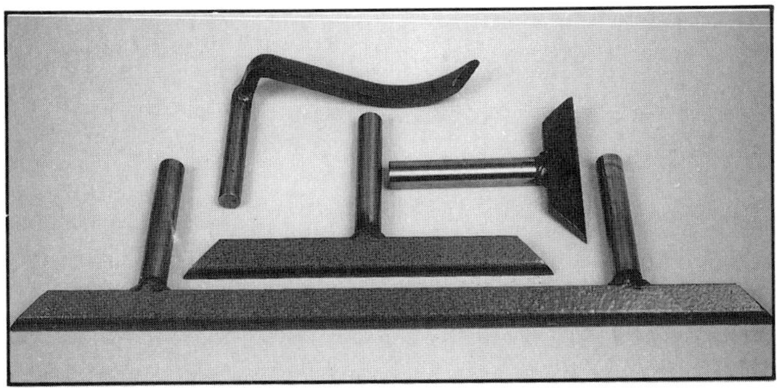

Bowlturning rest, short toolrest, standard toolrest, extra long toolrest

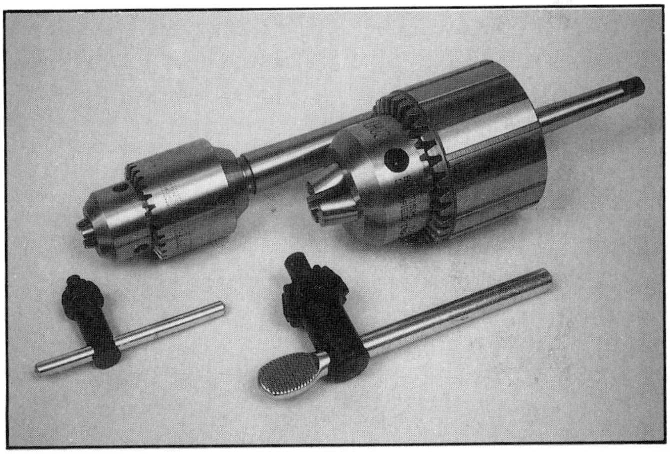

½″ and ¾″ capacity drill chucks
No. 2 and 1 morse tapers

Cup chuck set

The Hobbymat Variant Lathe available from C. Z. Scientific Instruments Ltd. in the U.K. Manufactured in Germany, it has a cast alloy bed with extension piece

The Variant Lathe

The Hobbymat Variant Lathe is purpose designed for small work with a between centres capacity of 650mm (a centre width of 300mm plus a 350mm bed extension which is supplied as standard). Its gap bed gives a bowl turning facility of 300mm. It has three speeds of 950 rpm, 1450 rpm and 2100 rpm. The motor is 370W–240v/50Hz.

It comes complete with a rotating centre, drive centre, tool rest face plate with woodscrew centre, egg cup chuck and tool kit.

A multipurpose chuck is available as an extra. It is a self-centreing 4 jaw chuck and the reversible jaws may be used to provide compression and expansion clamping and may be removed altogether, thus turning the chuck into a face plate. The chuck is supplied with a driving dog, fixed centre and woodscrew centre.

For the man working in the home without workshop facilities, this machine would seem to be the answer. It weighs only 30kg and needs a space of only 120 × 35cm.

The Tyme Student

The latest lathe which will be found extremely useful for the turning of small work is the Student Lathe from Tyme Machines (Bristol) Ltd. This lathe is moderately priced but has all the qualities seen in the higher priced machines from the same company.

The capacity is 10″ diameter with 30″ between centres. It features a ½ hp totally enclosed motor, speeds of 2,500, 1,000 and 540 rpm on a poly 'v' drive system. It comes complete with a No. 1 morse taper headstock and tailstock with sealed for life headstock bearings.

All the accessories shown for the Tyme Cub Lathe are available for this machine since the mandrel is screwed 20mm × 2.

The overall size of the lathe is 30″ × 15″ × 10″ high. For the user who doesn't need the length of bed, an adjustment with a good hacksaw will quickly affect a change.

The Student Lathe from Tyme Machines (Bristol) Ltd. Designed with the newcomer to woodturning and modelmaker in mind, it is constructed of cast iron with a solid steel bar

Tools for Miniature Work

Cutting tools

Cutting techniques for this work are the same as for normal size wood turning, but here we find the need for perfection in cutting. Indeed very little scraping is necessary or indeed possible.

Purpose designed tools called Sorby Micro Tools, made in High Speed Steels and of the same shape as their elder brothers have appeared on the market and these perform excellently. They are handled with the hand in mind, not the size of the blade, and are in polished Ash. No set is complete and to these must be added one or two which can easily be made. Roughing down can be done with a ½″ nose spindle gouge, although a ¼″ gouge could be ground square across and used for faster cutting. The latest High Speed Steel gouges will be found most suitable for this. They are deeper in the flute and therefore will cut faster.

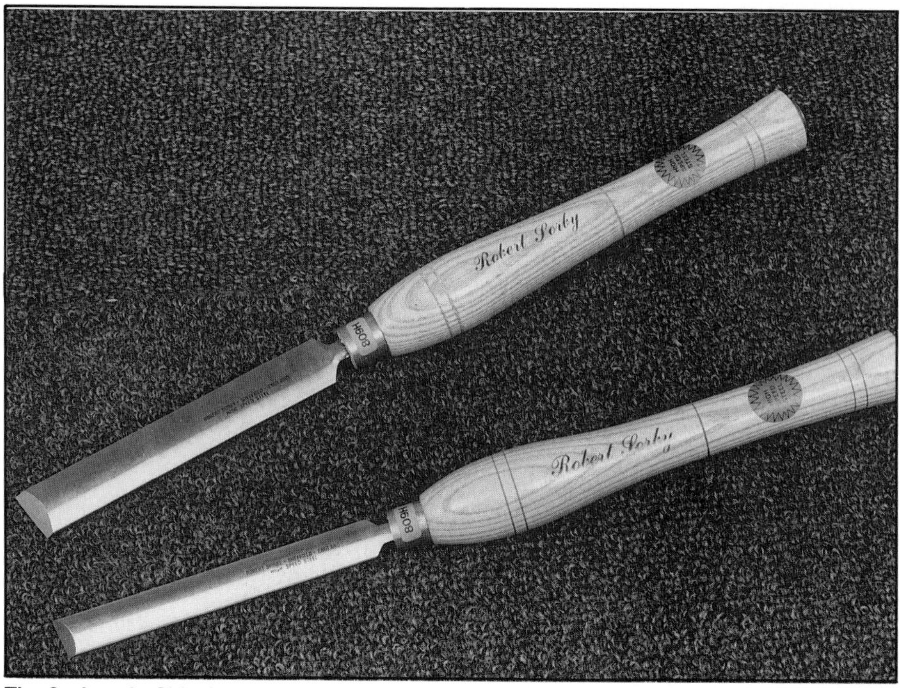

The Sorbysafe Chisel

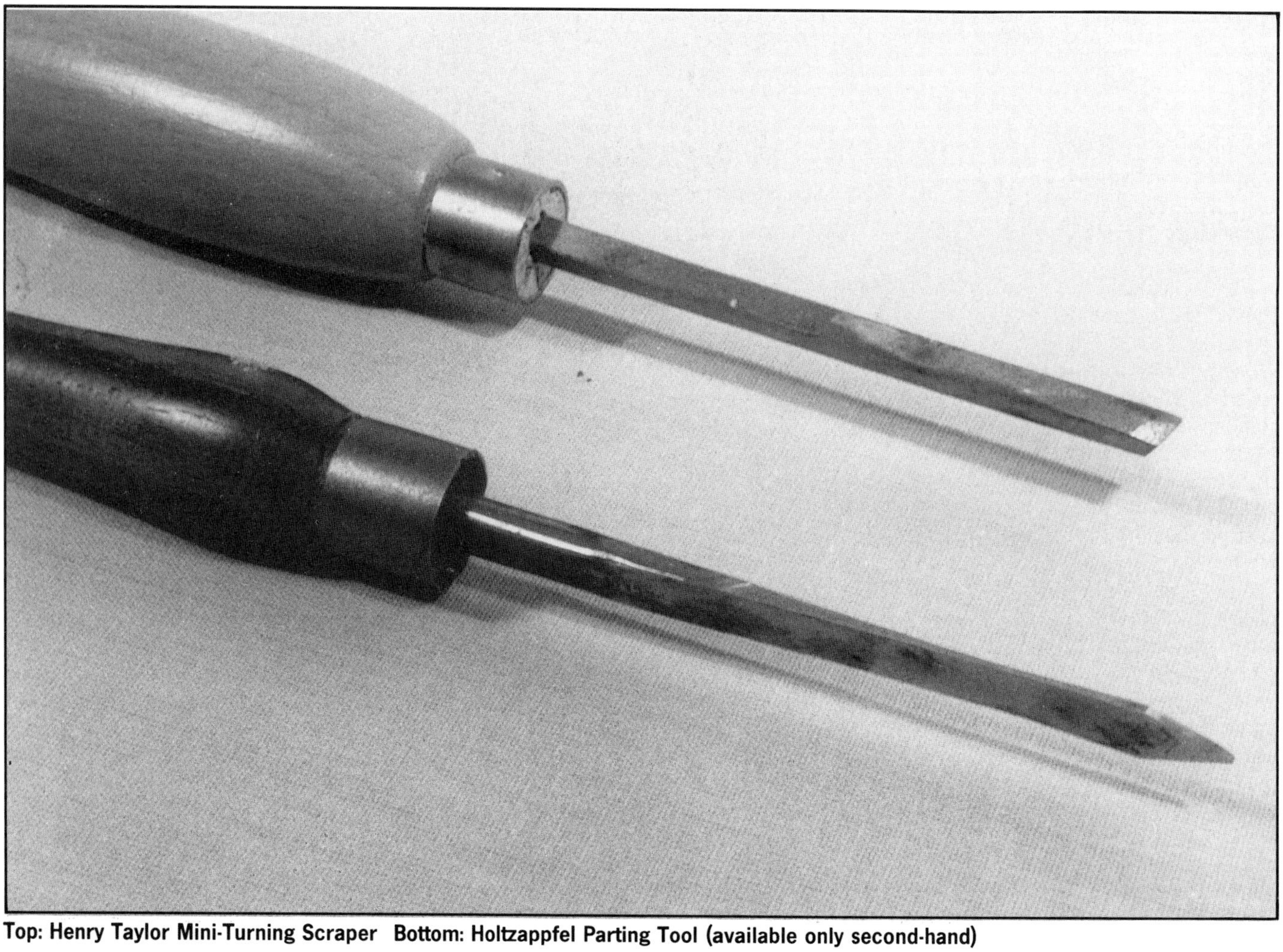

Top: Henry Taylor Mini-Turning Scraper Bottom: Holtzappfel Parting Tool (available only second-hand)

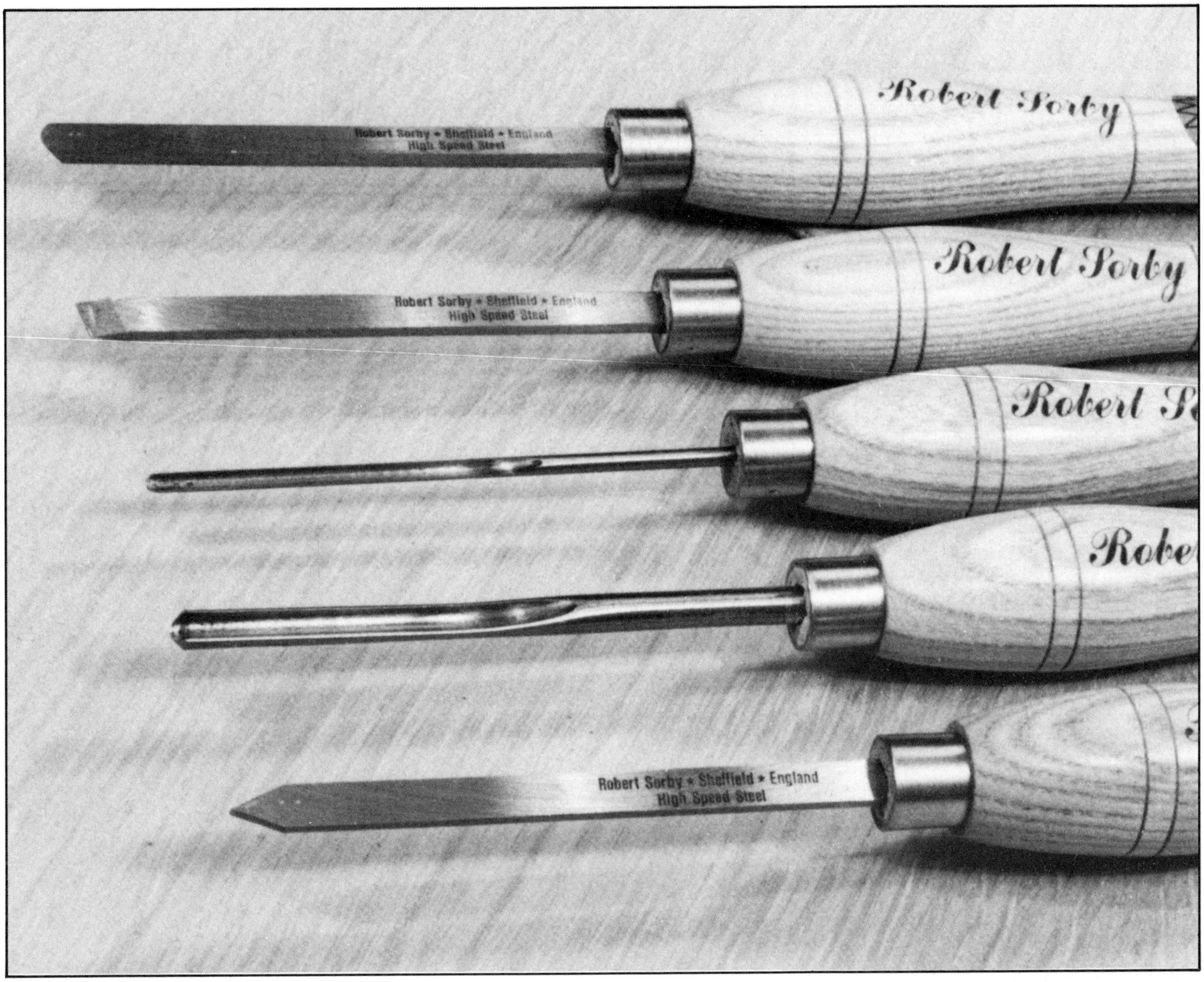

Sorby Micro Turning Tools

Planing should be carried out with the ¼″ skew chisel HSS or a ½″ one if the user prefers. The very latest chisel is the Sorbysafe, made from specially rolled 'U' sectioned steel, which removes many of the problems which people experience in using the traditional style of chisel. The ¼″ skew chisel, if ground square across, can be used for beading and other curved work.

Gouges in ⅛″ and ¼″ with round noses will be needed for coves and other small concave cuts.

A very thin parting tool is essential. This can be used not only for normal parting off but also as a beading tool and for cutting fine detail.

For faceplate work all the foregoing are used as well as a number of small scraping tools, the shapes of which are detailed in Figure 1. From time to time a form tool may be needed which can be made using the information in Appendix A.

Some of the cutting tools needed for miniature work

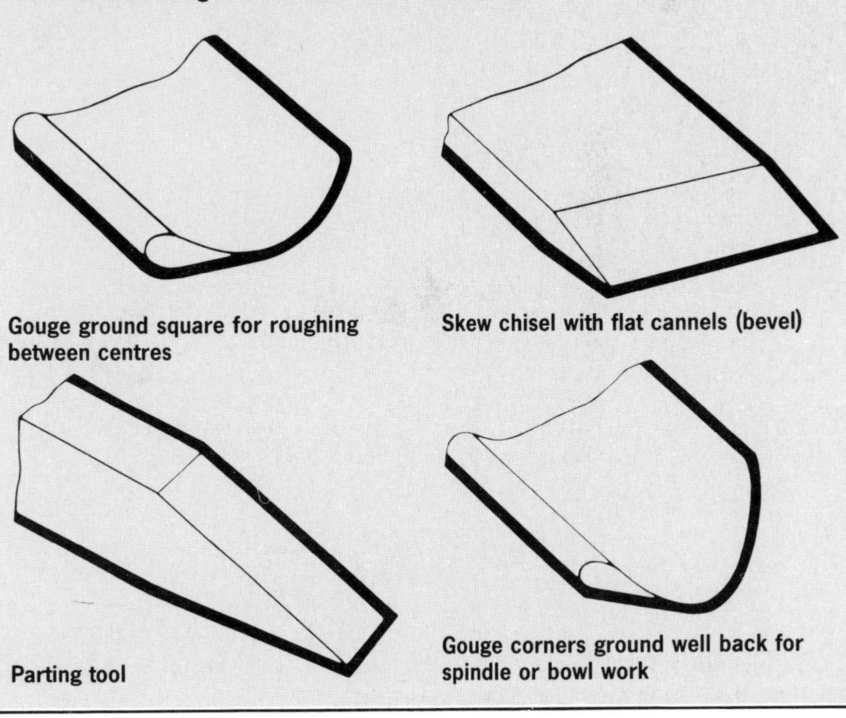

Scraping Tools

The tools in this group are not cutting tools in the strict sense. They do not cut and lift the shavings, they cut by scraping. They are ground at 80° and the technique of using them is the same as using the scraper on the bench.

Scraping on the bench is a finishing technique, yet many people when transferring this type of cutting to the lathe seem to regard it as a shaping technique – indeed a final action before the application of abrasives.

On the bench, the scraper follows the plane when it has been found impossible to arrive at a good finish after the finely sharpened cutter has been applied. The bench scraper has a hooked edge which engages in the wood when the scraper is tilted forward in the direction of movement. A fine lace like shaving is produced and the resultant surface will be flat and quite smooth. Only the finest of finishing paper will now be required.

Figure 1. Scraping Tools for Miniature Work

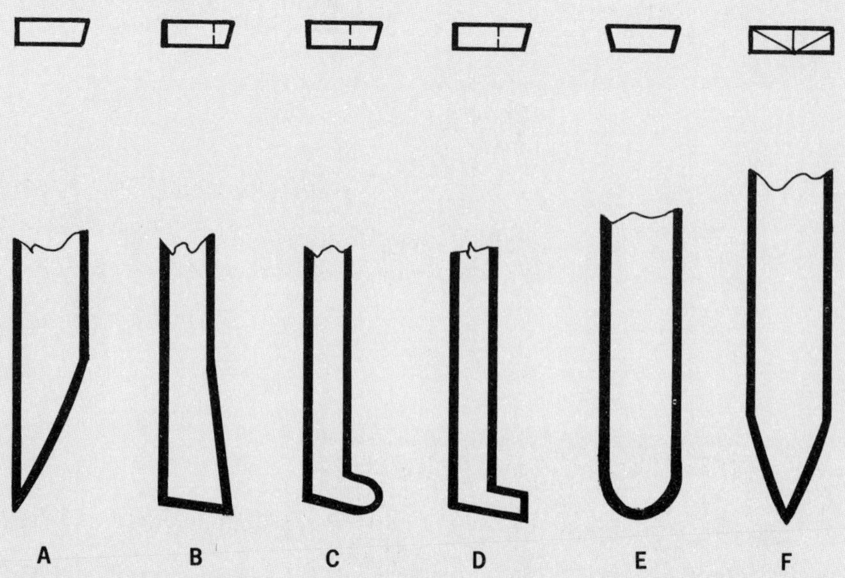

A. Side scraper and boring tool. B. Spade. C. Side Shaping D. Undercutting and parting. E. Round Nose. F. Chisel

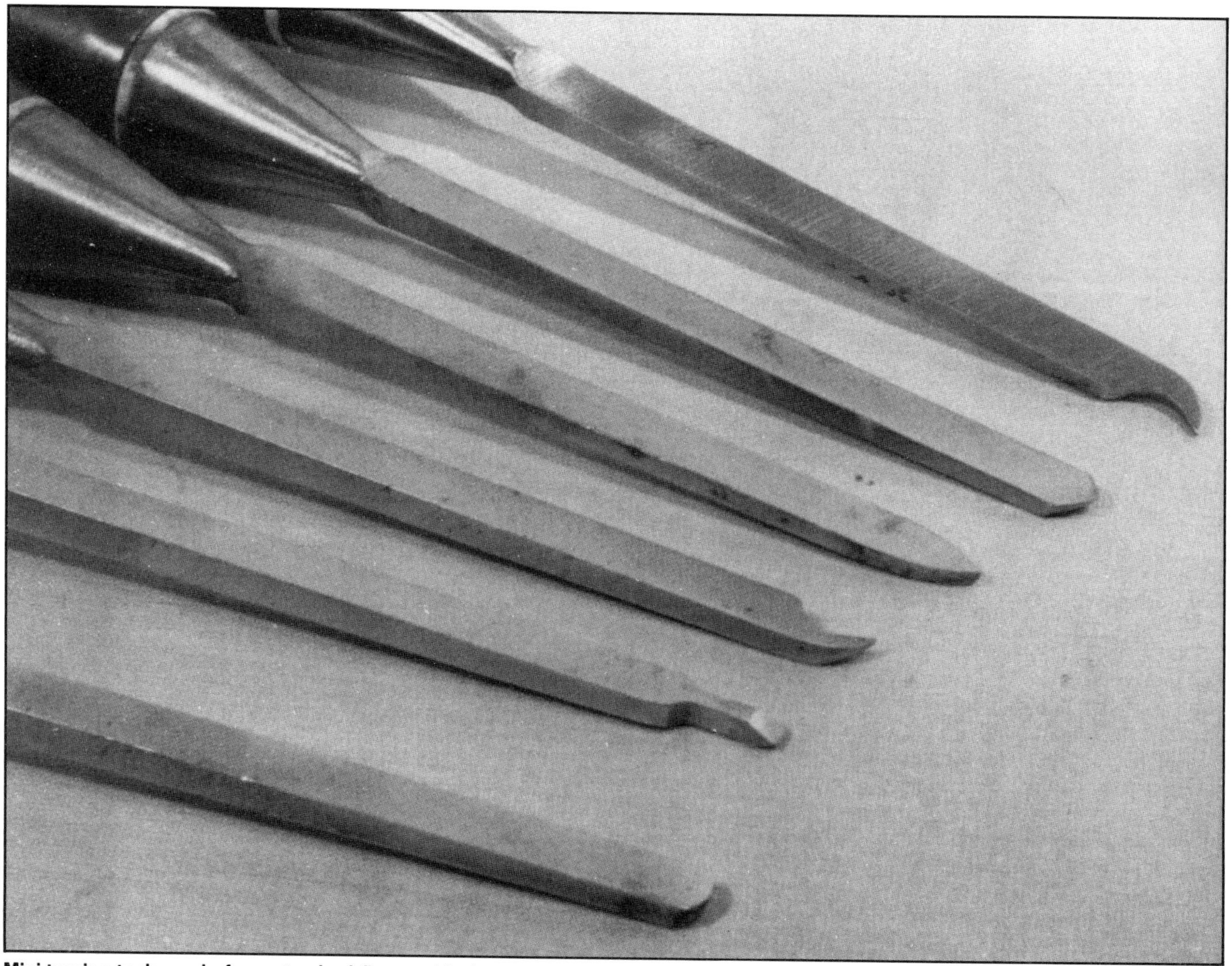

Mini-turning tools made from standard firmer chisels

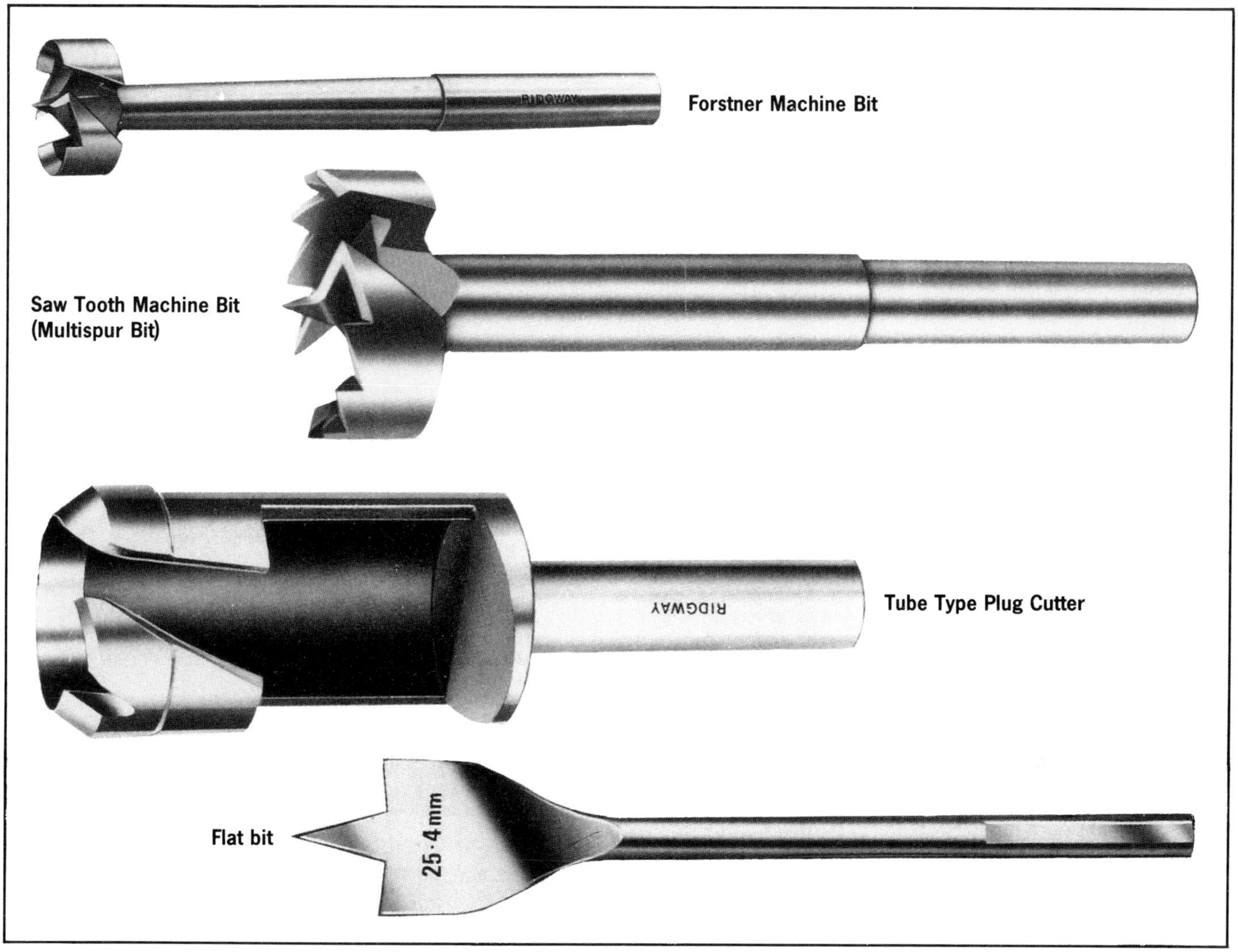

An exact similar approach should be made to scraping on the lathe, with the tools sharpened as described later in this book. The tool will be held flat on the tool rest and trailed slightly (cutting edge lowered, handle raised) to copy the bench procedure. The hook will engage in the timber and shavings will be taken from the work. Since the tool cannot produce a slicing cut and the bevel will be looking at the tool rest instead of the wood, there can be no polish from the tool either.

Scraping tools have been developed with certain basic shapes as illustrated in Figure 1. A number of manufacturers make them in Carbon Steel and High Speed Steel, and recently we have seen the introduction of Tungsten Carbide Tipped tools.

My own scrapers do not have the hook. They are finely sharpened on the stone, lie flat on the tool rest, without trail, and produce a much finer finish.

To scrape or not to scrape is a contentious question. In small work, very little scraping will be possible. Some timbers will defy cutting tools and therefore some additional work will be demanded. The purists, and I hope there are many, will sharpen and polish, then cut, and ask the doubters to emulate them.

Boring Tools

For the most part, the holes to be drilled will be of small diameter and the ordinary carbon steel twist drill of the engineer will be found to be suitable. Careful watch must be kept in case the flute becomes filled with wood chips.

Holes of ⅜″ and above can be bored with either the Forstner Machine Bit or the Saw Tooth Machine Bit (Multispur Bit in the USA).

Flatbits used with care and at high speed will produce finely finished holes, but it may be wise, if these are to be used frequently, to reduce the length of the brad point with a fine file.

Longer holes, in tiny diameter, can be cut with a diamond shaped drill made from a round of silver or similar tool steel. This type of tool could be fitted with a small handle and pushed through the tailstock for support. These I successfully used many years ago when teaching children to bore the trepanned hole for making brushes.

Plug cutters, either of the wing or tube self-ejecting type, will be found most useful for cutting plugs from waste exotic timber. These will make a useful store of turned blanks for mini-work.

All these boring tools will be held in the tailstock drill chuck.

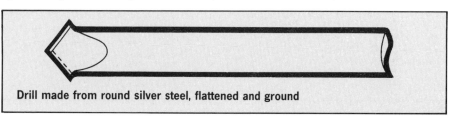

Drill made from round silver steel, flattened and ground

Equipment for Driving and Holding

Driving Forks
With morse taper to suit the particular lathe. They can be of two chisel or four chisel design. The point should be well forward of these chisels and the diameter of the fork itself should not be greater than ⅜″ across.

Dead Centre/Running Centre
Again a small size, certainly not greater than ½″ in diameter.

The screw chuck – improved screw thread

Mini four prong centre

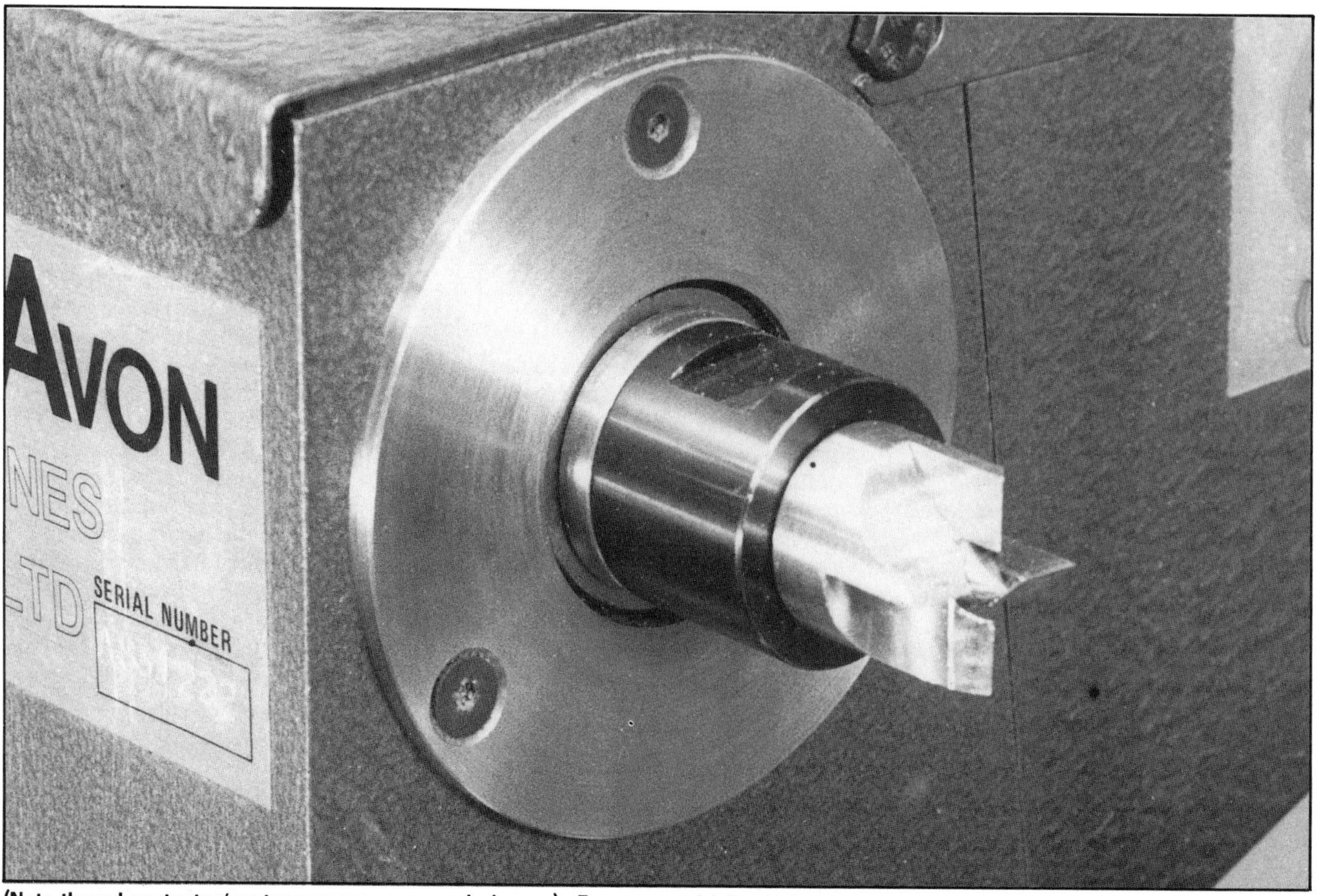

(Note thread protector/centre remover on mandrel nose.) Four prong driving centre.

Solid dead centre

Running centre

Screw chuck 40mm

Morse tapered screw chuck

Screw Chuck
This is probably one of the most useful accessories we can have for the lathe. The 1¼″ chuck shown is the most suitable chuck available for miniature work, but the small morse tapered one shown is perhaps the real answer. I've fitted it with a rod to prevent it drawing out of the headstock mandrel when in use. The small screw is held in a slot and is secured when the taper is drawn into the headstock. Screws of various lengths can be fitted.

Precision Combination Chuck
This type of chuck will always figure in any woodturning scheme. Here shown are the component parts and the assembled job when fitted in the expanding collet mode, with the smallest set of jaws.

Small work can also be held in the smaller of the collet/spigot jaws.

The chuck can also be fitted with the screw chuck but we shall have to get the makers to fit a smaller screw, even the ¼″ may be found to be a little too big.

Precision Combination Chuck as expanded collet chuck, showing smallest size collet. Underside of jaws shows smaller recess into which the small expander fits

Precision Combination Chuck fitted with smaller collect/spigot jaws

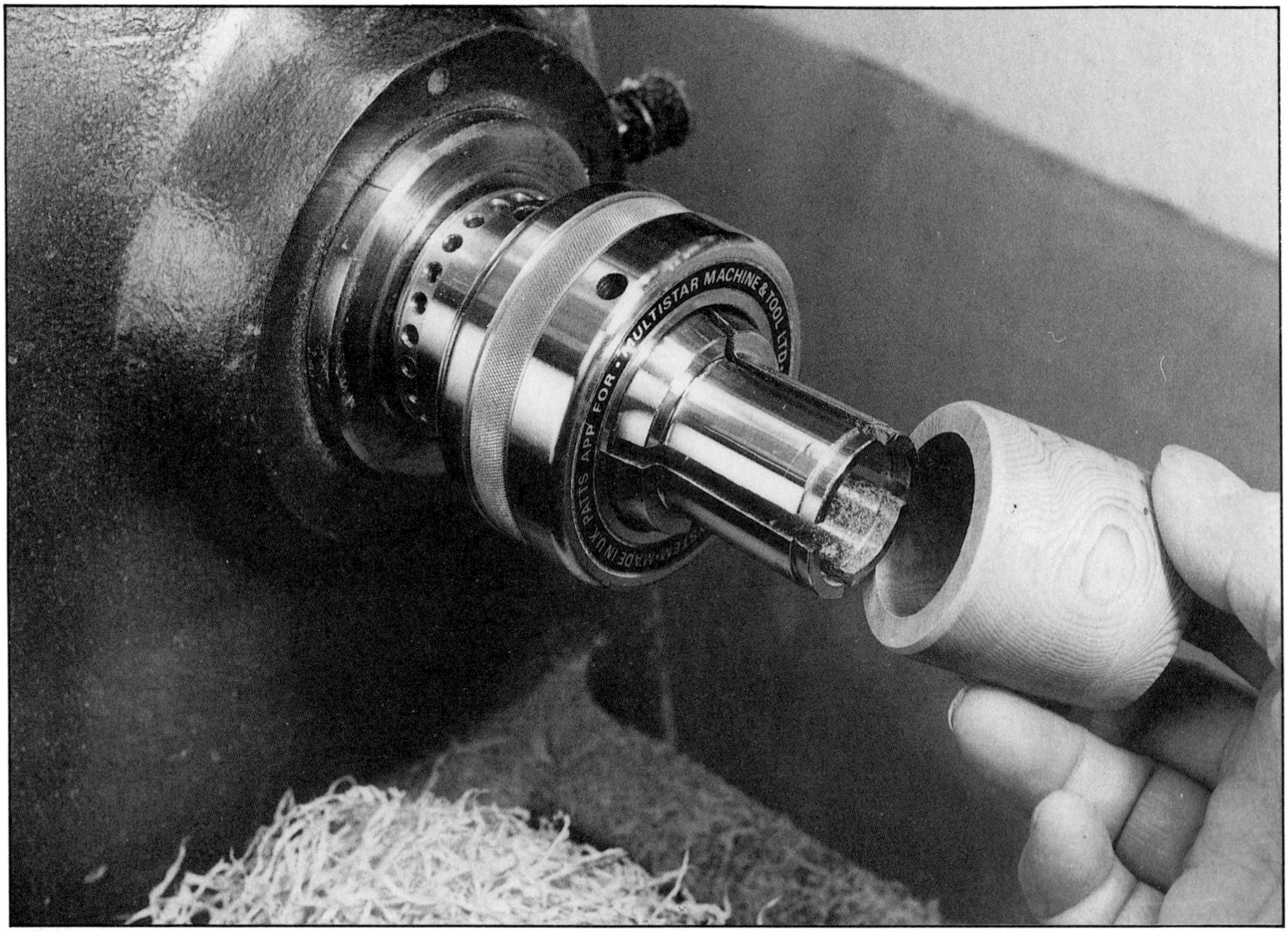

Multistar Chuck – smallest jaws used in expansion as a mandrel

The Multistar Chuck
Fitted with its smallest jaw can also be used.

Lace Bobbin Drive
A fairly recent addition to the accessories list, although I introduced this in wood many years ago with the children. It features a square pyramidic hole at the end of a morse tapered centre which serves to house and drive small pieces. Perhaps one day we shall see an even smaller hole.

Tools Rests
An oft neglected area. The ideal one has not yet been made. For my part I prefer the home-made variety, shown elsewhere, but the smallest supplied for the Cub is easily the best of the manufactured variety, not being bulky, but strong enough to support the tool and the hand.

Lace Bobbin Drives

Cone drive centre

Cone Centres

Small cone centres can be used for driving small pieces of rough stock or pieces already turned. Even completed pieces which need slight alteration can be returned to the lathe and driven without problems of centricity or damage. For owners of Coronet lathes, these screw directly to the headstock mandrel. Users of other lathes will need a screwed morse taper to suit their own particular lathe.

Drill Chuck

A drill chuck of ½″ capacity with morse taper to suit the lathe is essential. Not only may it be used in the tailstock with a boring tool inserted, but it may also be transferred to the headstock to hold small pieces of round timber. If constant use is to be made of the chuck in the headstock, the morse taper should be bored to receive a tie rod which passes through the headstock mandrel. The end of the rod is threaded to receive a washer and nut. This will prevent the chuck from moving out of the headstock mandrel when in use. This precaution also applies to any tapered addition to the lathe used in a similar way.

Drill chuck used in head or tailstock

Right angled tool rest

Holt melt glue gun

Right Angled Tool Rest
This is a useful addition to the lathe equipment and will be found to be a great time-saver. There are two versions, one in solid rod, the other in tube. They are available for both left and right hand applications.

Hot Melt Glue Gun
For miniature work the glue gun will be found most valuable. A block of faced scrap wood attached to either the screw chuck or the faceplate with a thin film of glue spread on the timber is sufficient to hold even sizeable blocks. The best gun is one with a trigger which pushes the glue in to the barrel, otherwise the glue stick is pushed by hand. Glue sticks are available up to 300mm in length.

Long thin knife
I use an old cobbler's knife to tap between the job and the hot melt glue chuck to separate the two. Any thin knife will be found suitable.

Double Sided Tape
Hardly a tool, but a roll will be found to be most useful as this material used between two flat clean surfaces makes a perfect hold. Extremely good for small, thin pieces.

Spigot Chuck
This chuck is smaller than the precision combination chuck and can be fitted with dual purpose jaws which function in both collet and spigot mode. Two sizes of jaws are available – 1″ / ⅞″ and 2″ / 1⅞″. Pin mandrels can also be fitted within the collet jaws for the holding of a pre-bored material. The spigot chuck may well prove, in some users' hands, to be *the* chuck for mini-turning.

Myford – 4 in 1 Chuck
This is the oldest of the combination type chucks and in recent years has been fitted with a small collet jaw.

Pin chuck used to maintain the spigot chuck at its correct diameter

Myford 4 in 1 Chuck – collet mode

Myford 4 in 1 Chuck – exploded with all components

50mm capacity Cup Chuck with reducer to give 30mm diameter

50mm capacity Cup Chuck

Cup Chuck

A number of these are available, the best being the one manufactured by Tyme Machines of Bristol. This is sold as a set of two sizes, the outer cup having an internal diameter of 50mm and the insertable or reducer cup one of 30mm.

> SAFETY NOTE
>
> When using morse taper equipment in the headstock, it is advisable to use a draw bar to secure the taper. The manufacturer is slow to recognise this need and you may have to either do it yourself or find a friendly engineer. The danger is that the taper can move out if the cutting is a little vigorous, with possible disastrous results for the turner.

Equipment for Marking

In working to scale, it is essential to have a number of measuring and marking tools. These need to be the smallest available.

Inside Calipers
These should be of the spring type, with the legs pivotting on a roller and tensioned by the action of a bow spring. Fine setting is obtained by a knurled split nut which gives a quick action. The smallest size is 3″. With very tiny work, often the calipers cannot be used and recourse will have to be made to the simple rule.

Outside Calipers
Of the same design as the inside calipers. Again a 3″ size is suggested.

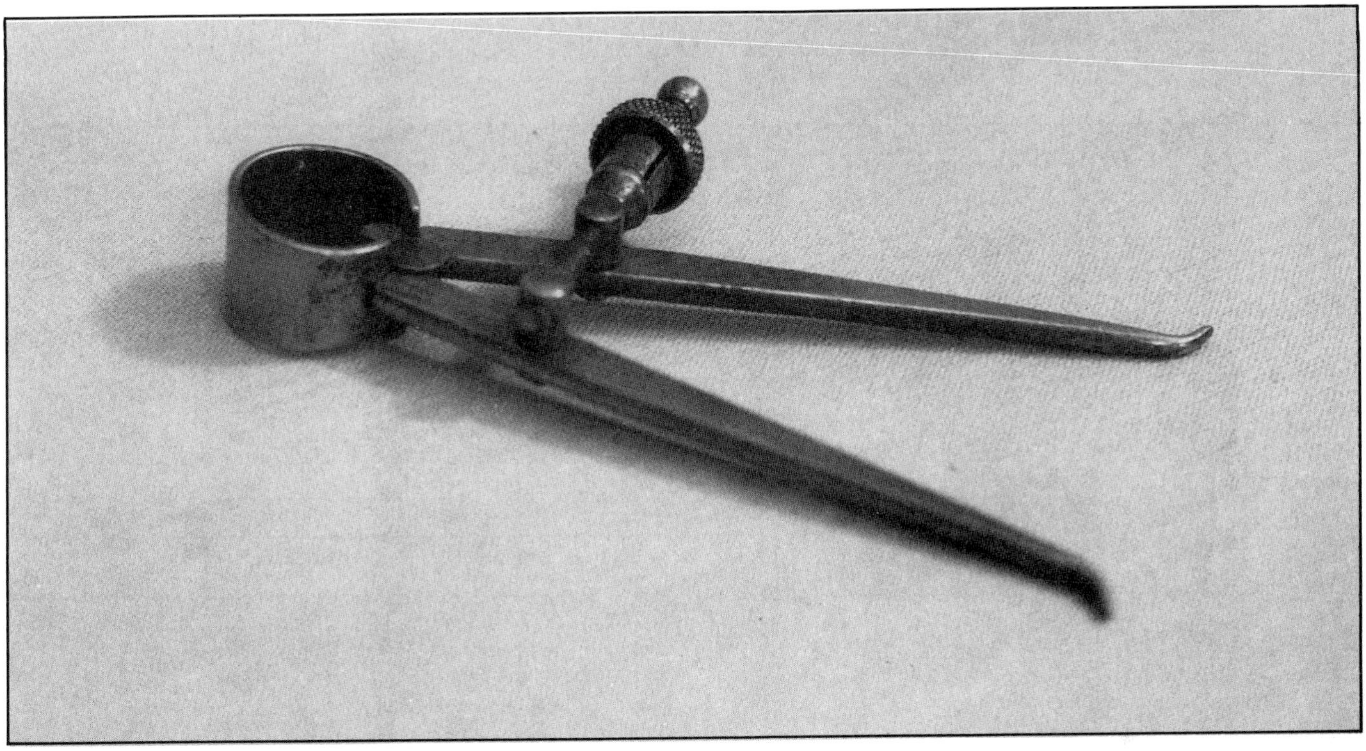

Inside calipers

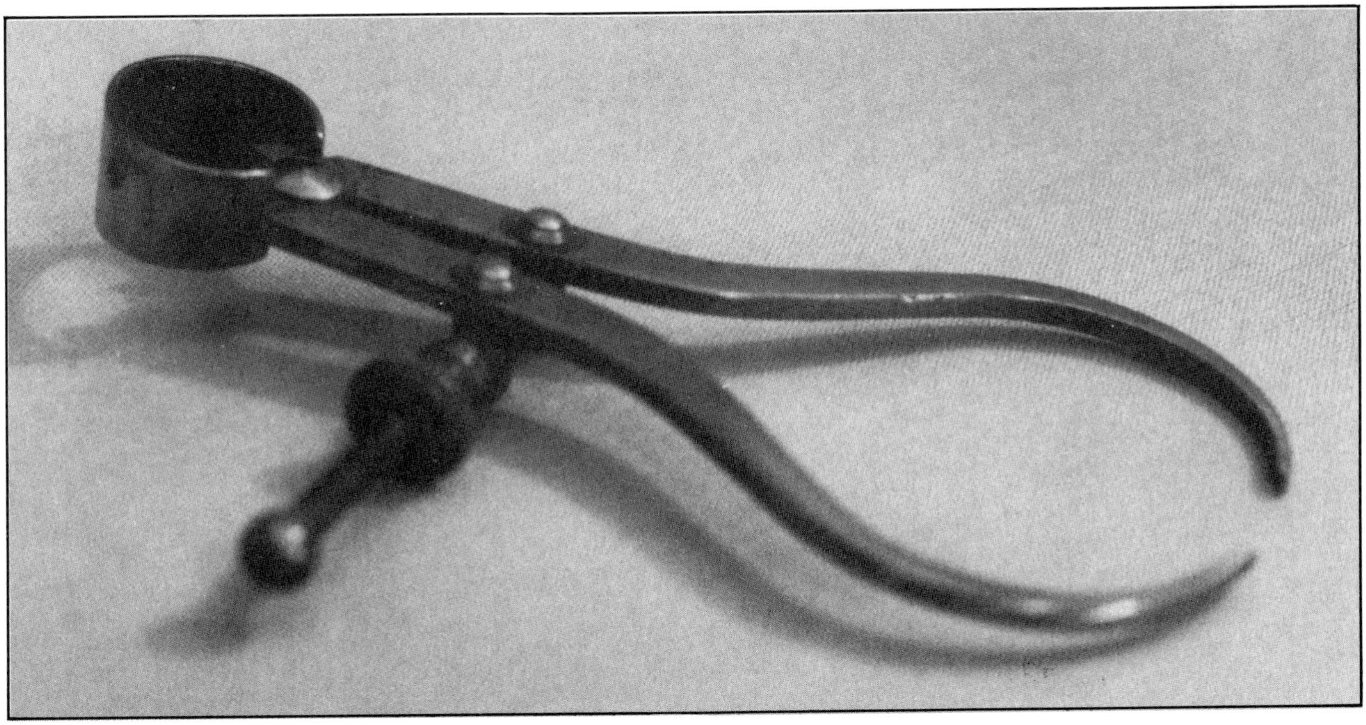

Outside calipers

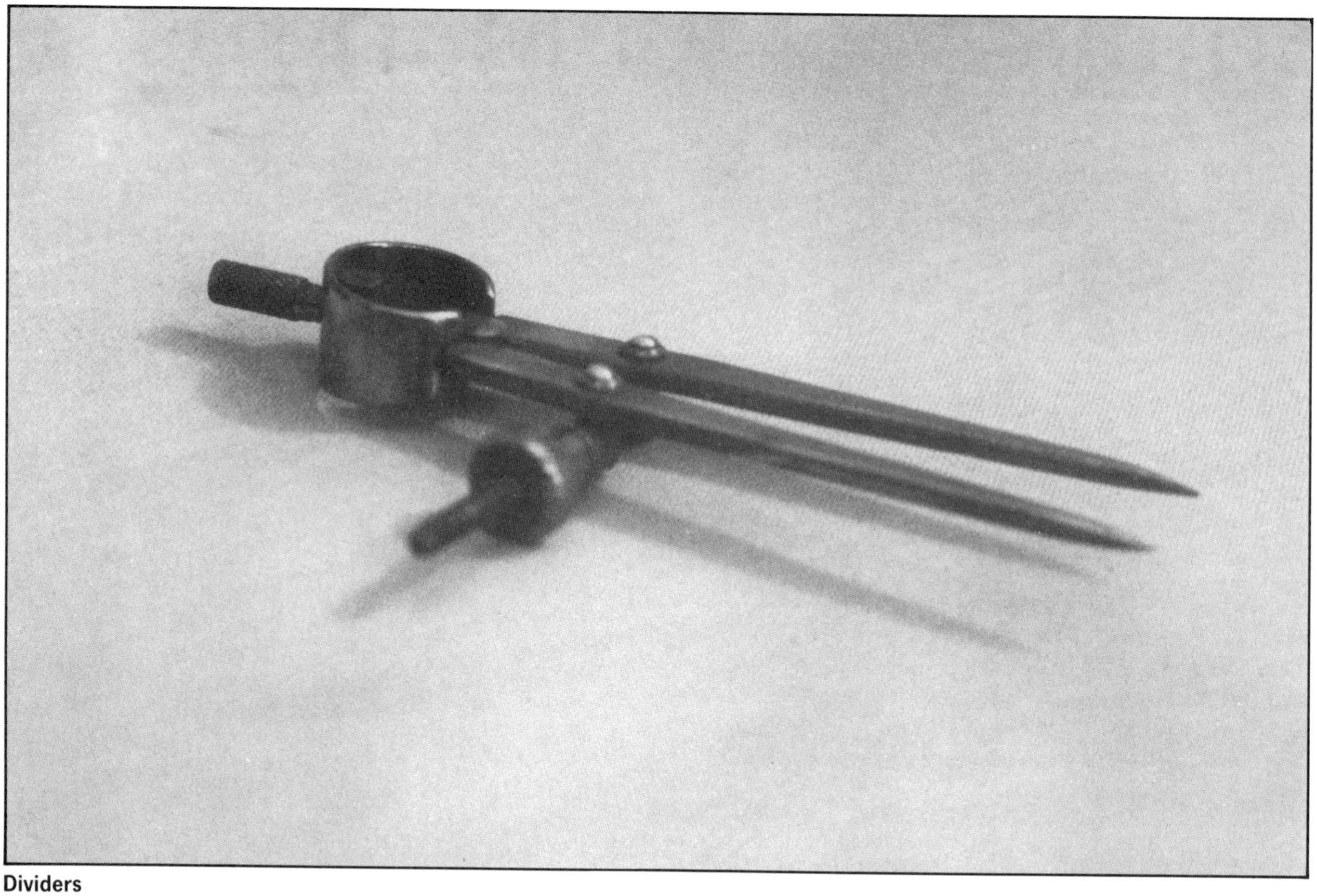

Dividers

Panel pin guide

Dividers
Useful for scribing circles and taking off measurements, their construction is similar to the calipers.

Pin Template
These can be made using thin strips of wood and transferring measurements from the drawing. Tiny holes are bored at important marked points and small panel pins pushed in. This is then held in contact with the work and the lathe turned by hand to score the marks.

Marking Knife
A marking knife point can be used to transfer markings from a drawing or a template onto the job. Really any small knife will be found useful for this job.

Cardboard Templates
Generally a cardboard template made from the drawing will be sufficient, but if many of the same design are to be made, it may be better to make a template from very thin metal, such as aluminium. The template will have to be filed in this case to cut in the fine detail.

Marking knife

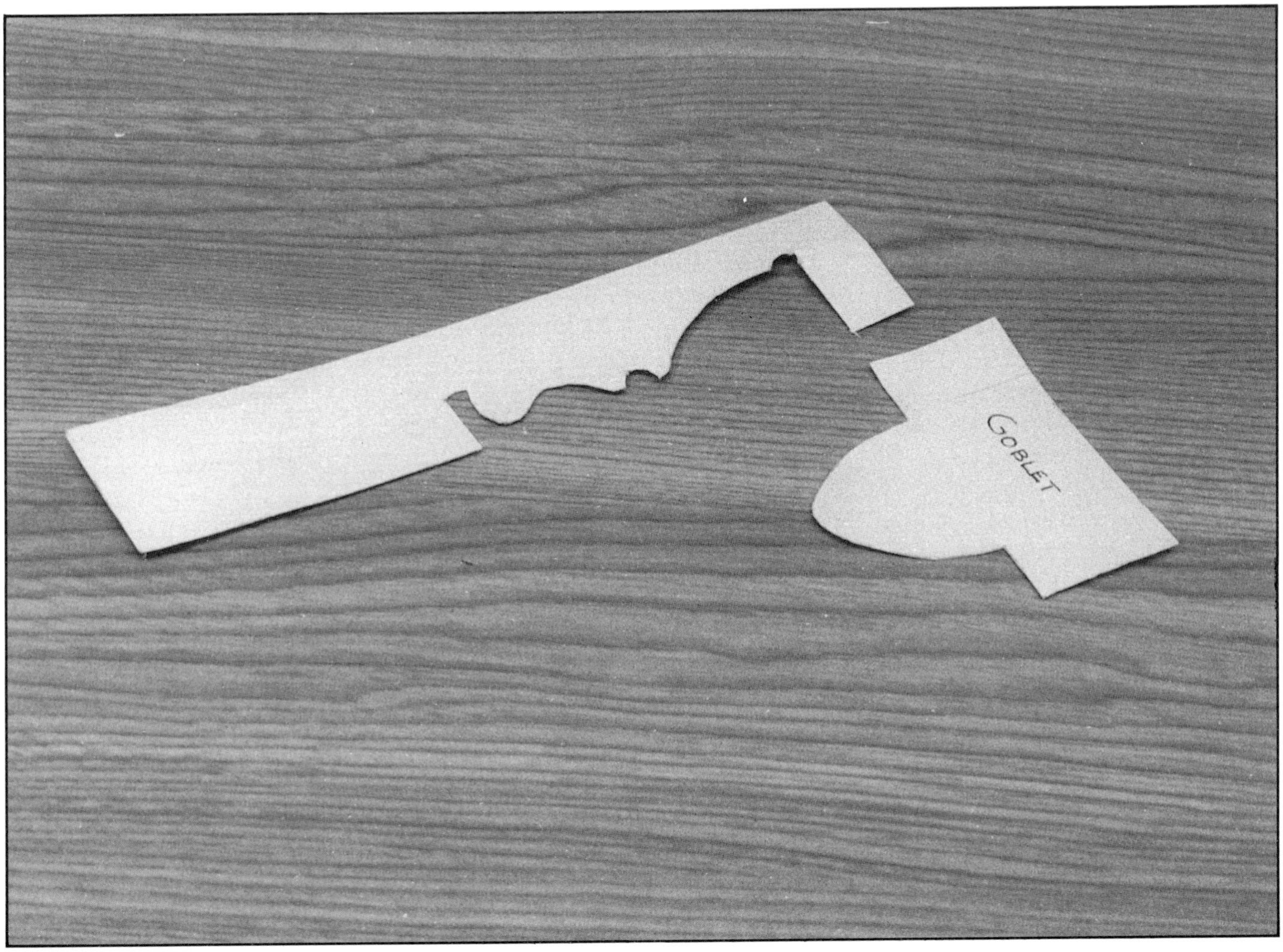

Cardboard template

Boxwood calipers

Vernier Calipers

A number of craftsmen work to such close dimensions as to demand the use of the vernier calipers. These are really fine. There are a number of cheaper types on the market, slightly less smart than the engineers' vernier calipers which will serve the woodcraftsman well. I have for many years used one made in boxwood by Rabone. It's accurate and good enough for most of the measuring tasks I give it.

Depth Gauge

I used a dowel pushed through a slat of timber for some time and then decided to make one in metal. It's of very simple construction and can be seen in the illustration. For measuring the inside of small boxes, it's really the answer.

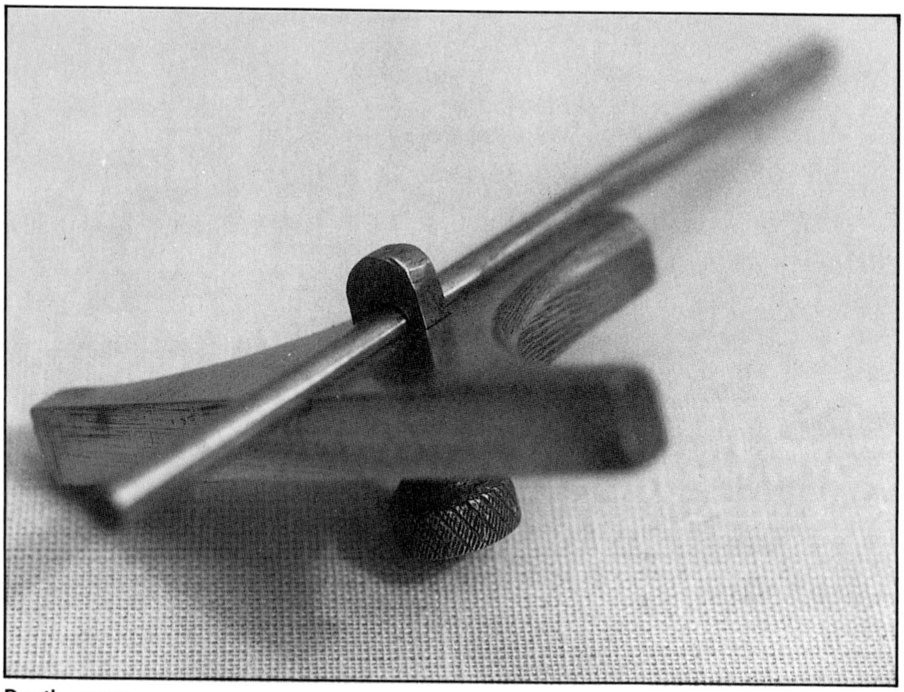

Depth gauge

Marking Awl

This is a tool often preferred by the craftsman for marking out, where there isn't the necessity of actually cutting the top fibres on the workpiece. The one shown was found in a roll of carving tools and I have never seen it on sale. There are a number of these made for marking wood and metal which are quite suitable for this work.

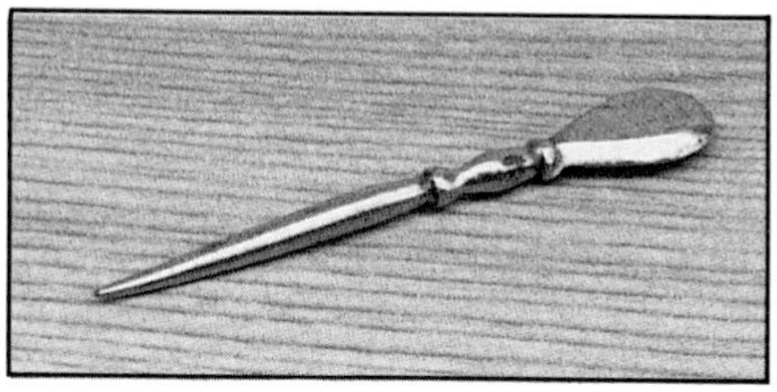

Marking awl

Equipment You Can Make

The completed tool rest, constructed as shown in the line drawing

Tool Rests

These never seem to be of the right length to suit the job on hand. They are often of bad shape or cannot be brought right up to the job. The old turners used wooden rests and these they changed frequently or straightened up with the plane.

For many years I made tool rests up using a piece of angle iron to which I welded a rod of size to fit the lathe. When they were bored for screws, I could fit them with long straight grained hardwood, shaped to fit the particular need. These are warm to the hand and I think much more comfortable in use.

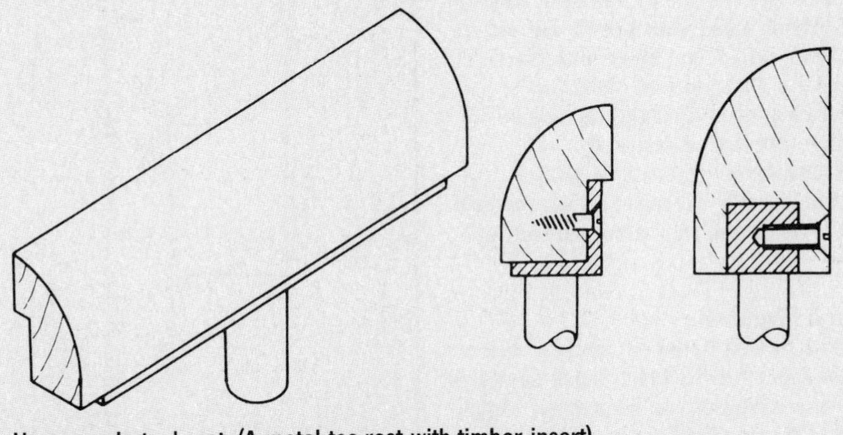

Home-made tool rest. (A metal tee-rest with timber insert)

Driving Taper
This particular aid was designed to meet the need for driving small pieces between centres, since the driving forks at that time were far too big for this task. I used Box for this, but any good long straight hardwood will be found suitable, tapered to suit the lathe. A small square pyramidic hole is cut to receive varying sizes of timber. This design has now been copied in metal and is shown in the chapter 'Equipment for Holding and Driving'.

Tapered wood mandrel

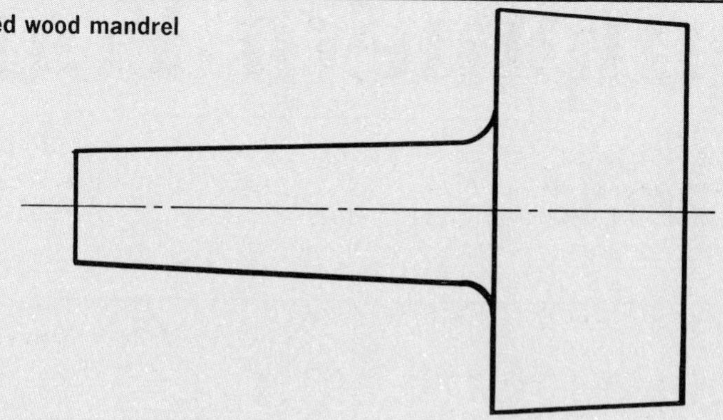

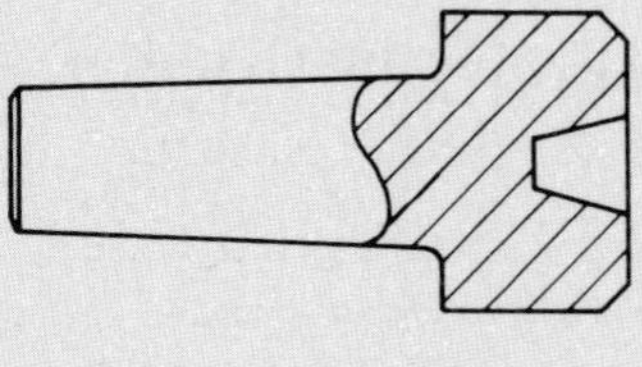

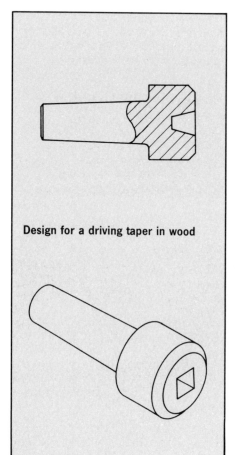

Design for a driving taper in wood

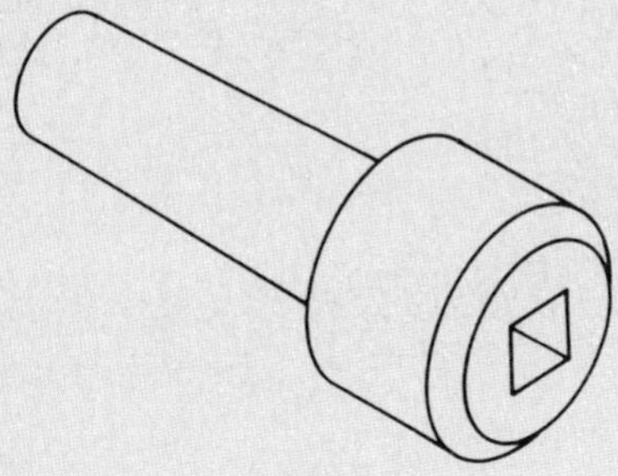

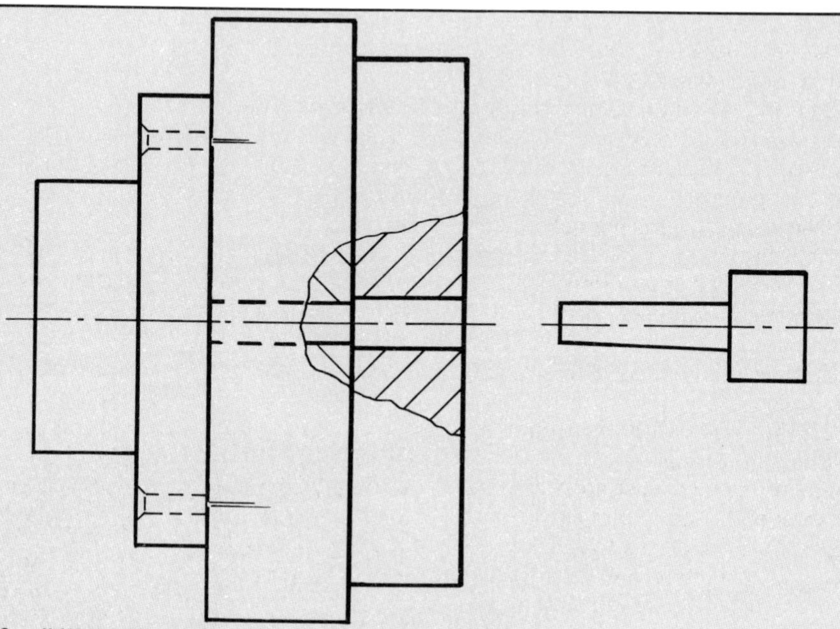

Small Wood Chuck, bored to receive small turning

Small Wood Chucks
These can be made in a similar way to the driving taper, but here a flat face is provided which can be recessed to receive a small turned piece, or accurately turned on the outside to receive pre-bored material.

Alternatively, a block of timber attached to the faceplate or screwchuck and prepared in the same way can be used.

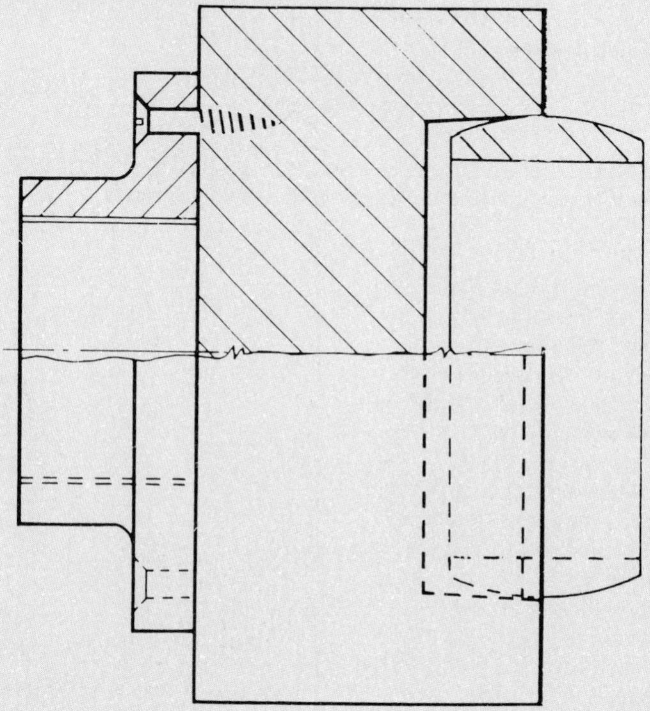

Wood Mandrel
This is turned between centres with a slight taper, on to which small pieces of pre-bored timber can be pushed. Small rings for a multitude of purposes can be turned using this device.

Grinding and Sharpening

Many changes have taken place in recent years in the manufacture of turning tools and in the materials used. High speed steel is now in common use and recently introduced are tungsten carbide tipped tools and cobalt alloy tipped tools.

The sharpening of woodturning tools is a subject of disagreement but the writer sticks to the belief all tools applied to the cutting of timber should in the first place be ground correctly and then sharpened either by using traditional methods or employing the latest available materials.

Schools of thought can be divided into four groups:

Sharpening by grinding only, on a fast moving double ended grinder.

Traditional grinding using a grindstone and sharpening on an oilstone.

Grinding, sharpening and stropping (Polishing).

Grinding, with sharpening and polishing in one operation.

The newcomer must appreciate that for tools to cut correctly they must be applied to the work so that the bevel rubs and as a result the timber polishes after the point of cut. It follows, therefore, that the bevel must have a very high quality of finish; indeed, it needs to be polished. The edge itself must be revealed as a black hairline completely free from flaw. Deviation from this maxim will tend to score the wood and abrasive papers will have to be applied in several grades to achieve a finish. The extra time spent on achieving this sort of finish can be placed against the time saved in papering.

The lathe cutting tools can be classified as:

1. Tools for cutting
2. Tools for scraping
3. Tools for boring. (Dealt with separately in the chapter 'Tools for Miniature Work')

> NOTE
> All lathe tools must be sharpened on the ground bevel.

Gouges

All the gouges for this small work should be round nose and they need not be deep fluted even for roughing. They should be ground with a 40° included angle and sharpened on the ground bevel.

Chisels

Chisels can be skew or ground square across, but the latter cannot be used for some of the cuts. They are ground both sides and have an included angle of about 30°. Parting tools are also included in this group.

Scraping Tools

These have a completely different cutting action and should be ground at 80°.

Before making a decision on which method of sharpening to adopt, first of all decide which you can carry out with the equipment available. Better still, decide before making any purchases.

It might be best to try all methods and make a decision after using them on the timber for some little time. Certainly do not accept my word but make a decision on sound findings.

The easiest and best method I have found for grinding is to use an abrasive belt or wheel. Choose aluminium oxide grit 120 and run at 350 rpm or close to that. For sharpening I almost always use the rubberised sharpening wheel, moving fairly slowly and with the wheel in a horizontal position if possible. My second choice for sharpening is the motorised Japanese waterstone.

Sharpening by Grinding

It is suggested that an 80 grit carborundum wheel be used and mounted to a double-ended grinder. This wheel should be 25mm (1″) across and 125mm (5″) or 150mm (6″) diameter. The wheels usually revolve at 3,000 rpm.

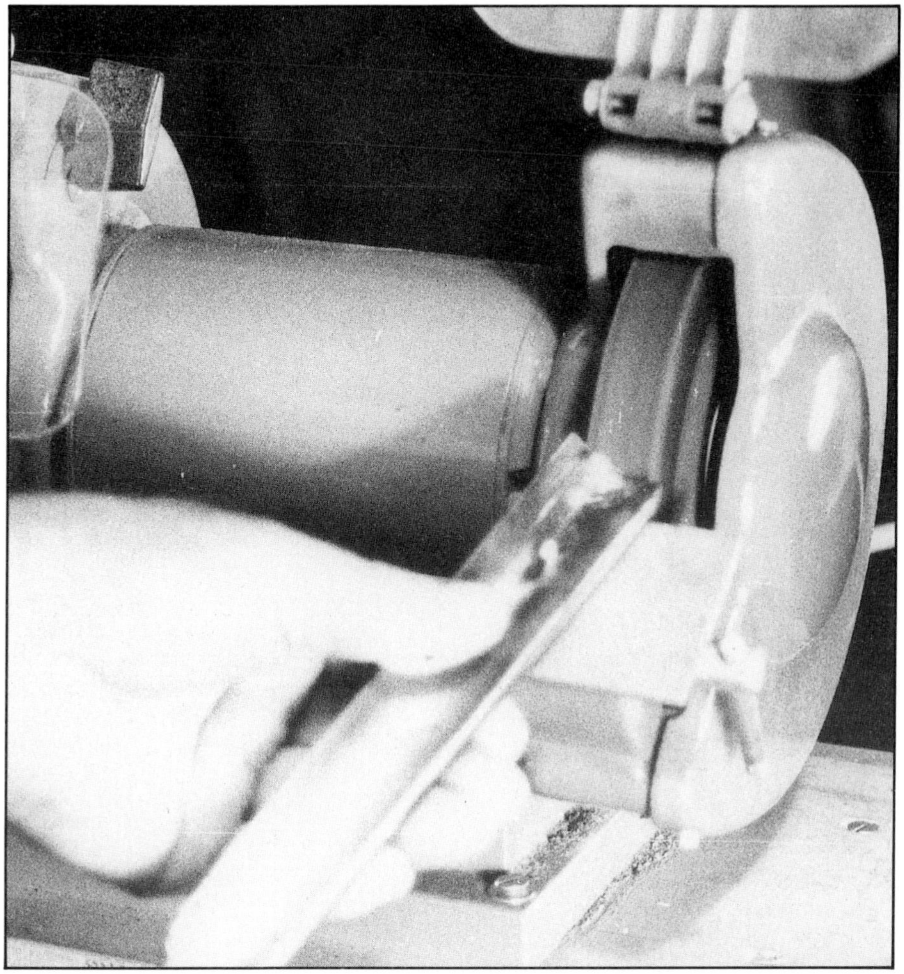

Gouge sharpening by grinding – using the double ended grinder. (In use always have the guard down)

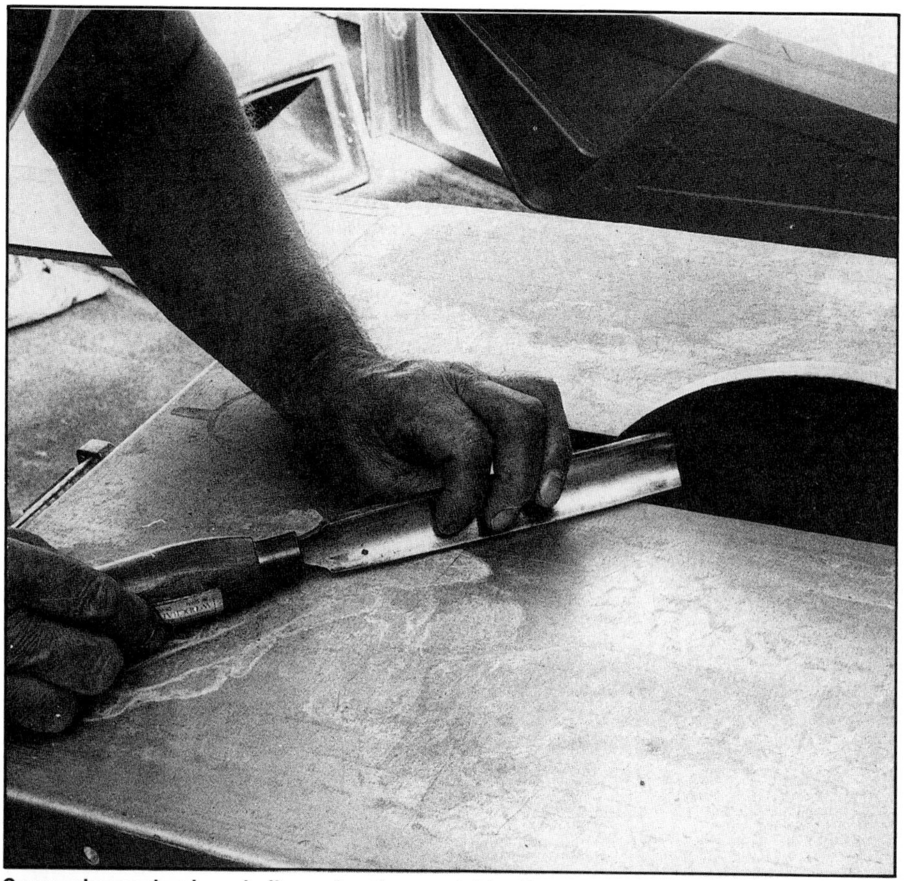

Gouge sharpening by grinding using the saw table disc

To Sharpen a Gouge

Place the gouge on the rest, which has first been set at the correct angle, and line it up with the wheel, so that they both lie in the same plane. Let the heel of the tool rub the stone and be prepared to roll the tool from side to side, so that grinding takes place over the full width of the bevel. Gently raise the handle, don't push, so that grinding moves towards the cutting edge. The gouge bevel will take on the curvature of the wheel. The moment before the cutting edge is reached, drop the handle. Great care is needed here because if a line of light appears along the edge, it will have been burnt and the tool will be useless.

The chisel can be sharpened in the same way, but if greater than 25mm (1″) in width, it will be necessary to slide it across the rest so that it may be equally ground.

A far safer (as far as the tool is concerned) method of sharpening by grinding is to use either a disc or bandfacer, moving fairly slowly (350 rpm). The abrasive belt-disc should be moving away from the operator, little pressure is needed and very little heat

Sharpening the long and strong turning chisel on the belt grinder

Grinding the gouge on the belt grinder

is generated. This method ensures flat bevels of quite high quality.

The small Picador is the cheapest of the machines, but perhaps the cheapest way is a disc on the electric drill.

Whichever method is chosen, watch the heat and the line of sparks. Hold the tool lightly. Tools sharpened in this way will cut well, but the poor condition of the bevel will tend to leave tiny grooves on the job.

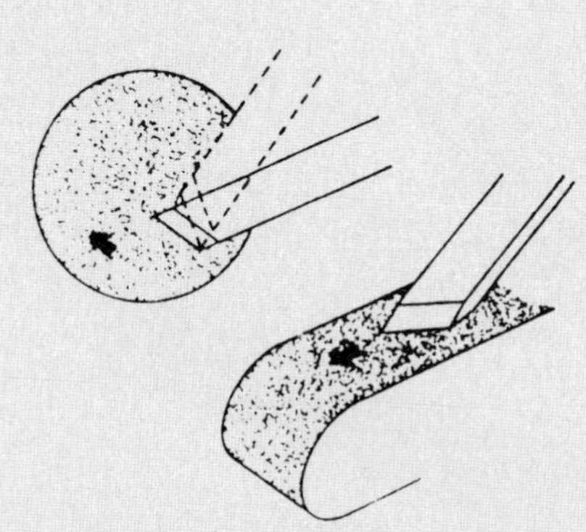

Sharpening the skew chisel on the disc or belt. Note the direction of rotation

Grinding the 3⁄8″ bowl gouge on the sanding disc

Sharpening by Grinding and Stoning

Choose the 200 × 50 × 25mm (8 × 2 × 1") stone and thin oil. Alternatively, use a Japanese waterstone of 1000 grit.

Grind only if the tool is nicked or badly out of shape, then proceed to use the stone. Many users hold the tool in the left hand and use the sharpening stone in the right hand – in the case of the gouge, moving it at right angles to the cutting edge and away from the user, angling the stone slightly across. Sharpen chisels in the same way, working on both bevels at right angles to the edge and away from the user.

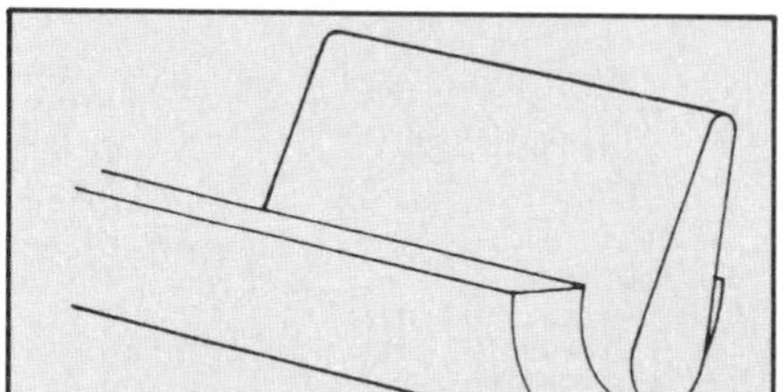
Removing the burr

The burr set up on the gouge is removed with a slipstone, moving it towards the edge and at the same time round the inside curve of the gouge.

The popular method is to place the boxed oilstone either in the vice or between the dogs on the top of the bench or on the oilstone bench. Hold the gouge with its bevel flat on the stone and, in addition to moving it forward and backward along the full length of the stone, rotate the gouge from edge to edge to finally produce a burr along the entire cutting edge.

The figure of eight movement, instead of straight forward and backward, may be used but this takes a little practice.

Complete the sharpening with the tool held at right angles to the length of the stone and rotating the bevel from side to side. This will remove any small flats which may have been made in the

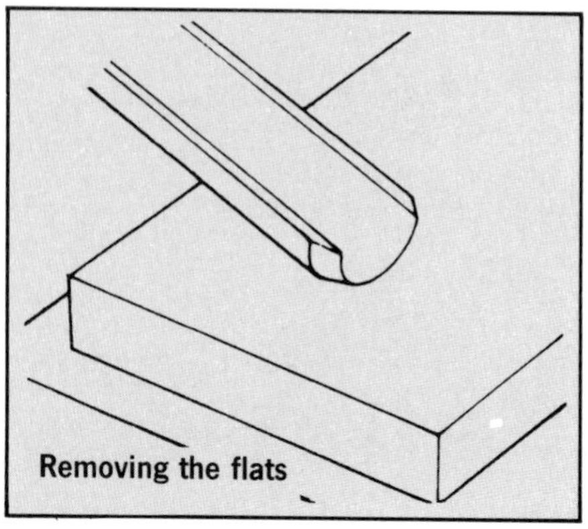
Removing the flats

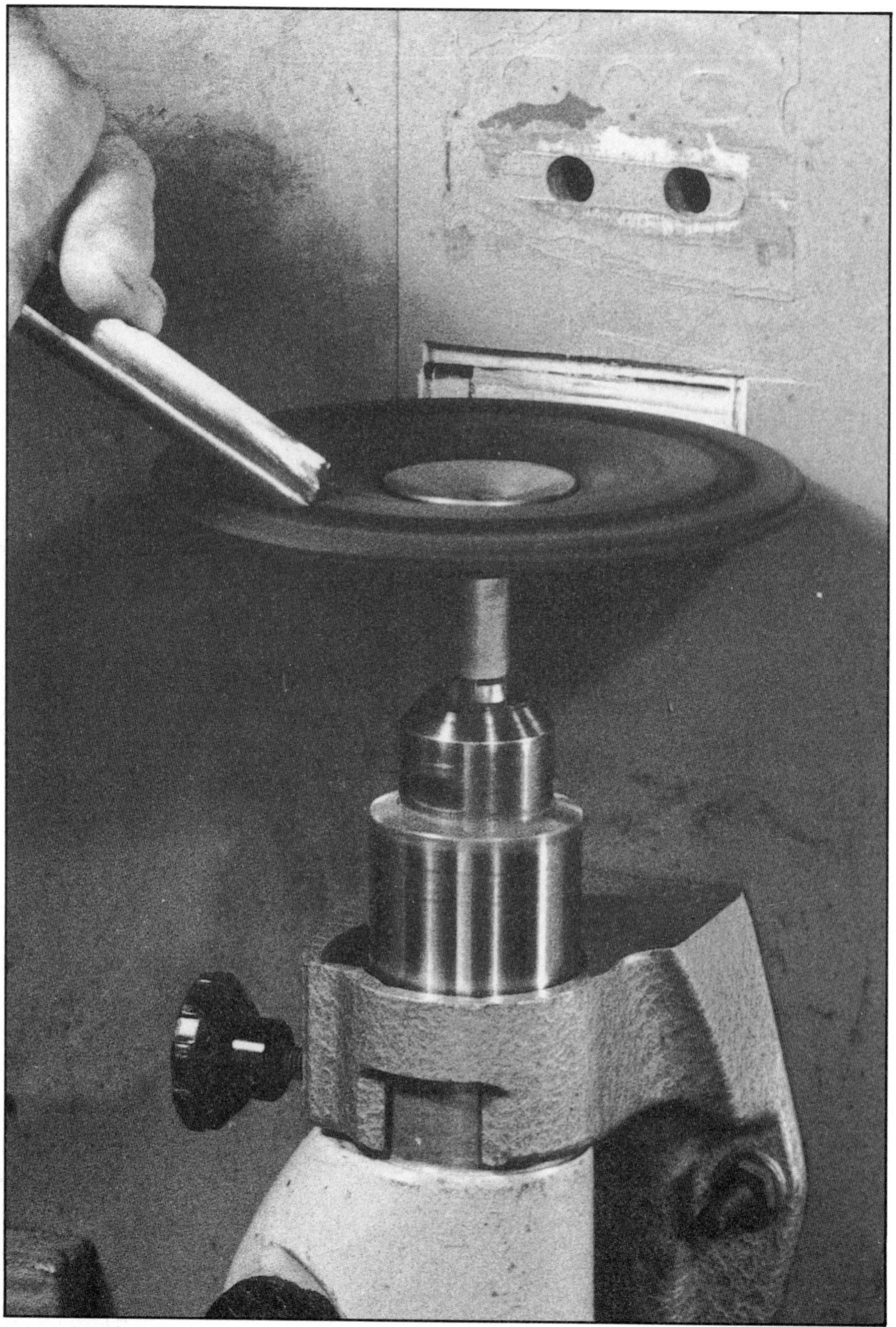
Gouge sharpening using a dressed rubber disc

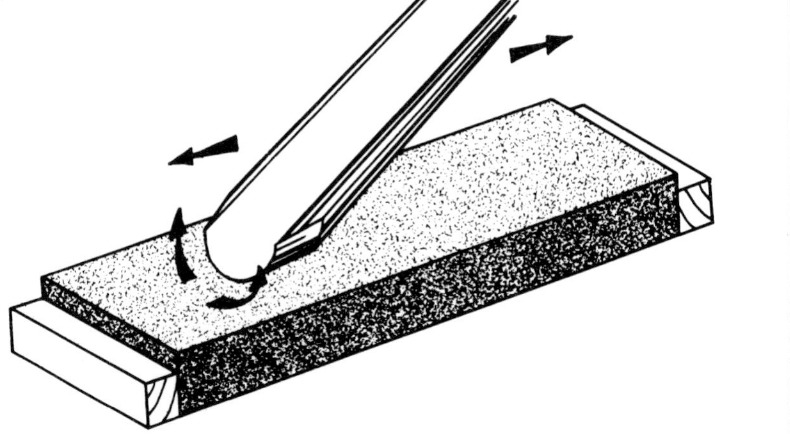
Sharpening the gouge on the oilstone

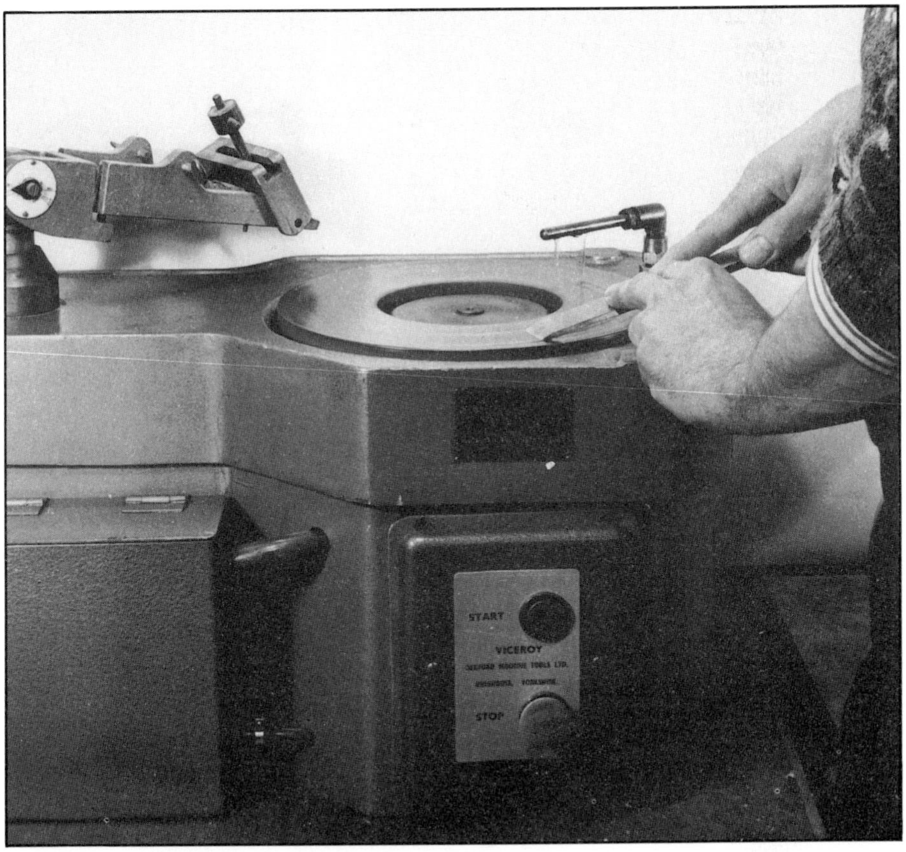

Denford Sharpedge in use – grinding the turning chisel

forward movement of the tool. It will also perfect the curve.

The chisel is sharpened in a similar way moving it forward and backward along the stone. Sharpening on both bevels, the burr set up will automatically be removed.

Grinding, Sharpening and Stropping

This method follows through from the previous two to offer the ultimate in edge and bevel. Stropping can be done, using leather dressed with a polishing compound or rouge. Many people use a piece of rolled leather in the hand. For many years, I used a strop glued to a board and finalised the edge using the board held in the same way as when holding the slipstone. Several machines are available to which a leather belt can be fitted – these are ideal for the purpose but always remember to hold the tool so that the belt is moving away from you. Another alternative is to fit the grinder with a leather wheel. The Craft Supplies Multi-head Linisher could be used to give excellent results.

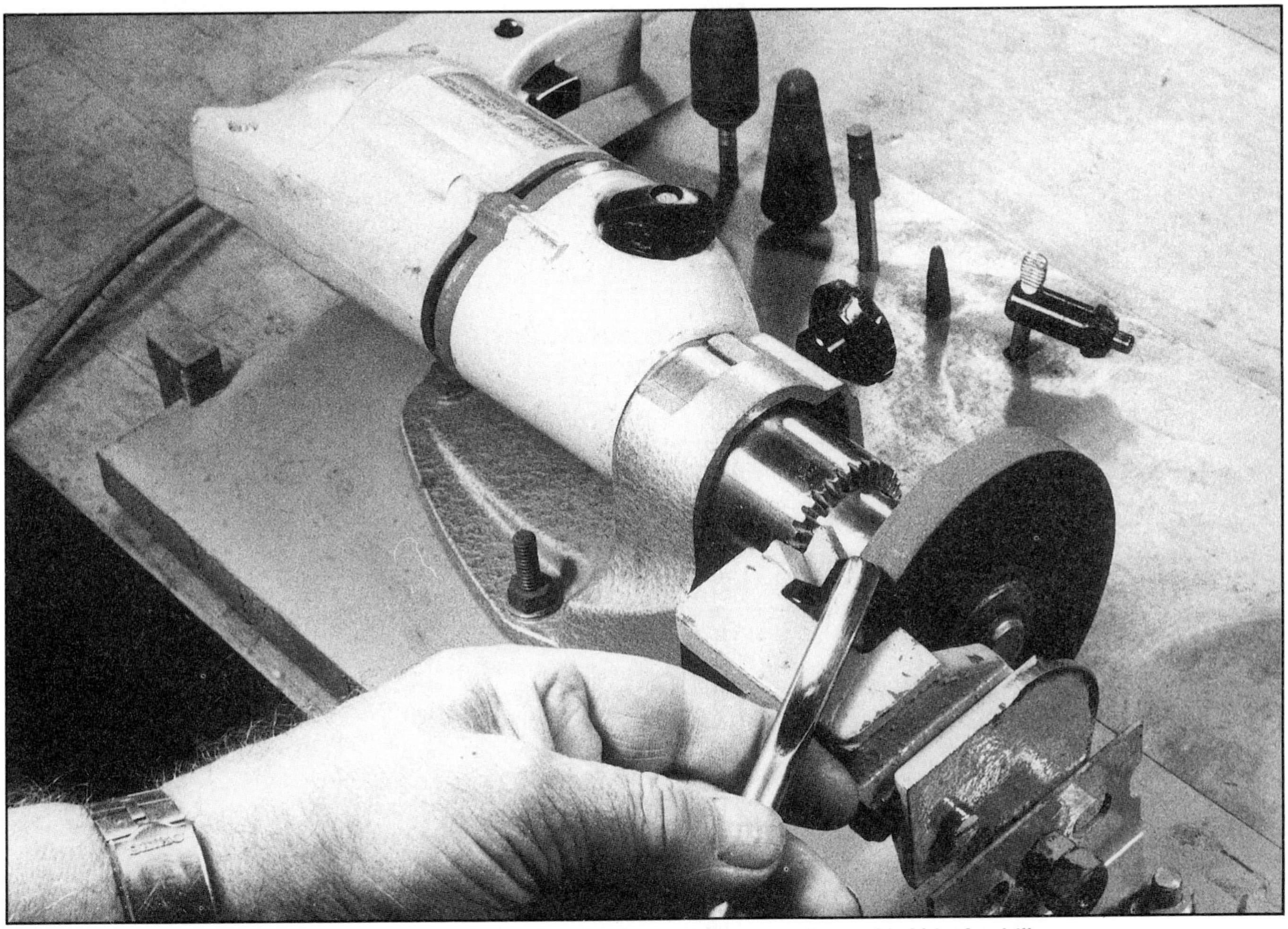
Sharpening the 3/8″ HSS gouge on the rubberised abrasive wheel, mounted on an arbor and held in the drill

Finishing the inside of the ¾″ deep roughing gouge with a rubberised abrasive point mounted in the drill

Grinding with Sharpening and Polishing in one Operation

Grind if necessary then move to the rubberised wheel, mounted in place of a vitrified wheel on the grinder or in the drill.

Ideally, the wheel should move away from the operator. In order to keep a flat bevel, angle the tool across the wheel and at the same time twist the tool so that the whole of the bevel is sharpened around the curve. This action will bring up a hair-line of cutting edge and a polished bevel. Remove the burr in the usual way but keep to rubber and use the rubberised abrasive slip. This will also serve to improve the quality of the flute, which must contribute towards producing the perfect hair-line of cutting edge. This method can be used for all gouges and chisels.

If the drill is being used, use it with the wheel in the horizontal. This is great, particularly when sharpening chisels. To improve the quality of the flute, use a rubberised point set up in the electric drill.

Sharpening, dispensing with the Grinder completely

This method is the result of the introduction of the motorised Japanese waterwheel. This is a fairly slow-moving machine, using water as a coolant. Fitted with 1000 grit stone it cuts quite fast and produces a polished bevel. Usually fitted with a tool rest, it is best used without, particularly with skew chisels and gouges. These excellent cutting properties preclude the use of the grinder at any time.

Final burnishing can be carried out with the rubberised slip stone.

All the high speed steel tools are sharpened in the same way. They are a fraction more difficult to grind but sharpen to a perfect polished finish without difficulty. The edges last much longer and are not greatly affected by frictional heat.

Scraping Chisels (Woodturners' Scrapers)

After buying your scrapers, make an exact copy of the profile of each tool, using either strong card or thin aluminium sheet. Check the angle of grind and make a note of it on the template. Refer to the drawing and make a template exactly to fit. (The drawing has been printed full size.) This will be used to set the rest before grinding. If your grinder isn't 6″, scale down to suit. To set the rest: slacken off the wing nut, hold the setting template against the circumference of the wheel and line up the rest, then tighten down securely on the holding nut. Being sure of correct setting every time will take the guesswork out of grinding, saving metal and time. It will also ensure the continuance of a perfect angle along the whole length of the cutting edge.

The traditional scrapers are made from carbon steel. Many have been made from old files which have the wrong steel and heat treatment. (If this material is used, it should be rehardened and tempered.) The modern scraper is a tool tipped with high speed steel. This can be sharpened in the same way and will hold its edge longer.

There are at least three different types of scraper edges:

1. Straight from the grindstone.
2. From the grindstone, to the sharpening stone with no hook.
3. Grinding, sharpening and ticketing to produce a burr.

Used straight from the grindstone, the scraper will cut, but the edge looks rather like a broken-down saw. It can be used for roughing out but will quickly break down. In any case, this tool completely misinterprets the intended use – scraping tools should be finishing tools.

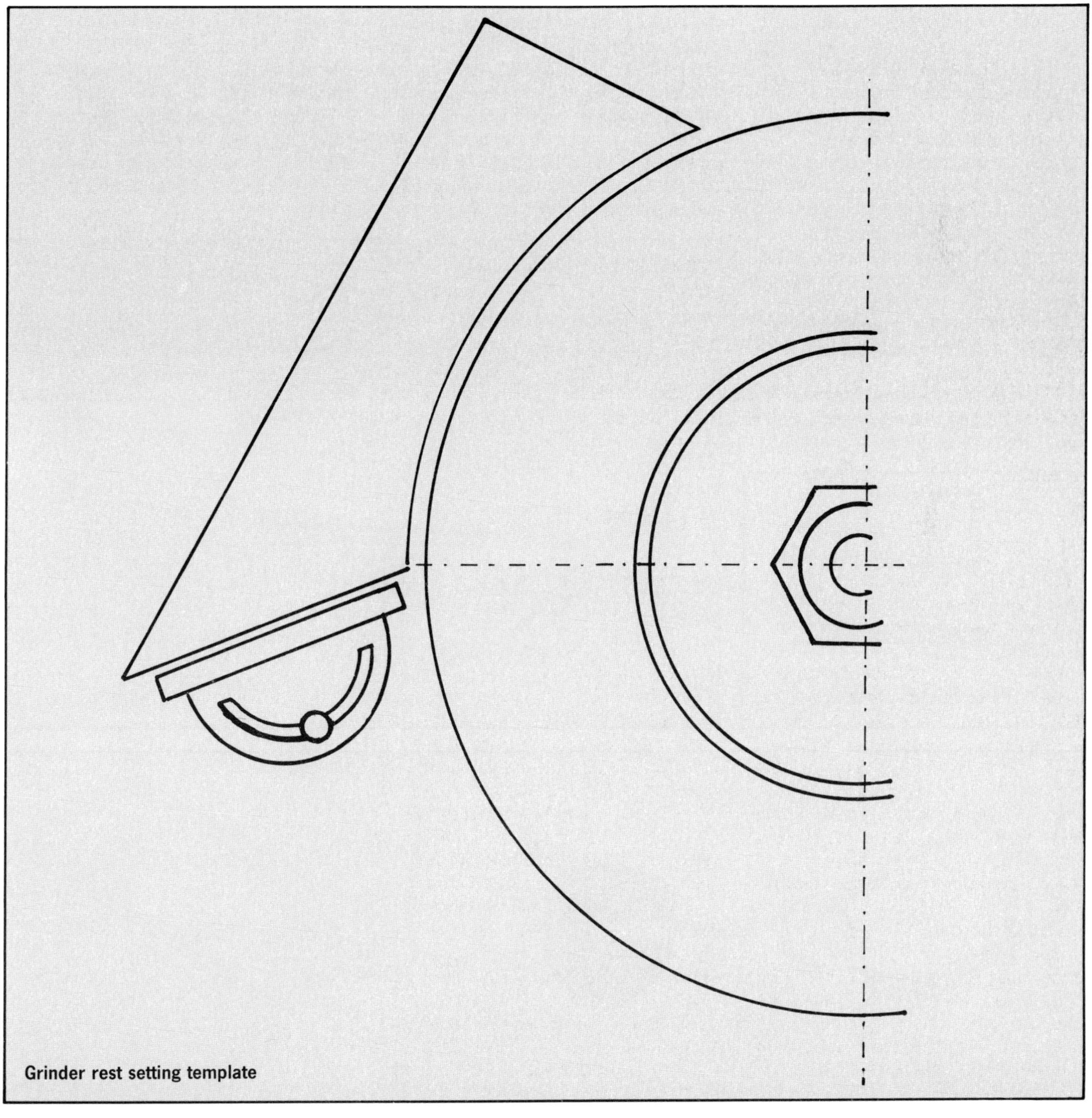

Grinder rest setting template

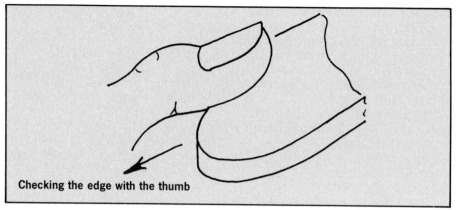

Checking the edge with the thumb

The second use is where first the scraper is ground to shape and angle on the grinder then moved to the bench sharpening stone. Lay the flat side of the tool, i.e. bevel uppermost, on the stone and bring this face perfectly flat and free from flats. Now with an oilstone in the right hand, hold the scraper in the left hand and carefully stone the bevel keeping it flat and angling it slightly to offer more stone to the bevel. When both faces have been brought together in a perfect edge, with a slight burr set up by the action of the stone, you will have a perfect cutting tool.

This edge will cut perfectly, but it must be held flat on the tool rest, NOT angled in any way.

The more common method is to first grind and shape to correct angle and form. Remove all traces of previous burrs by rubbing the flat side on an oilstone. Check this condition with the finger or thumb, drawing it lightly over the edge. Take a burnisher or ticketer; these can be bought, but any good hard steel will do. Mine is made from an old 4″ triangular file, with the teeth ground off and the edges rolled and polished.

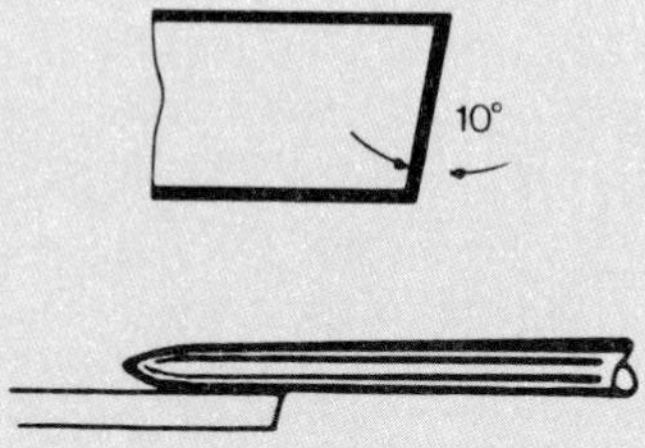

Keep the ticketer flat on the chisel

Rest the scraper on the bench (bevel down), hold the ticketer flat on the scraper face at right angles to the edge and move it backwards and forwards along the edge some 30 times. This is called consolidating the edge. Now place the scraper vertically in a vice. Place the ticketer flat along the bevel and draw it strongly along the edge with firm pressure. This will push up a burr which, if the flat face was flat and its edge properly consolidated, will give a perfect hairline of hooked steel which will cut perfect shavings. Here the tool is 'trailed' in use, i.e. the handle is slightly higher than the cutting edge when the tool is positioned on the tool rest. This, of course, is the action of the bench or cabinet scraper. It will serve as a finishing tool for the hardest timbers.

The wheel will need to be 80 grit, scraper bevel angle 80°.

ALWAYS keep the burnisher lightly oiled to retain its high polish and to prevent rusting.

Scraper blades require frequent sharpening, but they rarely become damaged. Nevertheless, be careful not to strike the edge against metallic objects.

Consolidating the edge

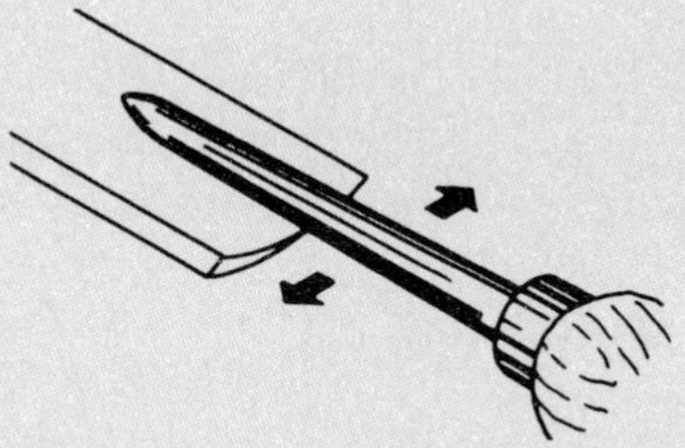

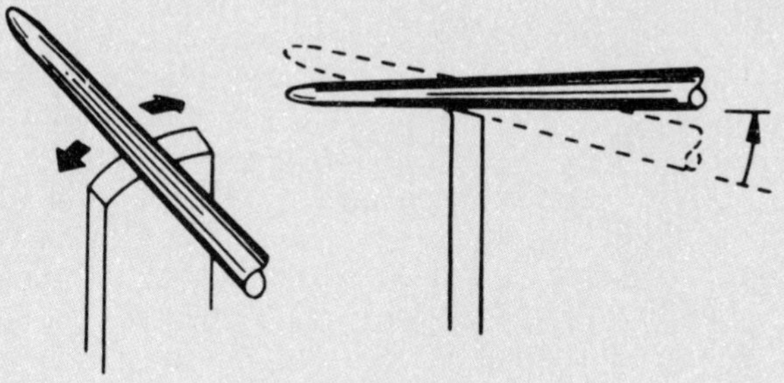

Ticketing the hook

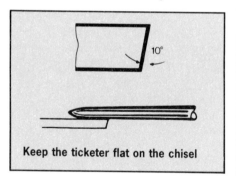

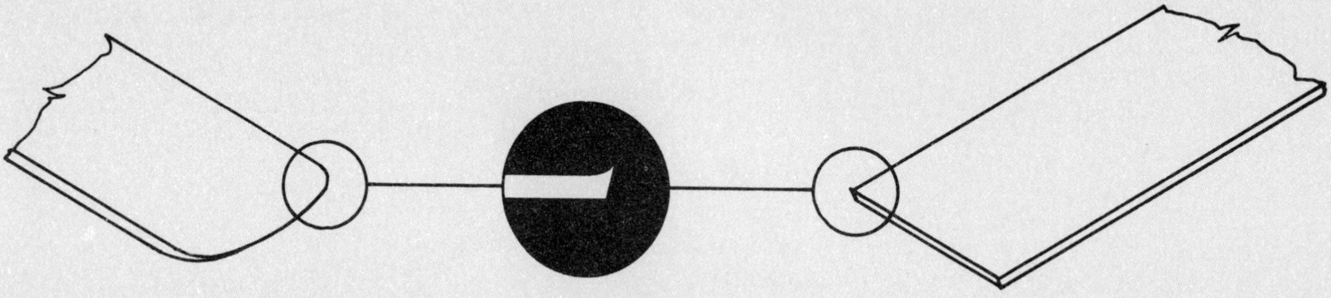

Finished woodturning scrapers

Diamond Slurry Sharpening

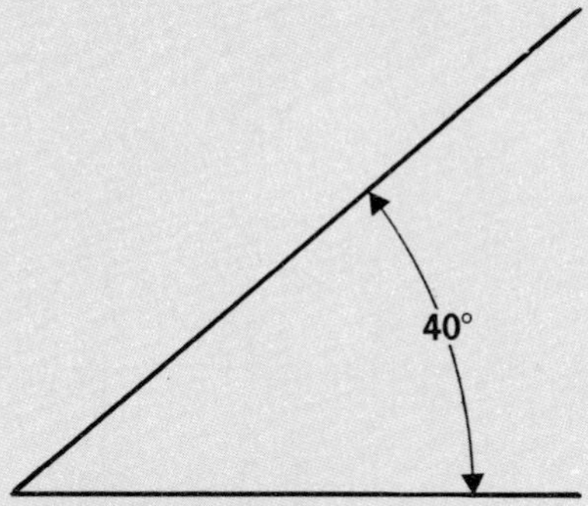

Gouge grinding angle

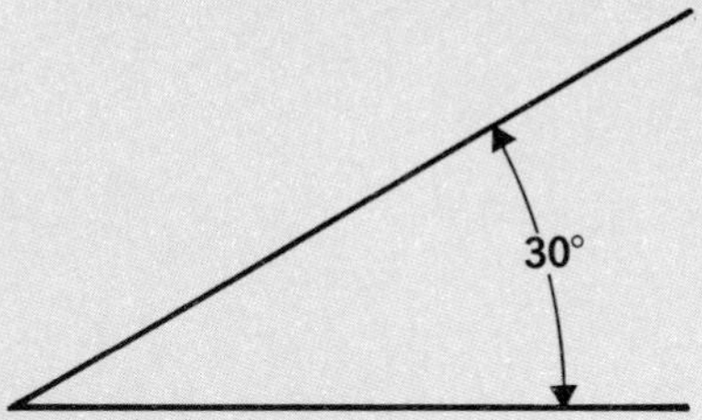

Chisel grinding angle

Diamond Slurry Sharpening

A completely new method of sharpening has recently appeared. This consists of a diamond slurry contained in a pressurised can which is sprayed over a plastic tile attached to a board for rigidity. The tile is specially formulated and repeated loadings of the slurry only serve to lengthen its life and maintain its efficiency. The tile is never wiped clean. Three grades of slurry are offered:

Medium	Coded Red	45 Micron
Fine	Coded Blue	14 Micron
Extra Fine	Coded White	6 Micron

The makers suggest that all the tools now in the hands of the woodworker can be sharpened using the slurry including TCT tools.

Sharpening is exactly as with the traditional oilstone and the results are splendid.

A note of advice

Many people find some difficulty in holding the tools at the correct angle for grinding and sharpening. Unfortunately, as tools are of varied shape and ground angle, it is impossible for any manufacturer to design a rest which will be universal. By far the best method is to practice holding with wooden mock-ups until the control of the angle is mastered – I know this sounds wearisome, but better to do it this way than ruin good tools. Perfection comes with practice and experience over a period of time and there isn't a quick and ready answer.

Holding Equipment for Boring

Holding Equipment for Boring

When boring pieces using the drill press, great care must be taken to hold them securely. Obviously the work should remain undamaged and holes bored accurately, but essentially with such small pieces the hands need to be protected, keeping them well away from the spinning boring tool.

Just a short time spent in making one or two fittings will pay dividends. A wooden vice can be made with VEE cuts in the wooden jaws to position and safely hold round and square stock, with a pair of folding wedges used to secure the job.

This wooden vice can also be held in the drill press vice if a small batten is screwed underneath.

The metal drill press vice can be used, but it needs to be fitted with soft jaws. Hard felt jaws can be bought with a magnetic strip to hold them in place.

Alternatively timber can be used, but if the strips are too thick then the vice capacity will be reduced. The vice shown in the illustration has a removable rear jaw, which in this case has been replaced with a wooden one.

For really small pieces a little hand vice can be used, again using folding wedges.

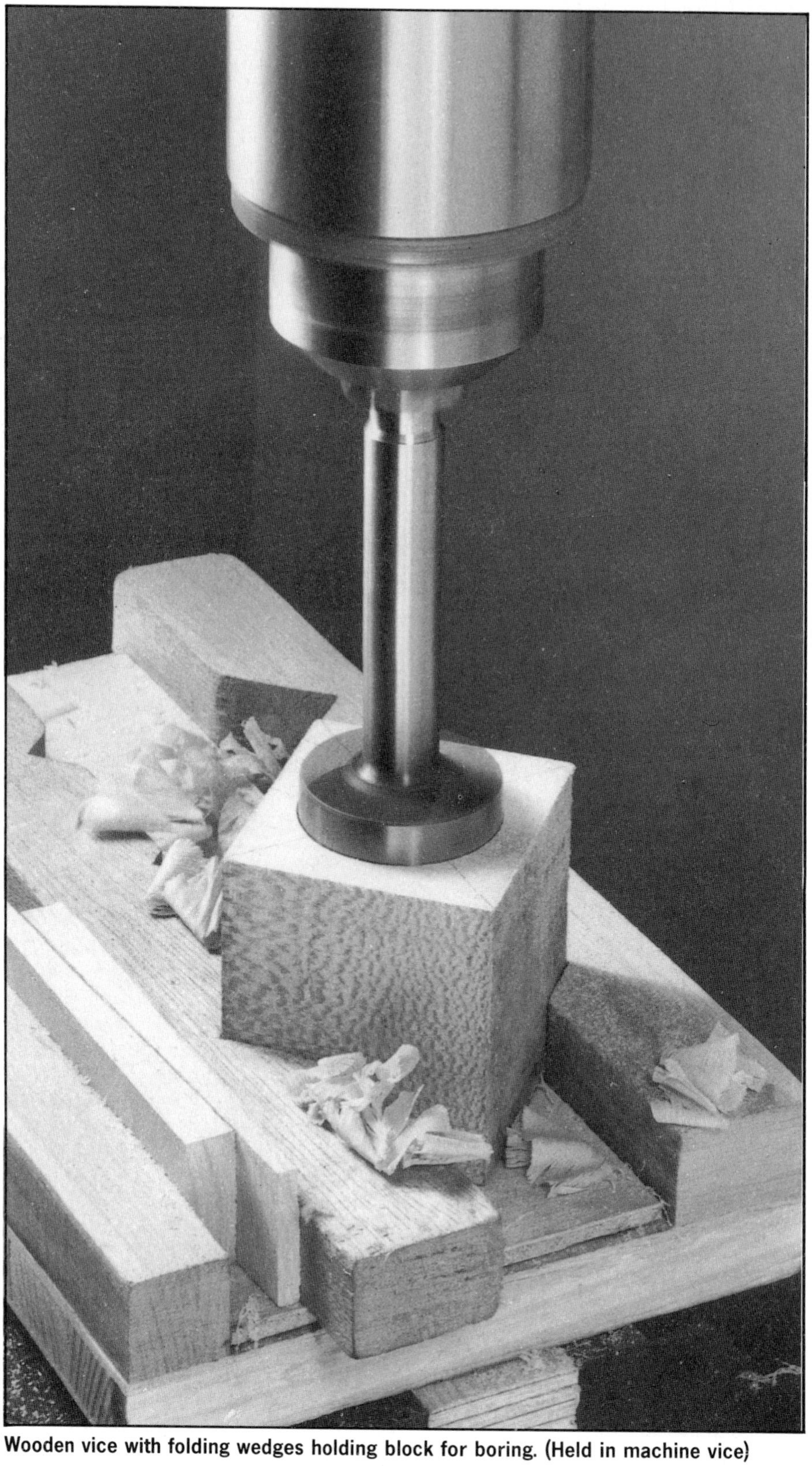

Wooden vice with folding wedges holding block for boring. (Held in machine vice)

Boring a block which is held in the machine vice. The sliding jaw has been removed and a wooden block substituted to give added space

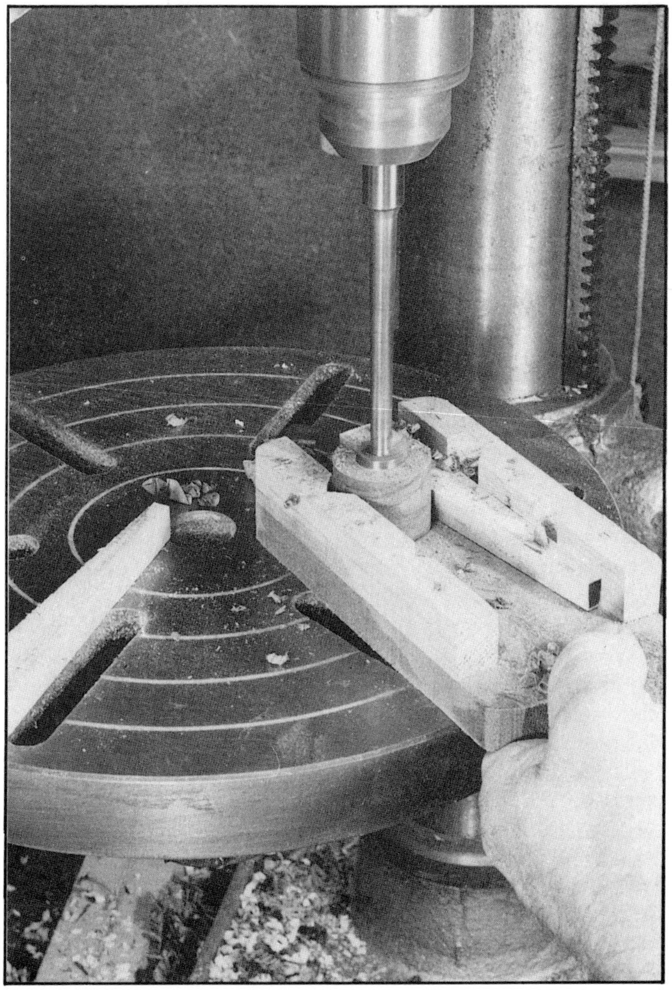

Wooden hand vice with folding wedges in use

Hand vice used when drilling small work

Timbers I Have Met

Miniature turning presents the opportunity to use up all those tiny pieces of exotics which one has had for years and refused to throw away. This also enables one to look at all sorts of pieces which one could not use in any other way. Here I refer to roots, knots, pieces from old furniture, butts of small garden shrubs and such like.

Work such as this will still need sound timber. For work between centres be sure to use timber which is long and straight, for short-grained timber will often be found to be accident prone. Small boxes and bowls, since they are to be brought to very thin section, will also need timber selected with care.

Most timbers can be used, but close grained ones will be best, bearing in mind the need to obtain finely-finished work straight from the tools. Excessive use of abrasives will result in lost detail and waste a great deal of real working time.

Make a collection of veneers, stringing and banding and also other materials which could be used for inlaying and contrast. Should any interesting pieces of plywood or blockboard come to hand, save them for experimenting.

Information about timber can be found in a number of reference books which are noted in the appendix.

However, much of the information given in a book on timbers is not of great interest to the craftsman working at home. He is much more interested in how the timber cuts and behaves, what colour it is, whether the colour is stable and the suitability of specific timbers for making a particular article. Much of this information can only be provided by someone who has worked and assessed many timbers. The notes which follow are an an attempt to share the writer's experience of different timbers. The majority are exotic timbers, for most users will be aware of the qualities of the well-known timbers in both the UK and USA.

The Most White

I used to think that the whitest timber was Holly, particularly if grown in the country. It's a lovely timber to turn and with sharp tools it will take some beating.

Yet, in 'the whitest' context there is a better one. It's Persian Ironwood, *Parrotia Persica,* which grows in the area from North Persia to the Caucasus. It is very close grain, slightly sticky when wet, and when in this state doesn't take kindly to glue. On the lathe the piece I had, from a home-grown tree, turned like a dream, required no abrasive and took kindly to sanding sealer and friction polish. Its grain isn't marked, but its cutting quality and its resemblance to ivory makes it my choice.

The Most Unusual Grain

This has to be Snakewood, *Piratinera guianensis,* which grows in Guyana and has been called Leopard Wood and Tortoiseshell. It has a grain which strongly resembles the skin of the snake and is deep mahogany red with dark markings. It comes only in small sizes and it's heavier than *Lignum vitae.* The tree itself has a very wide band of yellow sapwood, this being removed at conversion.

It isn't all that easy to cut and does split. Yet, it is a fun wood and fine for miniature turning. It comes to a good finish without too much work after the cutting tools and it certainly takes a high polish. I also understand that Hooboobali *(Surinam Snakewood)* is similar in grain, but somewhat more yellow in colour.

The Most Black

Most folk think of Ebony as the most black, yet there are many variations with streaks of brown and fawn and red. I really feel that there are a number of timbers which are blacker and the best of these is East African Blackwood, *Dalbergia Melanoxylon.* There are many others called blackwood which could not be classed under this heading. Scottish pipes were made of Cocuswood which took very fine detail, but with the disappearance of this timber, blackwood is now used.

A small mishapen tree, we thus generally find it in small billets. If it arrives in the wet state, dry it with care for otherwise it tends to split badly. Tough on the cutting tools, it nevertheless gives a smooth, slightly oily finish.

Eggcup in Mexican Rosewood

Another Black

There is another black, dyed by nature and unusual. I refer to Bog Oak, which is oak buried many years under the soil.

It comes up in the Fenland area around the Wash and sometimes good logs come out of the sea near Grimsby in Lincolnshire. It is really grey/black and its cutting qualities are quite different from the Oaks. It cuts like a soft Box giving fine shavings and a marvellous finish. I still have some from a log I found some 30 years ago.

The Most Startling Grain Variation

The accolade here must go to Mexican Rosewood, often called Grande Palisander *(Dalbergia Nigra.)* A really beautiful timber, rich brown with lighter stripes and black, the grain changes in such a startling way that one must wonder just what happens to the tree during its growth which gives it this strange change.

It polishes well, cuts without great difficulty, but at the same time it is hard. If, for the rest of my time I could only have one timber to turn, I think I should choose this one.

The Most Attractive Colouring

Tulipwood, *Dalbergia fruitescens variety tomentosa,* comes from Brazil. A small mishapen tree, it is rarely bigger in diameter than 20cms and produces a most attractive timber with stripes of yellow and rose red. These colours are best seen when the timber is first cut and unless a good finish is applied, it soon fades.

Its grain is long and straight, it turns well and takes most finishes. It is a favourite amongst the bobbin makers. Care in drying is essential since it can split badly, but it cuts and takes a good polish and has a very pleasant smell. Like most exotics, it's a little expensive.

The Most Attractive Timber After Long Exposure

Laburnum Vulgare. This is the golden chain tree, popular in our gardens. The timber isn't available commercially but it grows plentifully in the hedgerows of West Wales. It has a colour which varies from golden brown to dark green. In Scotland, this tree seems to yield a greener timber.

Small sizes culled from the garden are ideal for miniature work. It is a little more difficult to work than some of our native garden trees, but has a lovely variation of grain form. After turning and finishing, it's a golden brown, but unlike many timbers which tend to fade and lose their attractive colour, Laburnum does the opposite, becoming a deep rich brown and very attractive.

The Most Accurately Named Timber

Osage Orange, *Maclura Orantiaca.* This timber is very accurately named for it is orange in colour. Although this darkens on exposure, it is most striking. A tough old wood which turns well, it is very strong. I've not been able to turn large pieces but it seems easy to arrive at a finish and polishes well. It is common in the USA.

The Most Inaccurately Named

Partridge Wood, *Caesalpina grenadillo.* We dwellers in this sceptred isle know this wood bears no resemblance to the partridge. This timber grows in Central America and is sometimes known as Coffee Wood.

I first used it after being given split pieces which were piled for the making of truncheons for the South African Police. It is one timber which polishes directly from the tool. Deep brown in colour, it is extremely hard and heavy and I wouldn't want to be struck over the head with it.

Picture frame in Boxwood

The Most Pure Yellow

Years back the yellow timber which came most easily to mind would have been Boxwood, *Buxus Sempervirens.* This wood, popular for chisel handles and other tools, was largely found in Europe and Asia. It has become increasingly difficult to find in quantity and in good condition and consequently substitutes have been sought.

One of these is Pau Marfin. It grows in Southern Brazil, Paraguay, Uruguay and Northern Argentina. It grows to good size with a clean bole and has been found particularly good for rule making. Pure yellow in colour with no knots, it cuts beautifully, is pretty tough and takes a super polish.

The Brightest Mixture of Colour

I once had a small plank of Cocobolo, some 2″thick, which was given me in Edmonton in Alberta. I carried it home with great care and it eventually found its way to the lathe. It gets its name, *Dalbergia,* from a Swedish physician N. Dalberg. It grows on the Pacific side of Central America and isn't marketed in large sizes. It has many bright red hues which tend to darken on exposure.

Turning revealed an oily secretion which seemed to assist in polishing the wood from the tool. Indeed in some cases additional polishes could be avoided. Its colour seems to be quite stable. A word of warning – the dust can be poisonous and a peculiar orange stain sometimes appears on the skin.

The Most Pink

This has to be Pink Ivory, *Rhamus zeyheri,* which grows in South Africa (Zululand). This is really a most unusual timber and I found it to be extremely hard and the grain quite coarse. After some care, however, it polished well. Although the grain is not particularly marked, it is still a most attractive timber. It is quite difficult to obtain and comes only in small sizes.

The Timber That Looks Like Something Else

Olive Ash, *Fraxinus Excelsior,* really does look like Olivewood and could be substituted for it. The variegated brown heart is much sought, although at one time it was used up with the rest by the wheelright and the wooden vehicle maker. One tool maker in the UK uses it exclusively for turning tools. It cuts beautifully, giving a fine surface, and takes polishes well.

The Most Confused Name

Padauk, *Pterocarpus dalbergioides,* grows in an area from Africa to the Andaman Islands in the Bay of Bengal. The tree is very large; it is often found growing to a height of 60′ and to a circumference of 15′. In many parts it is incorrectly called Rosewood. A very good friend of mine has a Rosewood Dining Room suite made in Hong Kong – of beautiful craftsmanship – but the timber is padauk, which has bright purple colours which darken on exposure, sometimes to a reddish brown.

The Andaman seems a little more red and has little tendency to turn brown. It turns well and polishes without any problems.

The Last Letter in the Alphabet

Ziricote, *Cordia dodecandra,* grows in Central America and the West Indies. In colour, it is a rather flat brown with almost black streaks. The grain is fairly close and the wood turns without problems giving a smooth flawless surface which polishes finely. It can be found in fine cabinet work and has always been sought by the experienced woodturner.

Finally a Tree Which Shouldn't Produce Timber At All

Turu. *(Jessenia Bataua.)* This is a Palm and is therefore an indogen – all the trees which supply our timber are exogens. The end grain looks like bundles of wiry sticks lying closely together. It's black in colour and only obtainable in thinner planks, most of which will be shaped on one side as the tree itself. It turns, polishes *and* looks unlike any of the others, but it's an exciting wood to turn. So get some and have fun!

Disc of Turu

Other Materials

Small coins, cabochons, stones, slate, panels of dried flowers and such like material can be pressed into use particularly in box lids and bowl centres.
Discs of glass and silver.
Ivory pieces.
Bone.

Adhesives

Normal straightforward gluing will need the use of a PVA glue, or glues like Aerolite and Cascamite can be used.

Where glass, metal and other materials are to be attached, an epoxy resin glue like Araldite will be needed. Choose a fast setting one – those generally termed rapid will set in ten to fifteen minutes in normal temperatures. This type of glue when mixed with fine wood dust or sawdust will make an excellent filler for small identations and other flaws. Glue for the hot melt glue gun is essential. Sticks up to 300mm in length are available.

Finishing Materials

Abrasive paper comes in many trade names and in a wide variety of grit sizes. My favourite in recent years has been Lubrisil. This has silicon carbide grit and I have 80, 100, 150, 220 and 320 in use in the workshop.

Wet and dry paper is most useful but the standard glasspaper or garnet will serve.

Polishing Materials

Most work will need the addition of sanding sealer before final polishing. This will close up the timber and prevent the ingress of dirt, grease and oil. Always cut back with a fine grade of steel wool.

One of the standard finishes for miniature work will be wax. There are a number of proprietary waxes, the best of which in my experience is Briwax, but the reader may care to experiment. For many years I used a mixture of 90 per cent beeswax, 10 per cent carnauba wax, melted with a small drop of turpentine in a double heater. The carnauba hardens the beeswax and such a wax will be found excellent for most applications.

A number of friction polishes can be used. Speedaneez is well known and gives a high quality shine.

The old standby linseed oil will add lustre to the timber, but takes a little time to dry as also do Tung and Danish Oil. The latter has now become a very firm favourite with me.

The reader is advised to try a number of finishes, but at the same time take note of the intended use of the article and decide whether the finish will be suitable.

Finishing materials, such as cloths for applying the polish, must be chosen with care. They should be lint free and fairly soft, otherwise the latter may score the work. Burnishing is best done with hessian. Hessian does not mark the work and is hard enough to burnish the timber whilst removing surplus polish. Rolls of cotton cloth will be found generally useful.

Cutting back wet polishes is best done with steel wool in a fine grade such as 0000. If wet and dry paper is used, it is best applied with a smear of wax.

SAFETY NOTE
Cloths saturated with oils present a fire hazard and should always be disposed of outside the workshop.

Holding Methods Illustrated

There are numerous ways of holding small pieces of work on the lathe. Some are old and well tried, others make use of existing equipment designed for the holding of larger work.

Perhaps the most useful method of holding which I have used on both small and large pieces is the glue chuck. This consists of a suitable piece of soft hardwood, faced with the plane and attached to a faceplate or the screw chuck. If already round, it may well fit one or other of the combination type chucks. A thin film of hot melt glue is spread over the face of the wood and the piece to be turned is pressed into contact with the aid of the vice. Alternatively the job can be done on the lathe and the tailstock brought up to squeeze up the joint. This chuck, if undamaged during turning, can be used again and again. The glue can either be remelted using the gun, electric paint stripper or similar device. Do note that speed is of the essence in this work.

Another method is to use double sided tape. This should be of the thinner film type and pressure is also needed. My old friend, teacher and turner Russ Zimmerman of Putney in Vermont, uses this method for large pieces and has no problems.

To remove the finished work a thin knife is needed. This is placed at the joint and tapped with a hammer. Almost invariably the two pieces will part, leaving the glue still in place on the chuck. It is unwise to place glue on both pieces.

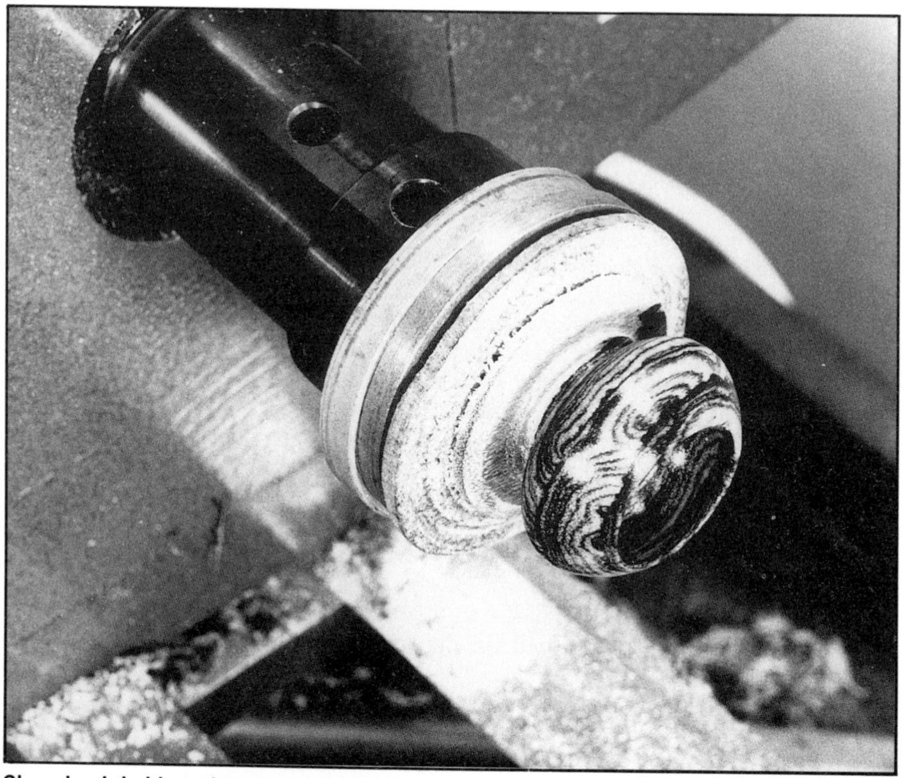

Glue chuck held on the screw chuck

Glue Chuck held on a Screw Chuck

The photographs show a small piece of *Grande Palisander* attached to a well-used glue chuck. The job is completely turned with a gouge, polished and removed with a knife.

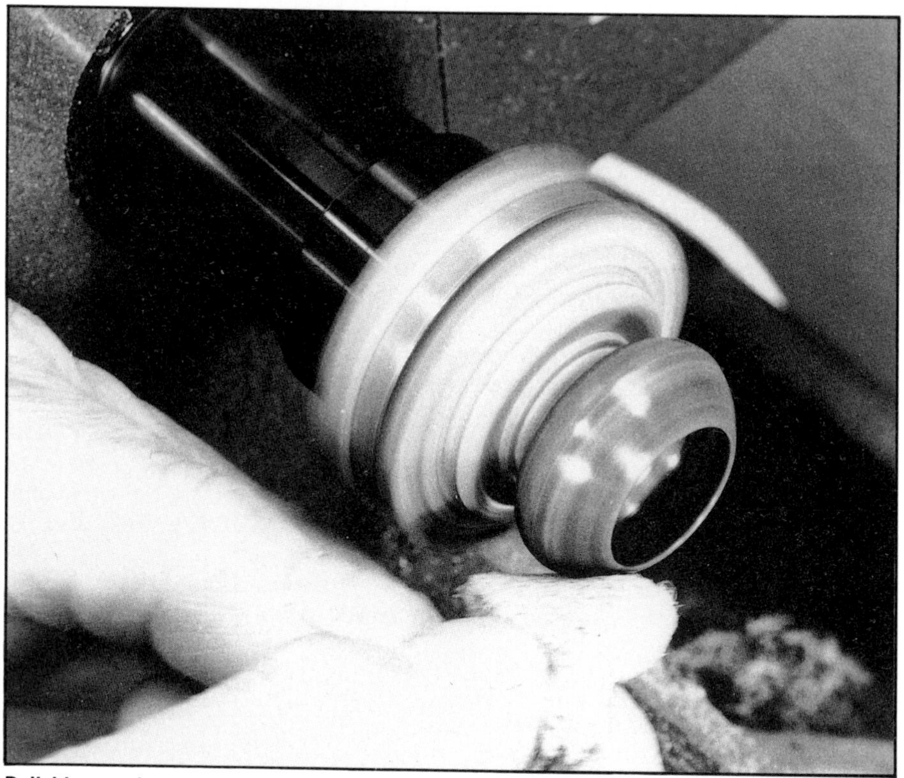

Polishing work attached to the glue chuck

Morse taper glue chuck

Glue Chuck Made with a Morse Taper

I used Boxwood in the case illustrated and turned on it a No. 1 morse taper to suit the Tyme Cub Lathe. The face of the piece was cut flat. A thin film of glue was smeared across the face and pressure applied with the tailstock centre to secure the working blank. Small chucks like this one also give access to the rear of the work, if sufficient length is given to the projection forward of the lathe mandrel nose.

The illustration shown is of a small plate made in Tulipwood which was cut from a piece of scrap using a plug cutter. The HSS ⅛″ gouge was used throughout.

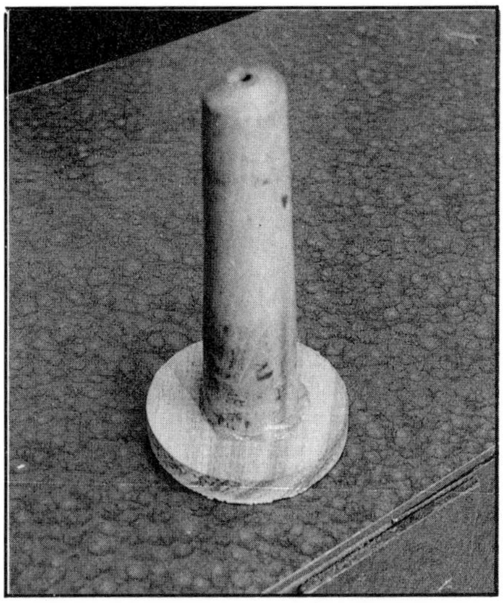
Taper removed to show the assembly

Pressure applied using the tailstock centre to secure the working blank

Plate shaped with the gouge

Turning down to size with the ⅛″ gouge

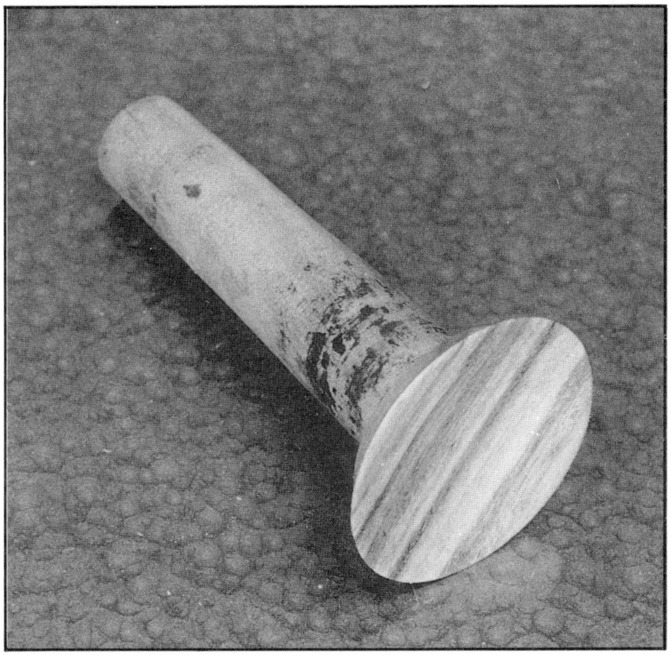
Completed plate attached to unit

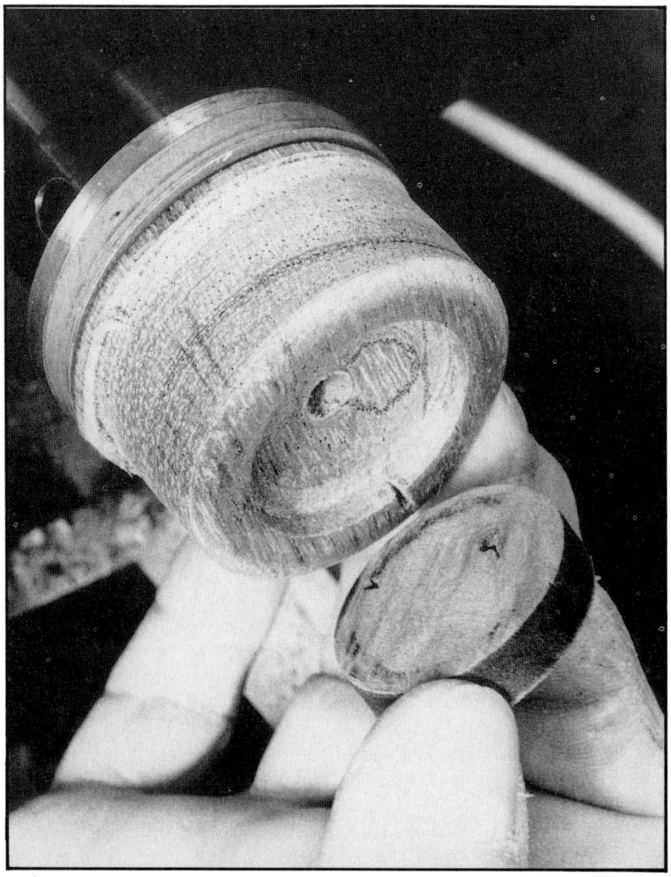
The work (a plate) is held in a wood chuck screwed to a screw chuck

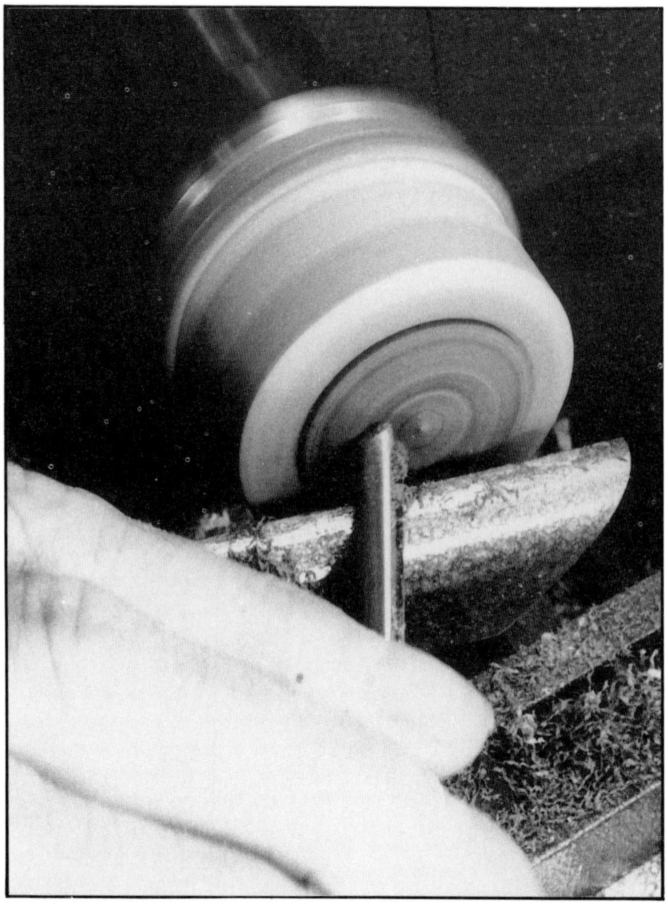
Using the ¼″ gouge to shape the underside of the plate

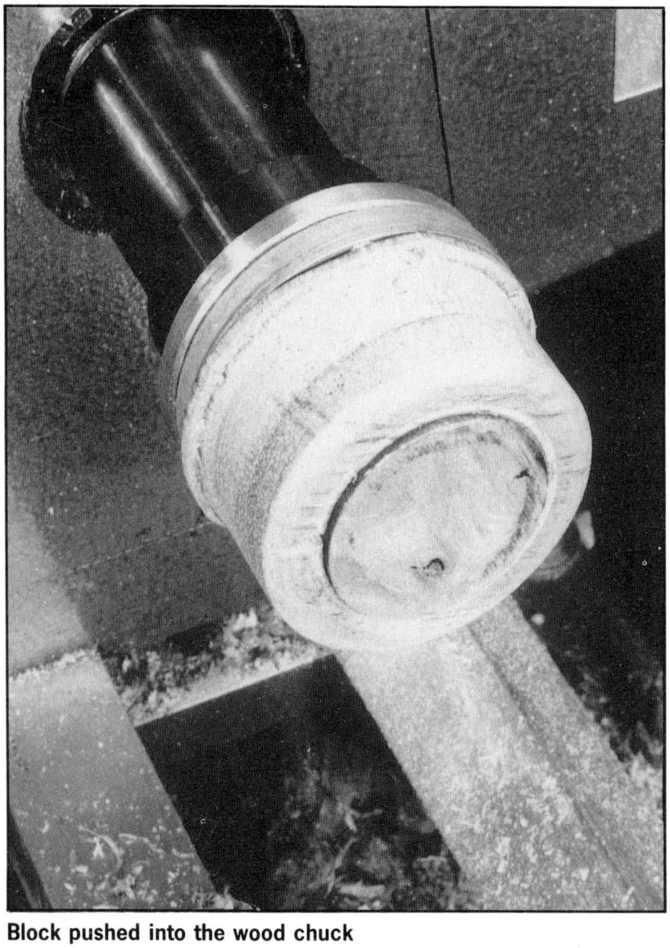
Block pushed into the wood chuck

Carefully removing the plate after completing the underside

Wood Chucks

One of the oldest methods of holding, used way back by some of the old woodturners, was the wood chuck. This was simply a piece of timber attached to the lathe using a face plate. Into the face a recess was cut to receive the workpiece. Often the job would be turned on the underside and finished to the polished state, then reversed for completion.

With small work, cutting small pieces using the plug cutter will save time spent on preparation.

Wood Chuck held on a Screw Chuck

The chuck block is screwed to the chuck and if the hole bored for the screw is brought right through the block, this will assist in removal of the work from the rear should an overtight fit of the finished job present a problem. In cutting the recess, it will be helpful if this is cut with a small taper to assist the fit. If a hole cannot be bored completely through, a tiny slot can be cut at the side so that a small tool can be inserted to act as a lever.

Shaping the plate to finish

The completed job

Wood Chuck on a Morse Taper
This was made once again in Boxwood. A number one morse taper was also cut and the chuck end was slightly tapered to an exact diameter of 1¼″. This can be used as a mandrel to hold pre-bored material for other jobs. Remember to give the recess a small taper to assist the fit.

Small wood chuck on a morse taper

Plate removed for turning round and re-inserting

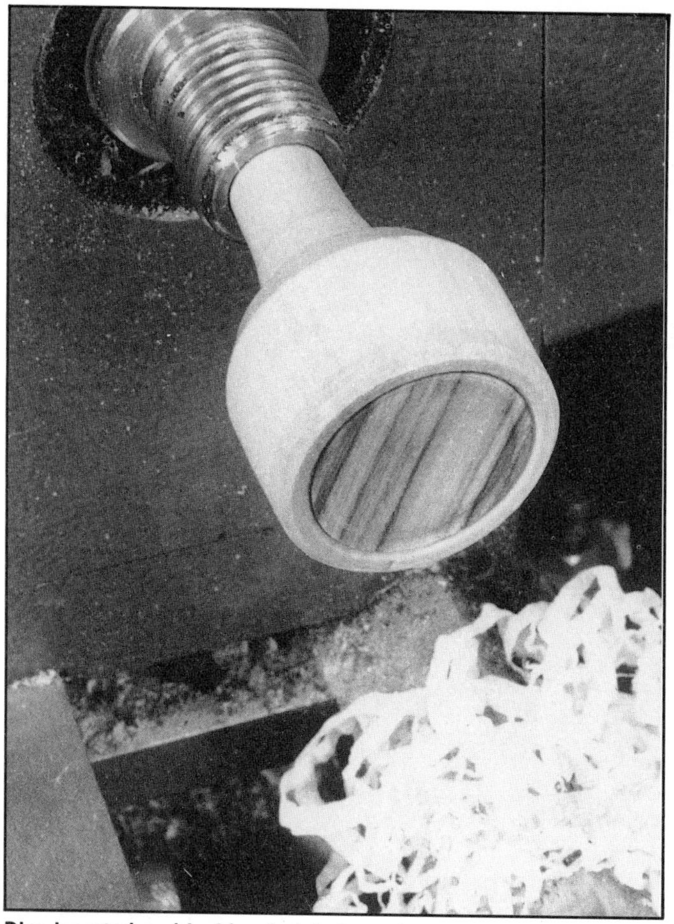

Disc inserted and inside of plate turned

Underside turned

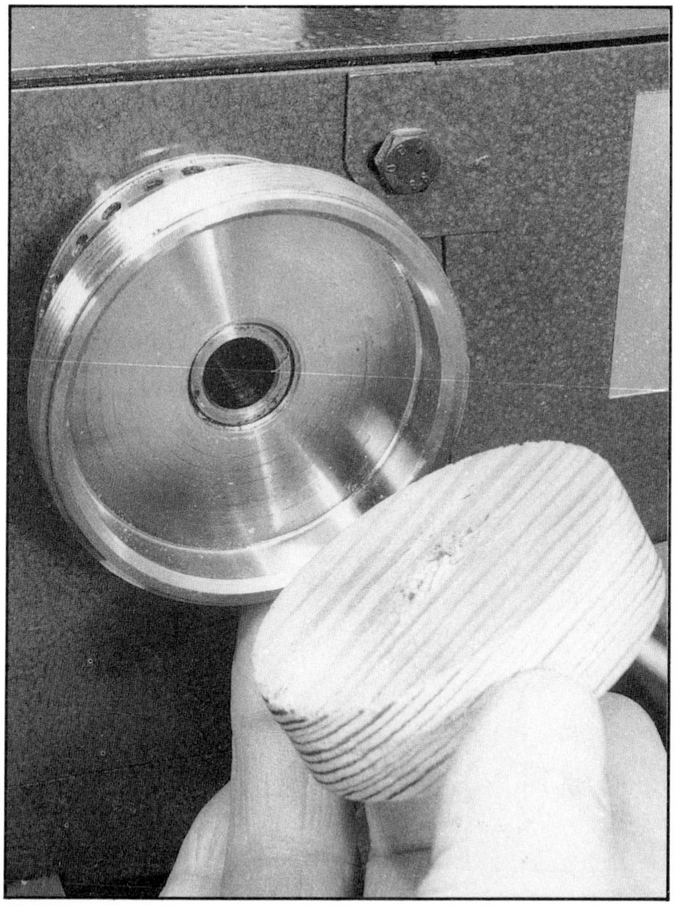

Multistar chuck body used to hold a wood chuck

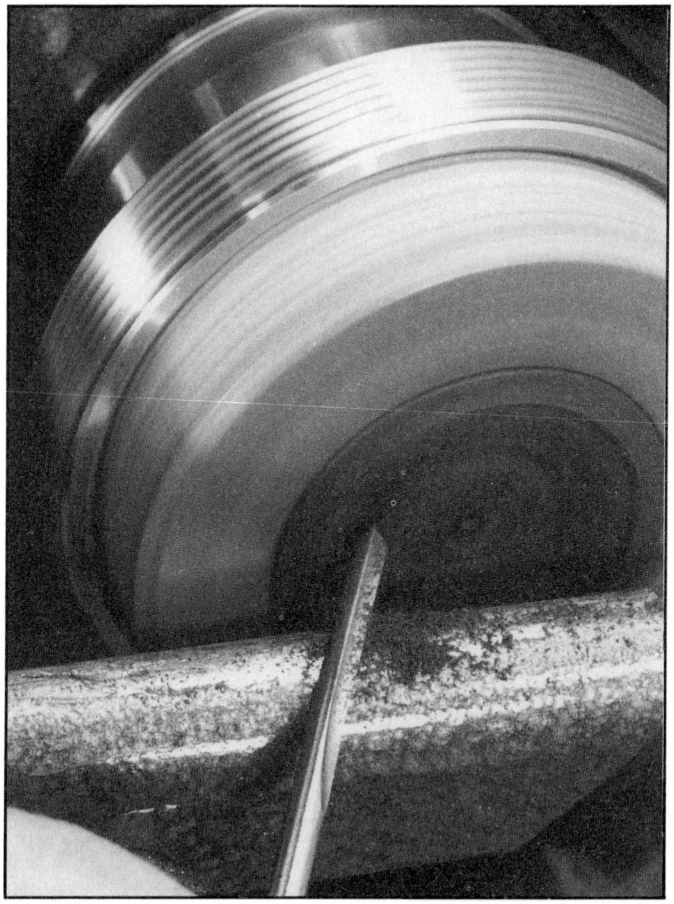

Using the gouge

Wood Chuck held in the Body of the Multistar Chuck

A disc of good hardwood is selected and turned to size to fit the chuck, either holding on the glue or screw chuck. The disc is then placed in the jaws and recessed as before. This insert can be used time and time again. Should the face be cut about, it can always be trimmed or cut to receive a different size of job.

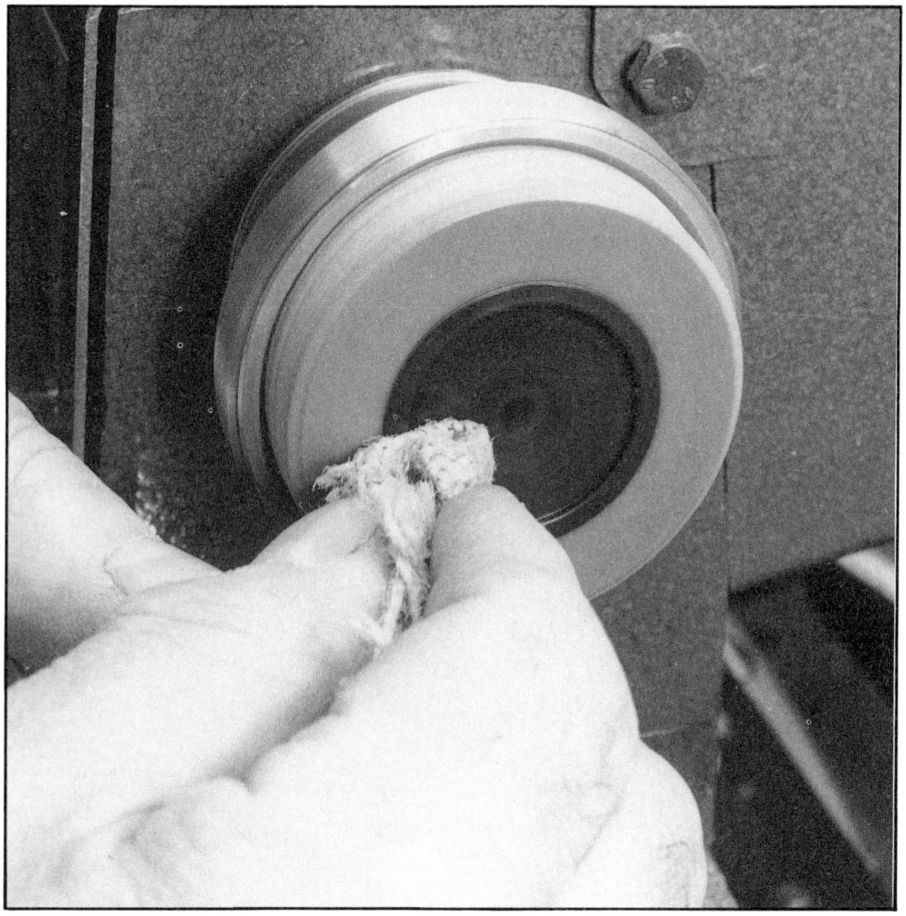

Polishing the plate

Wood chuck held in spigot jaw of precision combination chuck. (Preturned Ebony piece held by a spigot cut on its underside)

Wood Chuck held in the Spigot Jaw of the Precision Combination Chuck

Another chuck which can be used many times; just make sure that a good piece of hard-wearing hardwood is selected to make it. The jaws of this chuck are very accurately machined and there is little chance of loss of centricity of the wood chuck with repeated use.

The Ebony dish used to illustrate this was first turned on a glue chuck and given a small plinth. The wood chuck was then cut to receive this plinth.

Shaping the inside of the bowl of the dish

Completed dish

Metal cut chuck on morse taper

Metal Chuck held on a Morse Taper

This chuck is cut in aluminium and screwed to a piece of studding, which in turn is screwed to a steel morse tapered arbor. In the illustration the workpiece has been prepared for the making of a tiny bowl. All the turning was done with the ⅛″ gouge.

Bowl cut

Finished bowl

Wood Chuck held in the Collet of the Precision Combination Chuck
In this case the wood chuck, held in the collet jaws, is bored out with a saw tooth cutter to receive the blank for the making of a tiny goblet. The turning is carried out using the small gouge and a fine parting tool.

Completed goblet

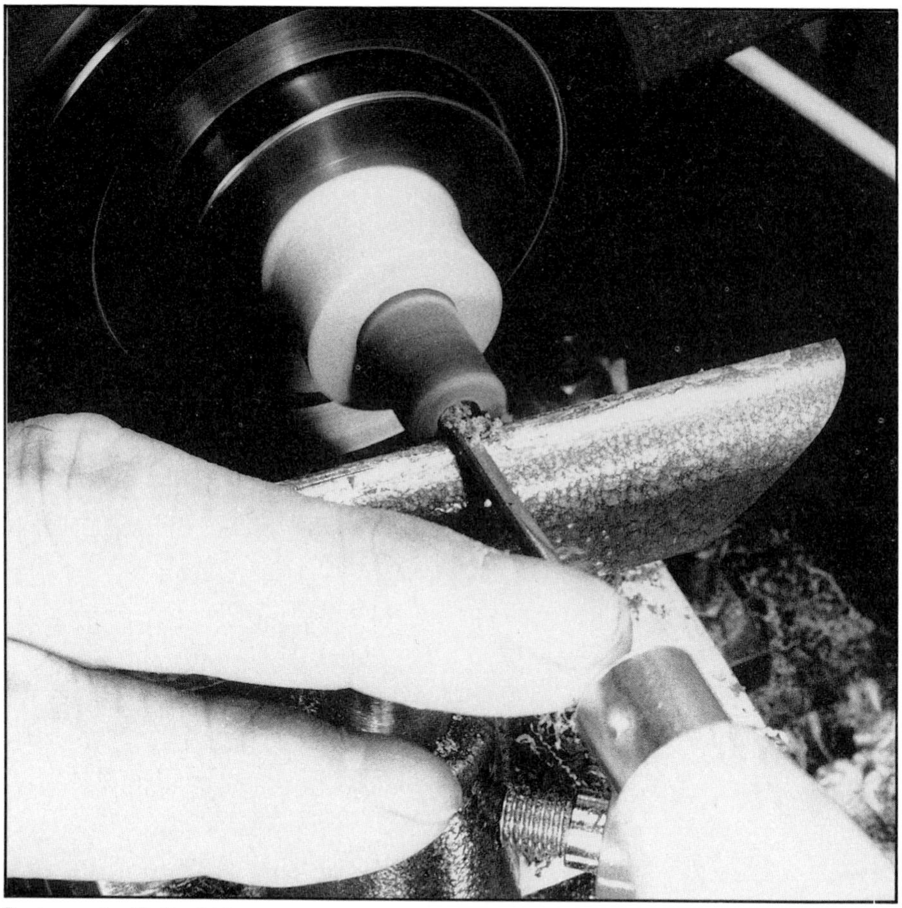
Boring out with the ⅛″ gouge

Wood chuck held in spigot jaw of precision combination chuck

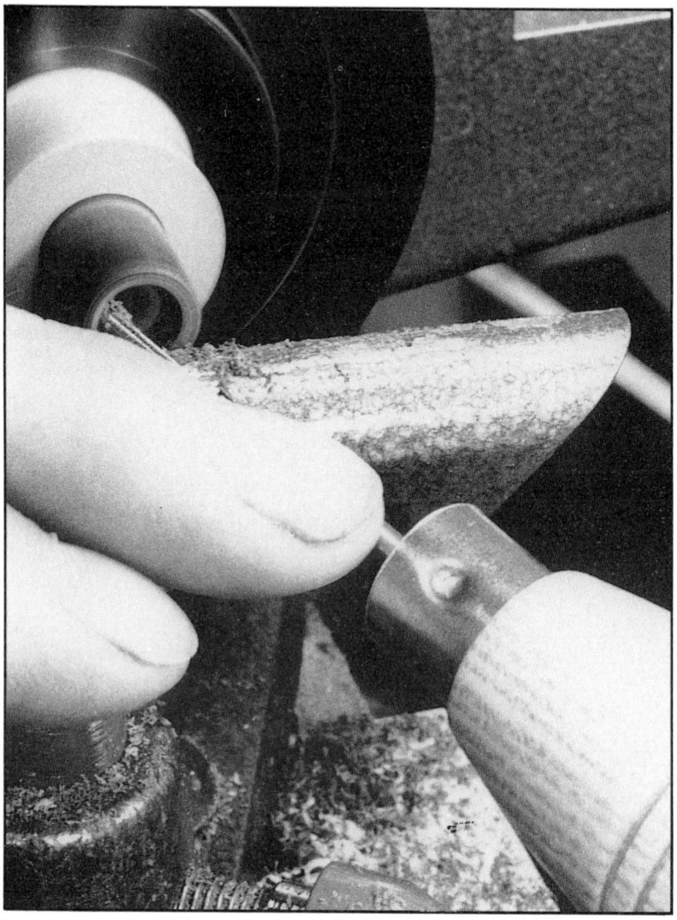
Turning the bowl of the goblet

Multistar Chuck fitted with its smallest jaws

The wood can be prepared between centres and convenient lengths cut. This is a perfect method of holding for mini work with good depth capacity.

Completed bowl

Multistar Chuck with smallest jaw holding in spigot mode

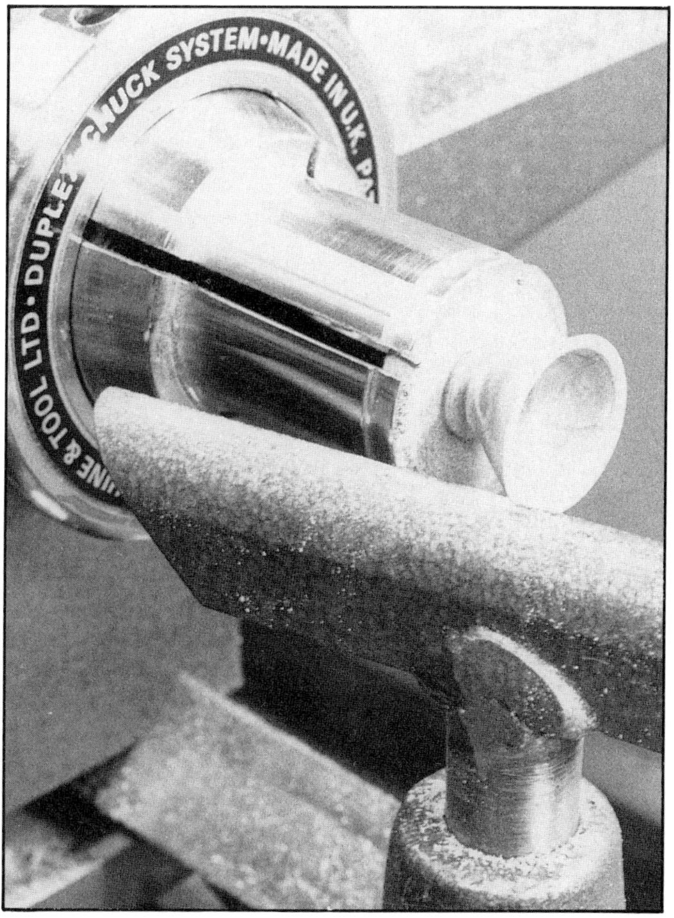

Small bowl turning

Coronet Collet Chuck. Mexican Rosewood, turned between centres, then secured in the collet

Coronet Chuck with Collet Jaws
The self-centreing spring-loaded jaws provide a firm grip and accurate centreing.

Completed box

Box turned

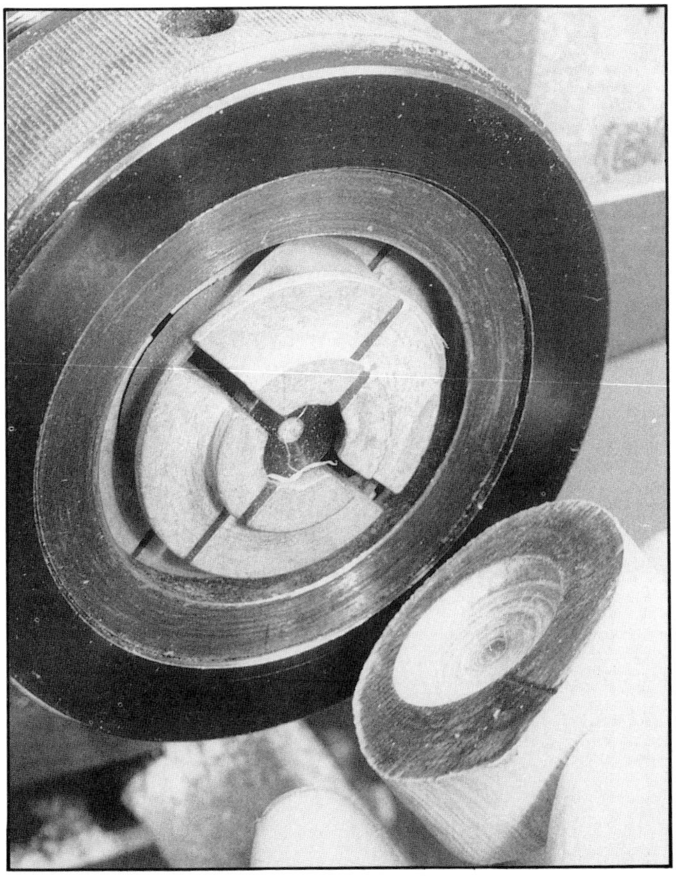
Small expanding collet used in pre-bored recess

Block secured

Precision Combination Chuck fitted with smallest size of expanding jaws
Here the block is bored in the drill press using a multispur bit to cut a shallow recess to receive the jaws.

Spigot chuck. Timber with small spigot cut with a plug cutter

Spigot Chuck
This chuck can be used to hold material bored with a plug cutter. The cutter makes a groove into which the spigot jaws fit.

Small Screw Chuck on a Morse Taper

This manufactured item consists of a split morse taper which has also been bored to receive a small screw. When inserted into the taper of the headstock, the split taper acts like a collet closing down on the screw to hold it firmly in position.

Screw chuck on morse taper

Block assembled

Turning to round

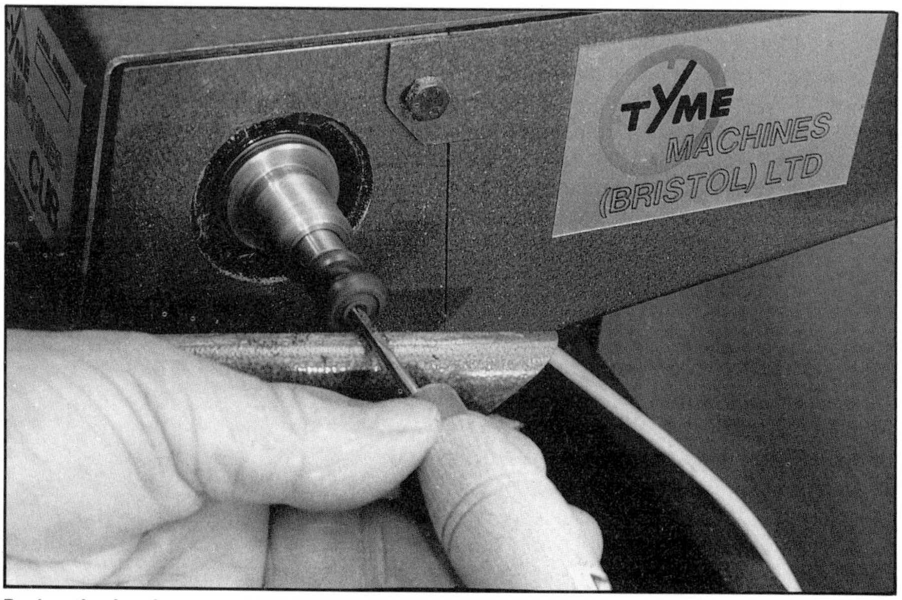

Boring the bowl

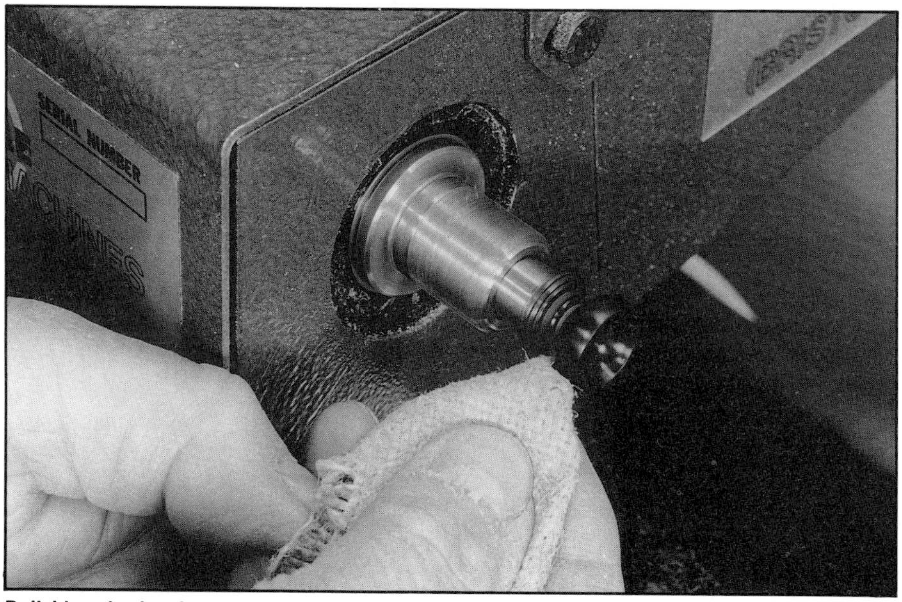

Polishing the bowl

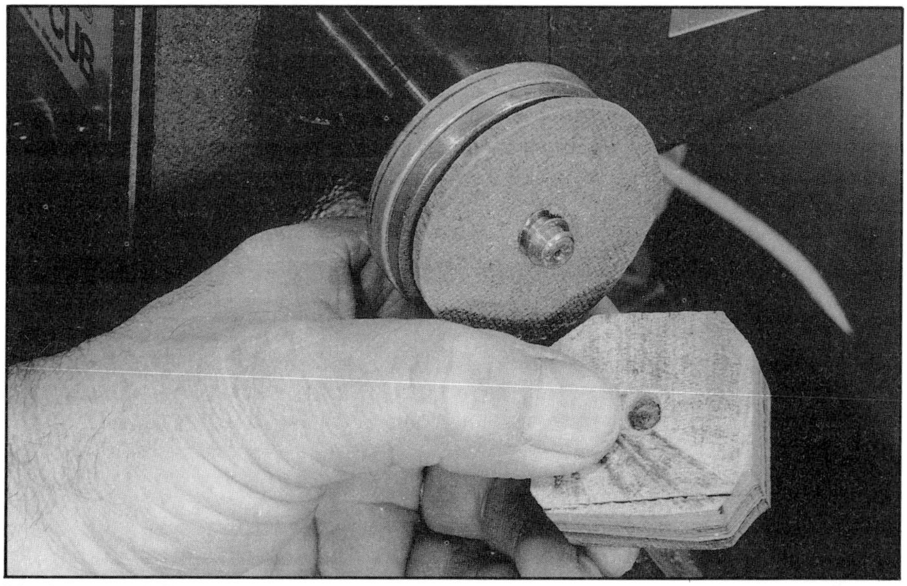

Block screwed direct to screw chuck

Roughing to size with the gouge

Chisel for planing and shaping

Screw Chucks

The screw chuck is probably one of the most useful chucks not supplied with the lathe. No turner should be without one. Indeed, if I were able to influence the makers, I would have one supplied as standard.

They are often made in several sizes. The smallest is the one for this work. Look for those which have an almost parallel screw for they have the best holding facility, particularly important in this work where often the piece is so small that only a fraction of the thread can be used.

The best one, and the only one which has an adjustment to limit the protrusion of the screw beyond the face, is the Coronet which is made in two sizes. Most others will need small discs placed over the screw to limit the penetration. The combination chuck, the Myford, the Woodfast and the Multistar all have a screw chuck mode. The Tyme is produced as a set having a common body. Material is best prepared by boring a hole the core size of the screw for soft woods and slightly greater for very hard woods.

Completed bowl

Blank held in drill chuck

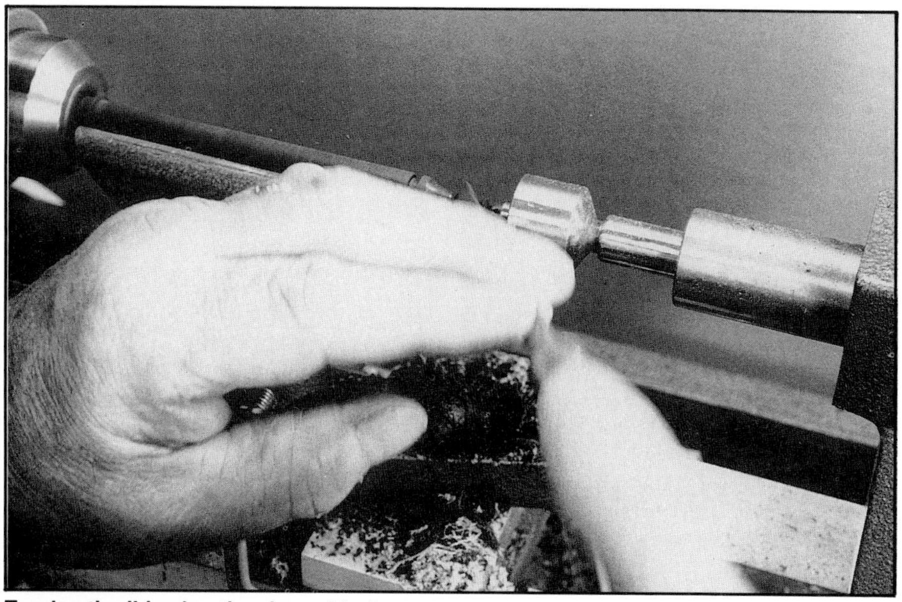

Turning the lid using the skew chisel

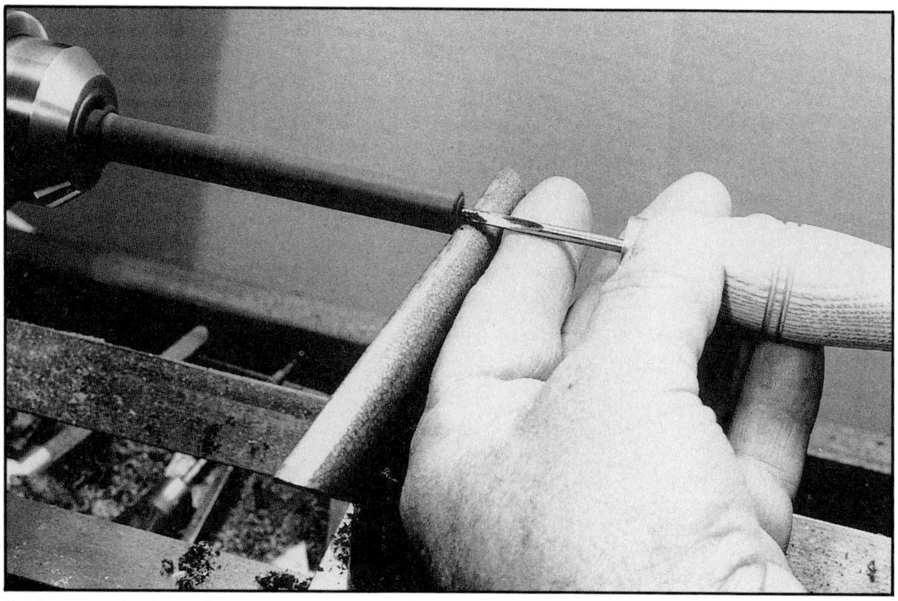

Boring out the box, first stage using the ⅛″ HSS gouge

Drill Chuck

Coronet were convinced of the usefulness of a chuck at the headstock and made one to screw directly to their lathes. If one uses the ordinary drill chuck, an arbor must be fitted so that it can be placed in the headstock.

Here the rough piece has been inserted in the drill chuck, with the other end supported by the small running centre. When turned to round, suitable pieces can be parted off. In this case, after the lid was turned, the ⅛″ gouge was used to centre bore and the ¼″ gouge pushed in to bore to depth. The lid was placed in position before the turning was finalised.

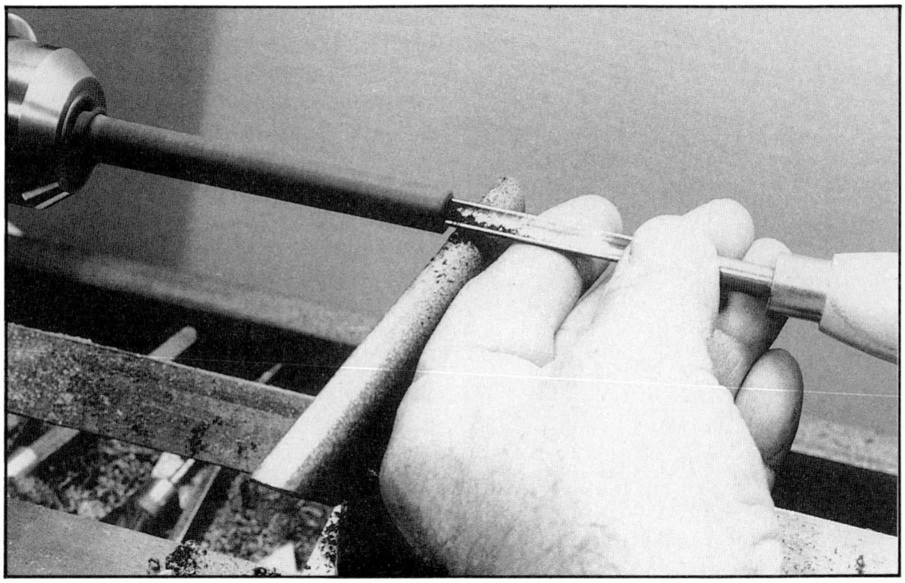

Final boring with the ¼″ HSS gouge

Turning completed

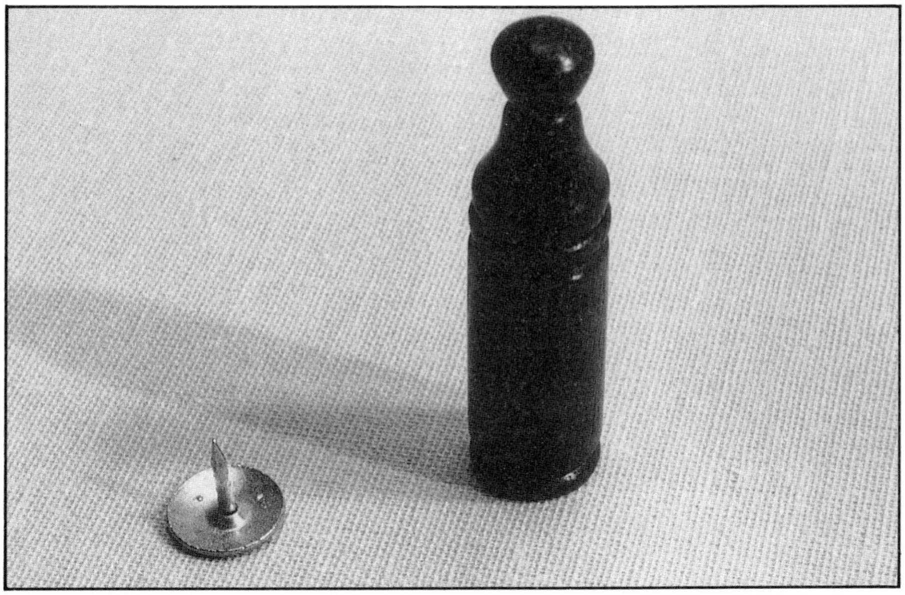

Finished box

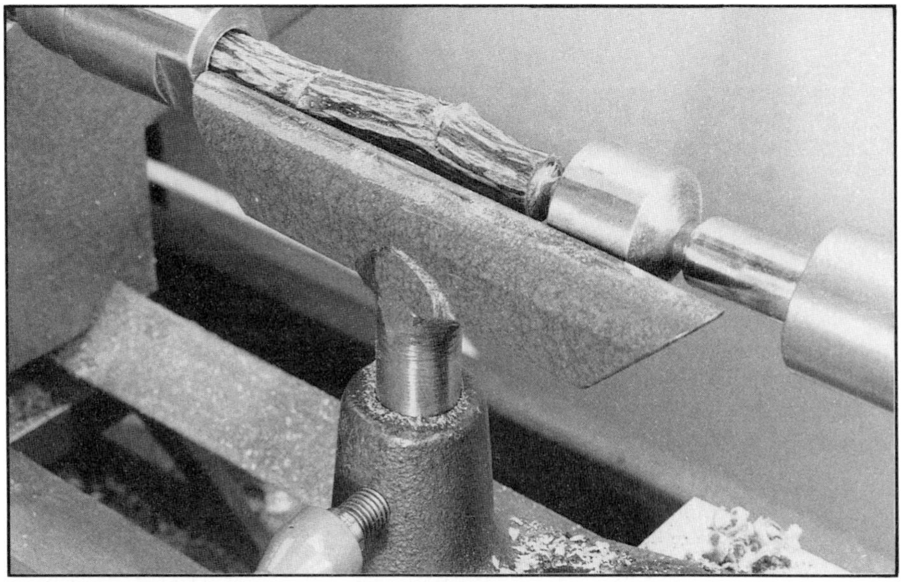
Work held between cone centre and running centre

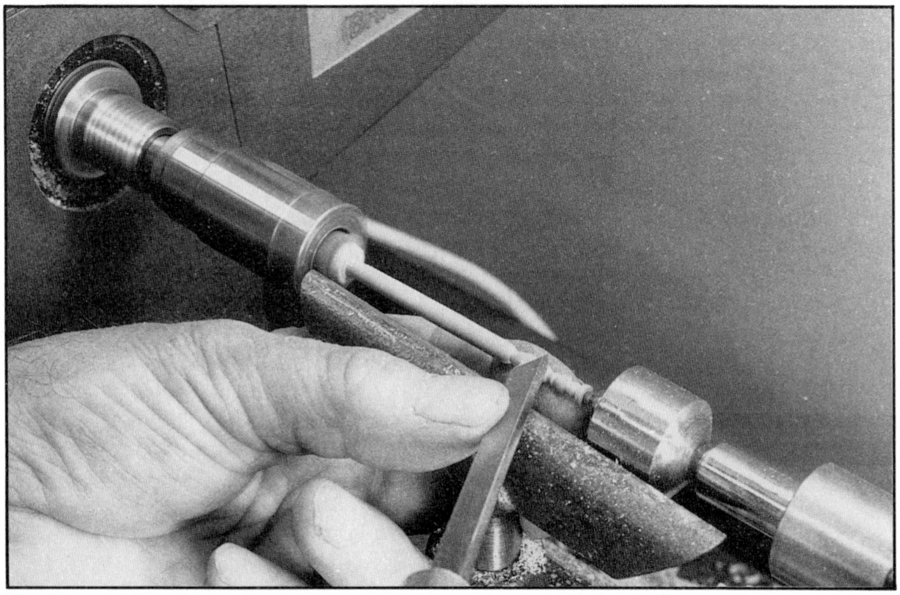
Shaping with the ¼″ chisel

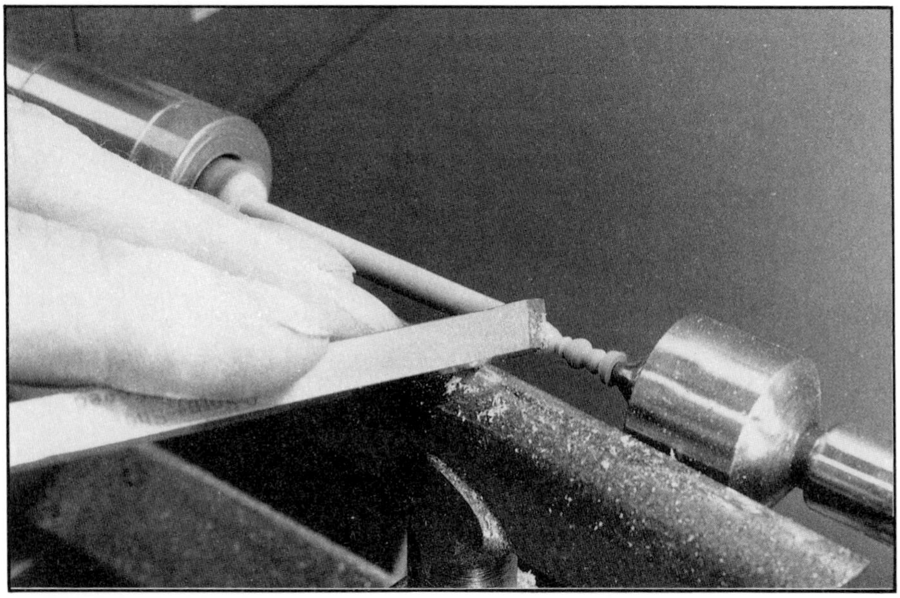
Shaping with the ½″ chisel

Spindle Turning

The standard equipment for this work is supplied with the lathe, but the serious may care to invest in the smaller versions available. The small running centre illustrated in the photographs I made many years ago. Perhaps one day someone will manufacture one like it as it's a most useful accessory.

In the section on tools we can make, I show a small driving centre which I made for children to drive small pieces. This was simply a tapered piece with a small pyramidic hole in which the timber was located for driving. I failed to get a manufacturer to make these, but Coronet came up with a substitute – the Cone Centre. The smallest of these I have in constant use but they made sizes up to 2″ capacity, and also had a running cone for the tailstock. They will drive round, square and odd shaped timbers and are useful for a number of other tricks.

Projects

PROJECTS
Offset dish/tray
Small box
Bud vase
Picture frame
Goblet
Candleholder
Another goblet
Vase
Bottle
Teapot and sugar basin
Box with a difference
Bowl, teapot and other handles
Square dish
Table
Fruit ring
Nut tray
Square boxes
Wine carafe
Beaker
Flower vase
Table lamp
Cup, saucer and plate
Rolling pin
Eggs
Egg mallet
Salt spoon
Lace bobbin

Introduction

The greatest of care must be given to the position of the tool rest in miniature work, since the tools will often be of greater girth than the turnings themselves. The general rule of placing slightly above the centres for spindle work and placing slightly below for faceplate work must be ignored. The tool rest should be set to suit each particular turning.

Often the work will become so thin that it must be supported by the index finger of the left hand, in the case of right-handed turners. The finger can be brought over the top as seen in the illustration on page 110. However, a correspondent of mine and an expert in mini work, Mike Darlow, who lives in Australia, brings his finger up from underneath.

Mini turning is an ideal way to sort out the cutting problems. I recommend it to anyone who has such difficulties, particularly with the skew chisel – there just isn't enough wood spinning around for that long corner to dig in.

Most of the work will involve cutting, not scraping which is impossible with some work anyway. It will also serve to underline the need for really sharp tools, since abrasive paper work is out, certainly at least with spindle work.

Offset dish in Purpleheart

Offset Dish

The basic design incorporates a simple dish with the centre turned offset.

Wood Any good hardwood will do, but it will be most attractive made from one of the exotics. In this case a piece of Purpleheart was chosen.

Method of Holding Must in this case be the glue chuck or double sided tape. Turn up a disc of scrap timber and face it flat. The glue chuck is held in either the screw chuck or faceplate.

Lathe Speed The top speed will be needed here, anything over 2000 rpm.

Tools The ¼″ and ⅛″ HSS gouges with the fine parting tool.

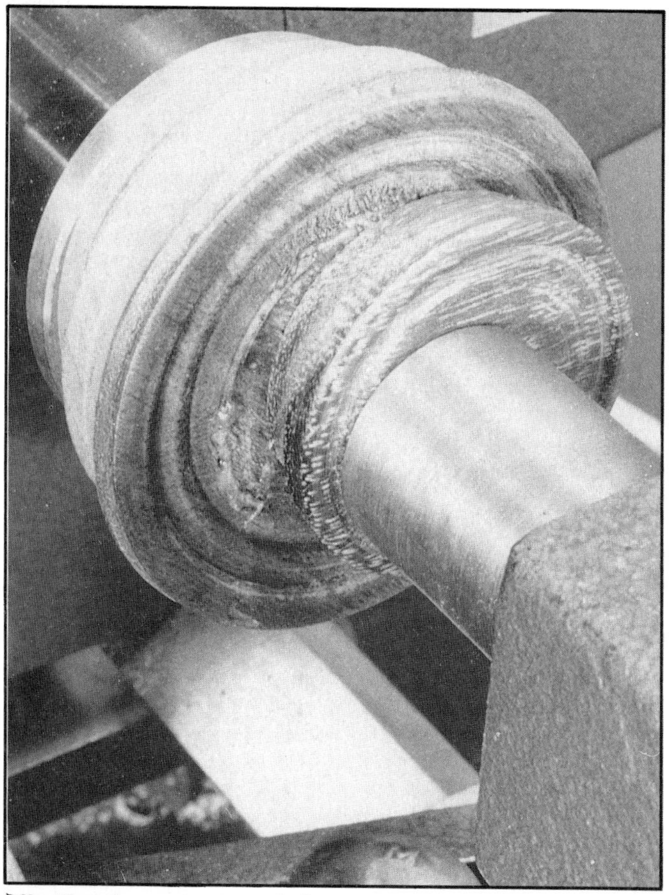

Offsetting the centre turned piece – use pressure to assist the glue from the tailstock

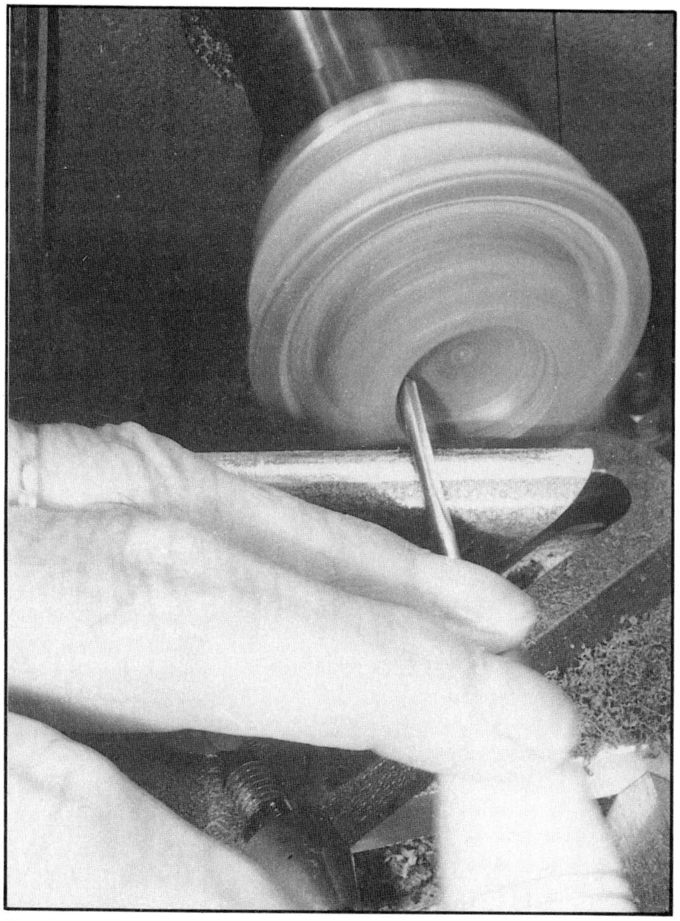

Turning the bowl of the offset dish – ⅛″ HSS gouge

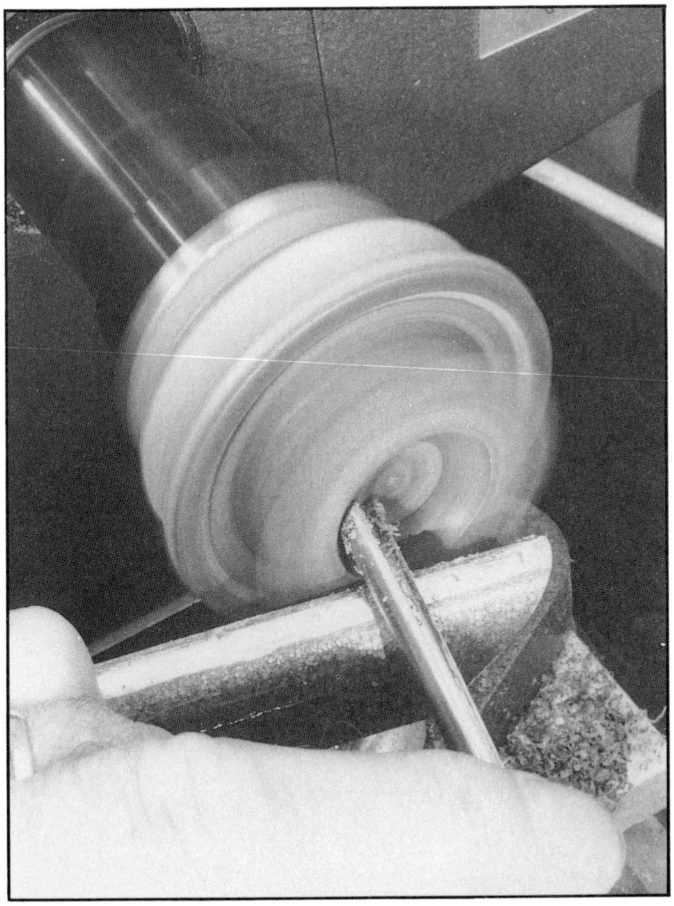

Turning the offset dish to finished depth

Offset dish – cutting completed

Method

First turn the blank down to size, then shape with the larger of the two gouges. Change the position of the tool rest to place it cross the face, face and shape as necessary. The turning up to this point must be completely finished and ready for polishing.

Stop the lathe and using a thin knife give a tap with the hammer to push it through the glue joint to separate the work from the chuck. Soften the glue already on the face of the chuck with either the gun or hot air and replace the work, offsetting it the required amount.

Using the parting tool, carefully mark out the final diameter of the inside turning with a shallow cut. Make sure you have the fine parting tool for this job. With the ¼″ gouge, bevel looking at the wood, make cuts from the groove into the centre. The bevel will rub after the point of cut and the purple heart will polish. After arriving at an acceptable shape, burnish the work with shavings, then seal with sanding sealer and polish to suit.

A great variety of shapes and offsettings can be carried out. Indeed we might end up by calling this sculpting, not turning.

Offset dish – polished and ready for removal from the glue chuck

Small Box

A box such as this would be ideal for the doll's house and the method can be used for others which will stand no more than ⅝″ high.

Wood Really go to town with the scrap for this work. The piece chosen here is of Indian Rosewood which should give a splendid polish from the tool.

Method of Holding Once again the glue chuck can be used since the piece is so small, but I prepared the timber by boring it to receive the screw chuck. On the face of the screw chuck I placed a number of washers to reduce the penetration.

Lathe Speed The faster the speed, the better the finish.

Tools ⅛″ gouge, ¼″ skew chisel and thin parting tool.

Small box in Rosewood

Box in Rosewood – completing the lid

Method

First turn to round, then carefully mark out the work remembering to leave enough timber between the lid and the box body for parting off the lid.

Use the gouge and chisel to shape the lid and box body before parting off the lid. Face the body with the tool rest across the face, then with the rest reset slightly below the centre, use the gouge to cut a hole to the depth of the inside. This is not difficult, but the tool does need to be held quite firmly. The gouge cuts like the old-type shell bit used by the carpenter.

Have it on its side and a small groove just inside the full diameter of the body will act as a stop should the gouge slip sideways. Clean up the inside and the bottom corner with a small spade scraper. Use the same tool to cut back to the final diameter. If glasspaper has to be used to arrive at a perfect finish, allow for this. Even the smallest amount removed at this stage will ruin the fit.

Insert the lid and bring the whole job to completion and final polish. Part off. Use an abrasive board to rub up the base and inside of the lid before polishing these also.

Polishing the small box

Parting off the small box

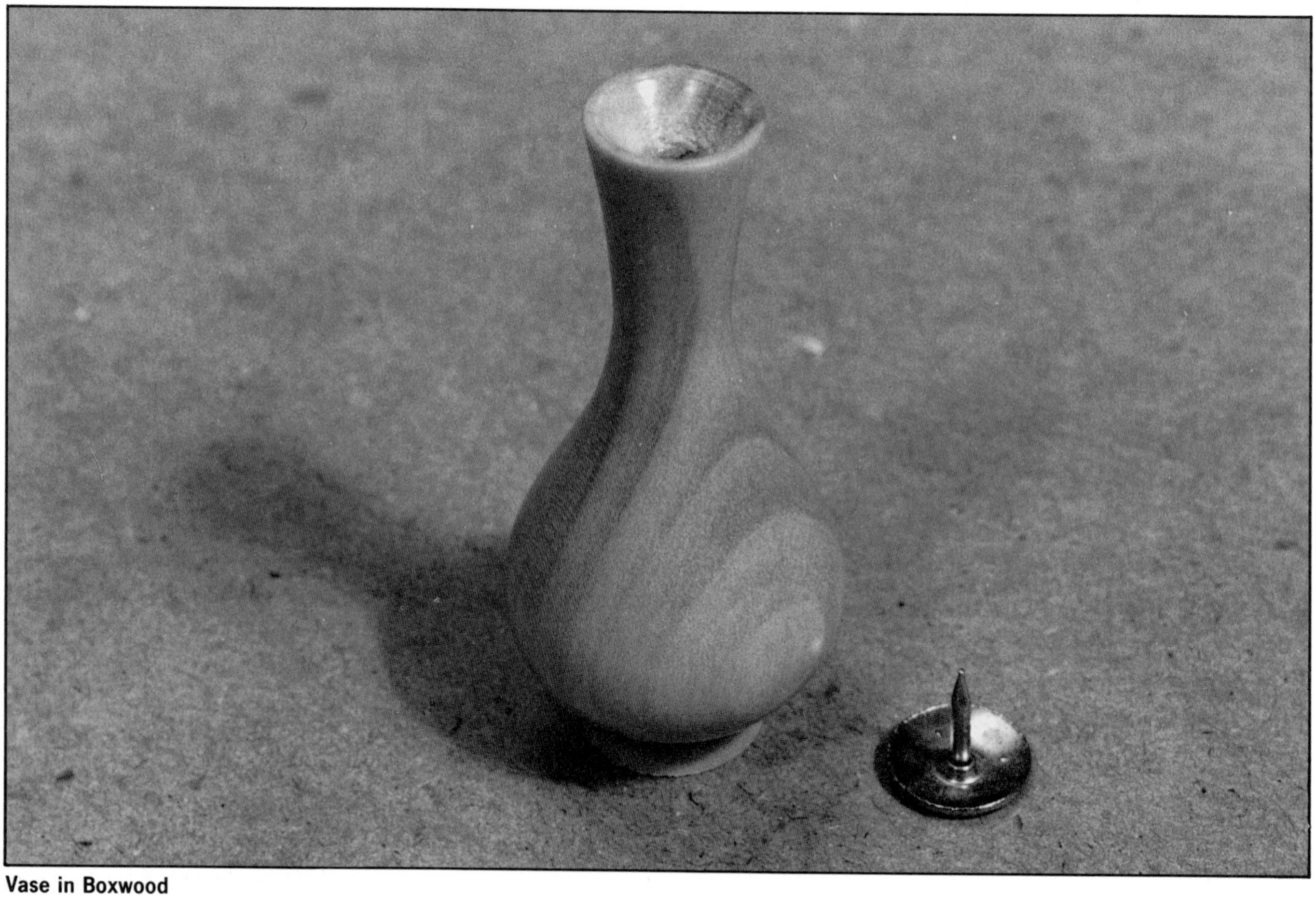

Vase in Boxwood

Bud Vase

This is intended to be a fairly long, slender item, parallel bored with the gouge.

Wood Be careful to choose a piece of timber with fairly long grain, to avoid any possibility of breakage after boring and to permit slender turning to be carried out on the neck. The piece chosen here was Boxwood, *Buxus Sempervirens,* which gave beautiful, long-ribboned shavings and a perfectly finished surface.

Method of Holding The glue chuck is not for this job, but any of the chucks outlined previously could be used here. Whatever method is chosen, be certain of a foolproof hold.

Lathe Speed Again, quite high.

Tools ¼″ gouge, ¼″ skew chisel and parting tool. Should the hole be bored with a saw tooth cutter or similar, the tailstock drill chuck will be needed.

Method

Rough down with the gouge. Turn to shape with gouge and chisel, bringing to an acceptable finish from the tools. Bore out with the gouge, first placing the rest ⅛″ below centre and keeping the tool in line with the centres. The tool will tend to run in towards the headstock without any pushing with the right hand.

Alternatively, mount the boring tool in the tailstock chuck and advance it slowly into the work, taking care to clear the shavings if there is any possibility of a jam. If a flatbit is being used, remember to locate the flatbit in the work before running the lathe.

Carefully face off the top of the vase. Clean up if necessary, polish and part off. The polish need only be wax, particularly if the work isn't to be handled frequently.

Vase in Boxwood – shaping with the gouge

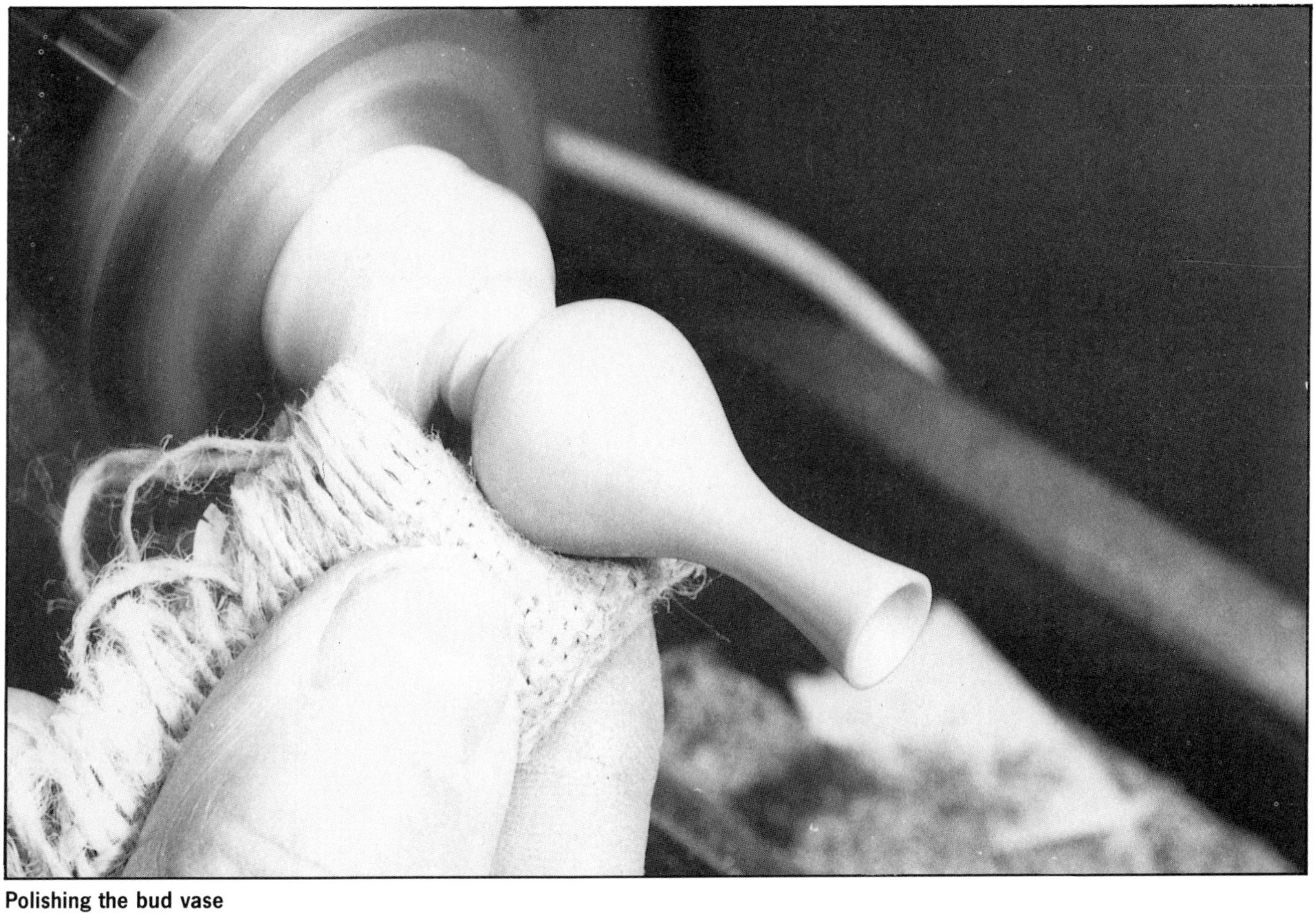

Polishing the bud vase

Picture frame in Boxwood

Picture Frame

Whenever a small piece of wood remains either on the screw chuck or the glue chuck, an opportunity is presented to use the remainder for making a small piece. Such a piece could be a picture frame with a small recess cut in the back, exactly as with the full size job.

Wood The stump of boxwood was used not only for the job itself, but also for making the mandrel for reversing the frame to cut the rebate.

Holding The timber is already mounted on the screw chuck in this case.

Lathe Speed As fast as the machine will allow.

Tools 1/8″ gouge and fine parting tool.

Picture frame – parting off after shaping the face

The picture frame – parted off

Method

Face off the stump and shape up the frame with the gouge and the parting tool. The finish can be scraped, but paper will have to be used which may destroy fine cuts. Then with the fine parting tool, push in to define the internal diameter and far enough back to permit the insertion of the parting tool from the side to finally part the job off.

Come to the side, touch up the diameter, polish the job and part off. The parting tool will meet up with the groove cut by the parting tool on the face.

With the picture frame in your hand, carefully use the gouge to cut down the remainder of the stump to the internal diamter of the frame. A tiny taper will also help. Now slide the frame onto this mandrel, back to front, and use the parting tool to cut the small rebate to receive the picture.

Picture frame reversed – cutting the rebate on the mandrel

Work finished – shows rebate on the picture frame

Goblet in Yew

Goblets

These will make demands, both in regard to design and cutting.

Method of Holding *Almost* always these are held on the screw chuck, but the collet facility of the combination type chuck can be used. The use of this type of chuck will ensure absolute safety of the material with little or no chance of losing the centricity of the work during turning.

Lathe Speed Depends on the size, but most can be done with speeds of 2000 rpm.

Tools ¼″ and ⅛″ gouges, ¼″ skew chisel and small parting tool.

Method

The tailstock centre can be brought up to support the work when in the rough state, but this really isn't necessary. Rough down to size. (Although it isn't noted in the tool list, a larger gouge could be used here for this stage.) Use the chisel to plane to final marking out diameter.

Mark out the proportions with the chisel, then with the parting tool. Change over with the tool rest across

Goblet – boring to centre depth

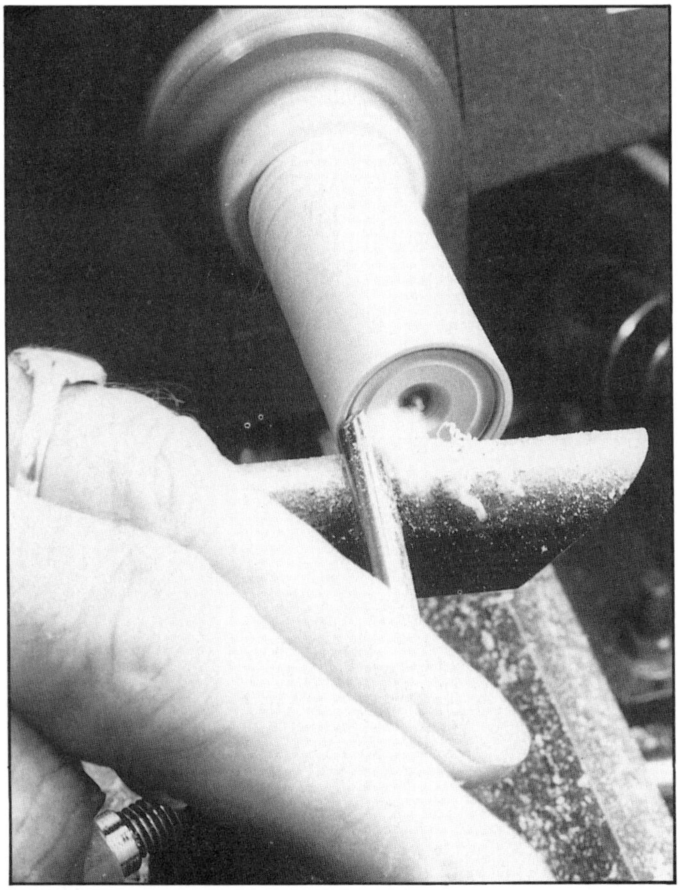

Starting to cut the bowl of the goblet from the groove (point of start)

the face and slightly below centre. Use the parting tool to cut a groove at the internal size of the goblet. This groove will serve as a point of start for the gouge, which lies on its side with the handle well down.

Now use the ¼″ gouge to bore a hole in the centre which serves as a point of finish for the gouge and also gives an indication of depth. Do this with the gouge on its side, give a little lead in to start, then bring the tool in line with the centres and let it run in to the required depth.

The same gouge can now be used to remove the waste and shape the bowl of the goblet. Bring this to perfection. Many prefer to use the scraper for this work, but try out the gouge and stick to the rule of letting the bevel rub. Thus the wood is always supporting the tool bevel and safe cutting is assured.

Always cut the bowl first. It is the heavier turning and is best done while there is a great deal of wood in the stem area.

Change the position of the rest and use gouge and chisel to shape the base and the stem. Finish as with previous jobs and maintain a good finish from sharp tools.

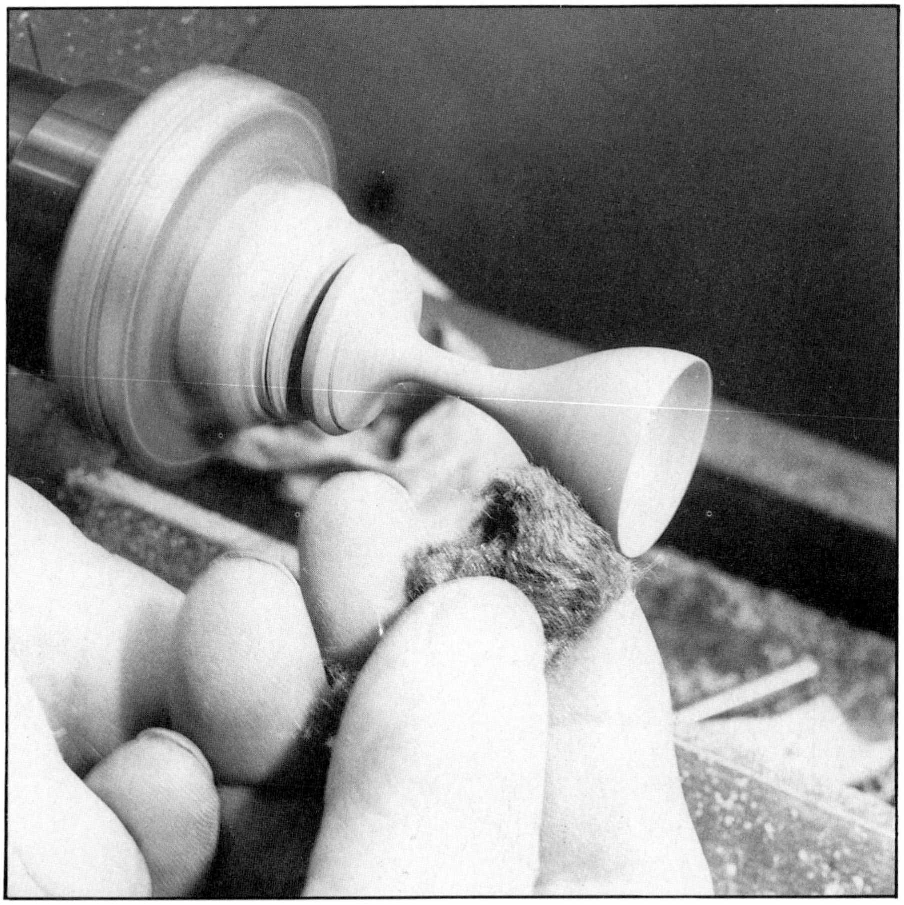

Polishing the goblet

Candleholder

A minute turning exercise where anything is possible.

The one shown comes from a fraction of timber left behind on the glue chuck from another job. Only the ⅛″ gouge was used and the job completed in seconds.

Much of this can be fun, but the turner will have to rely almost entirely upon sharp tools, a keen eye and a total loss of memory as far as glasspaper is concerned. Otherwise the whole job will disappear in a whiff of dust.

Candlestick in Laburnum

Completed candlestick on glue chuck

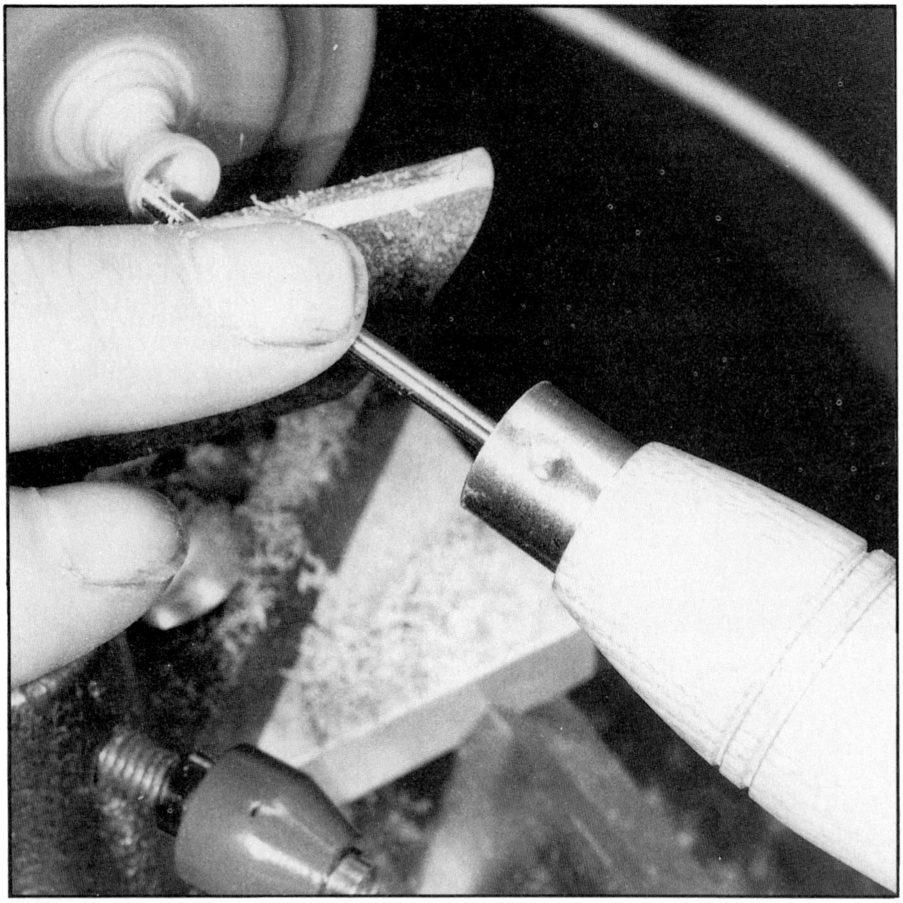

Tiny goblet in Laburnum – cutting the bowl

Another Goblet

Goblets can also be an additional job after a major one has been completed, using the small stump remaining on the glue chuck or the screw chuck. If the latter, don't get too close to the screw.

Only the ⅛″ gouge will be needed. If a scraper is used, it will need to be very small and thin otherwise it is impossible to get it into the bowl of the goblet and just one little push will destroy the job.

Cut the bowl first. Work from the outside to the centre and for safe cutting let the gouge bevel rub against the wood. Even here a very tiny groove near the edge will prevent slip. Bring the bowl to completion and paper at this point. Don't leave it until it is an acceptable surface.

Shape the outside carefully with gouge or tiny skew. Bring to a finish. If paper is used, take care or the job will disappear. Polish and part off with the long point of the skew.

This type of job emphasises the need for great care and *cutting.*

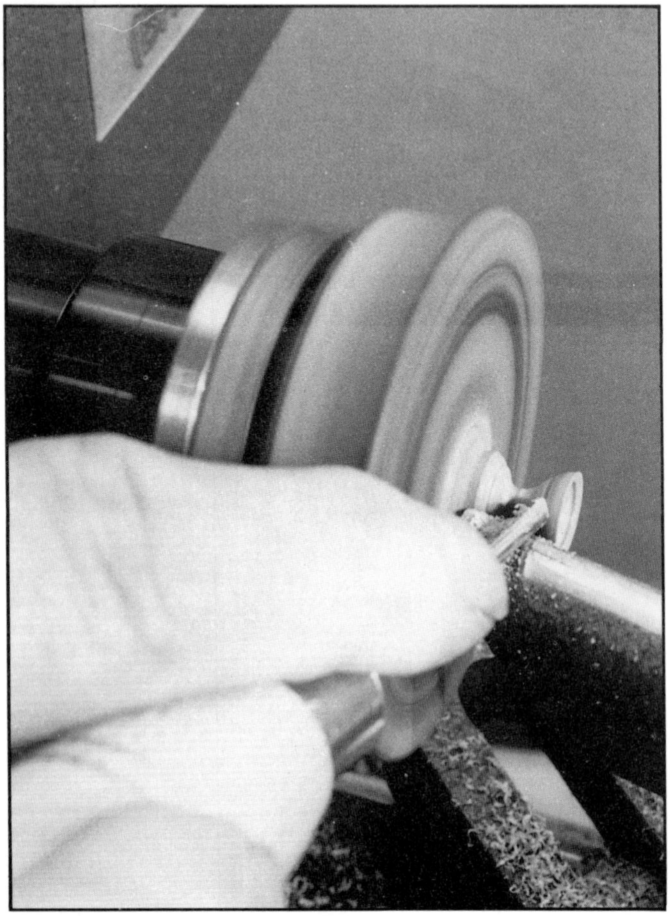

Shaping the stem of the tiny goblet

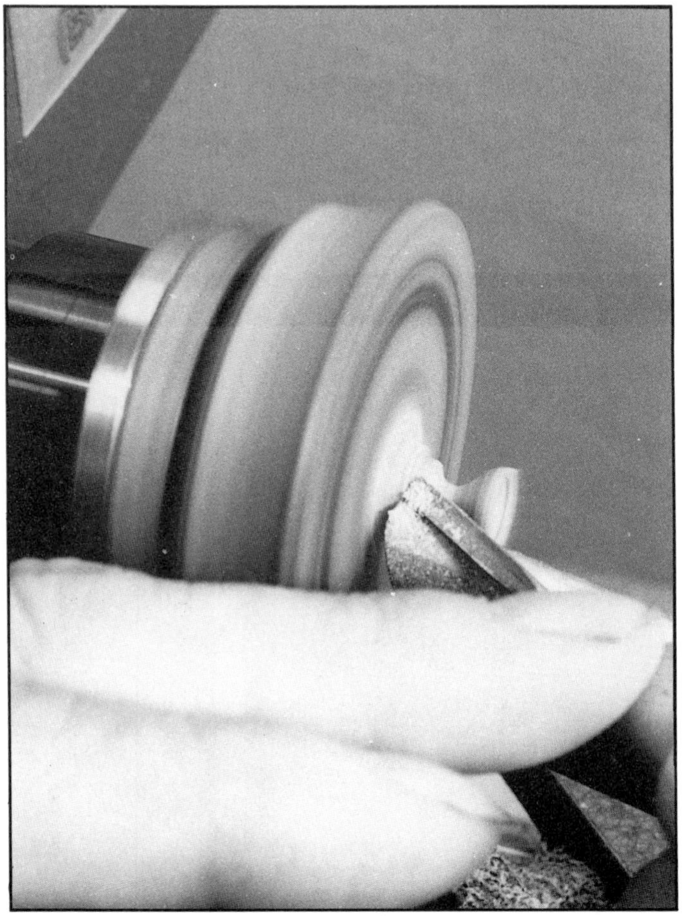

Goblet in Laburnum – finishing the base

Vase

This small vase has its inside cut entirely with a purpose-made scraping tool.

Wood Don't choose too hard a timber, especially with an untried scraping tool used for the first time. I chose Mexican Rosewood.

Method of Holding Use a screw chuck with a disc of hardboard. This gives protection to the tools should they inadvertently strike the face of the chuck.

Lathe Speed 1500 rpm, particularly for early scraping.

Tools ¼″ gouge for roughing down. ¼″ skew for planing and shaping. Purpose-made side cutting scraper for inside work.

Vase in Grande Palisander

Method

First turn down the blank to size and face off the end. Set the tool rest across the face and half the shank size of the ¼″ gouge below the centre. Take the ¼″ gouge, place it on its side and close to the centre – give a little sloping lead into the centre. Carefully line up the gouge on the line of centres and let it run into the job to the total depth of the vase. It may be necessary to remove it at least once to free the shavings. This method of boring will be quickly mastered and become a standard cutting technique for holes.

With the tool rest still in the lower position, take the side scraper, rest it in the trailed position (handle up) should it have a hook, and push it into the hole as far as it will safely go without jamming. Move it slightly to the left so that it begins to cut and draw it backwards out of the hole. Continue to cut in this way to the full width and depth. Take care at first until you become familiar with this type of working, since you cannot see the tool cutting – it can only be done by touch. The thickness of the wall must also be judged by sight and touch.

Clean up using a piece of rolled up paper. Again watch how much you are removing. A touch of paper wrapped around a small piece of dowel rod may assist.

Change over the tool rest and use the gouge and chisel to shape the outside of the vessel. Bring to a finish, polish and part off.

The scraper in position for internal boring of the vase

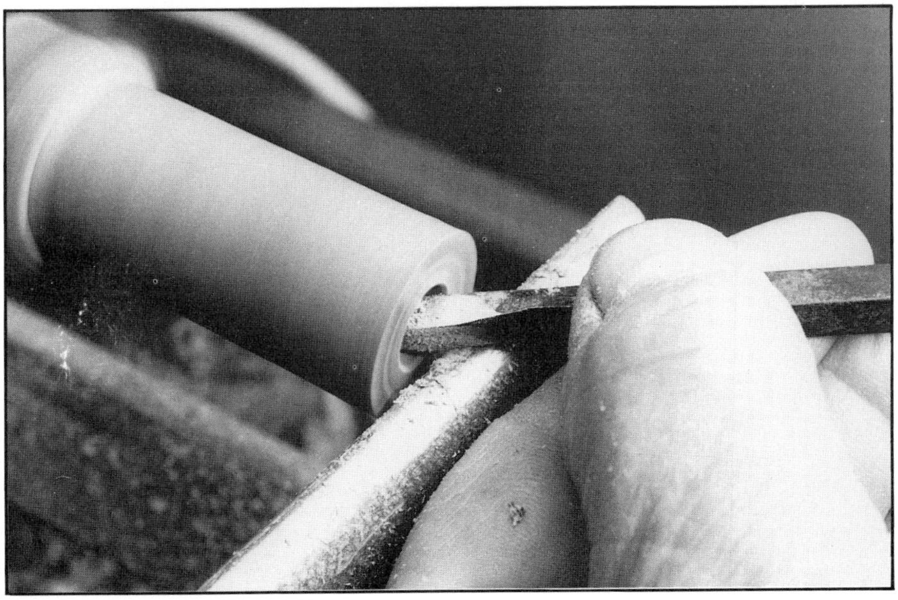

Scraper at work on the vase

Bottle in Laburnum

Bottle

Small bottles can be made in a one-piece turning, but the inside must be bored first and then the point of entry closed with a plug before the outside is turned.

Wood Choose the timber carefully, since the walls will be thin. A fairly close, long grain will be best.

Method of Holding Precision combination chuck fitted with the smallest collet jaws is an ideal method.

Lathe Speed 1500 rpm.

Tools 1/8″ and 1/4″ gouges, 1/4″ skew chisel and parting tool. Saw tooth or flatbits of size to suit the inside bore of the bottle. Tailstock drill chuck.

Boring out the bottle from the underside

Gluing in a plug to close the bore of the bottle

Method

Place the timber between centres and turn it down to the inside diameter of the collet. Remove from the lathe, screw on the selected chuck and secure the blank in place.

Place the drill chuck in position in the tailstock and select the drill to cut the inside body size. Move the drill up so the brad point of the drill just locates in the work. Secure the tailstock and advance the boring tool, carefully at first to ensure it centralises properly. Bore to the agreed depth, remove the drill and substitute a drill which is the exact size of the bottle mouth.

Bore this hole through the piece, beyond the total length of the bottle. This will ensure the bottle will finally part off, leaving the mouth open. Plug the hole with a previously turned or cut shallow plug. Use a quick setting glue.

The bottle itself can now be turned using the gouges and chisel. Completely finish the bottle up to the polishing stage and part off – do the latter with the skew chisel if possible so that the point of part is polished from the tool. This saves cleaning up on the bench when completing the job.

The stopper can now be turned using the remaining stump of timber. Be careful to cut for a good fit and part off as cleanly as possible.

Bottles can always be done in this way, but careful planning of the design to allow for the internal boring is necessary. The project can be done in reverse, cutting the stopper first, then boring out the inside, but this presents the problem of inserting a scraping tool into the job and having to cut without sight of the actual cutting.

The bottle sealed

The bottle shaped and ready for polishing and parting off

Finished teapot

Teapot and Sugar Basin

These are a matching pair. The handle and spout are turned separately, shaped to suit the curves of the teapot by hand and finally glued into position.

Wood Chosen for effect, in this case – Mexican Rosewood.

Method of Holding A piece of turned stuff from a previous job was used here on the precision combination chuck for safe holding. A wood chuck would serve the same purpose, provided it's a good fit.

Lathe Speed 1500 rpm.

Tools ¼″ and ⅛″ gouges and ¼″ skew chisel. Parting tool and round nose side cutting scraper.

Sugar basin

Teapot lid turned

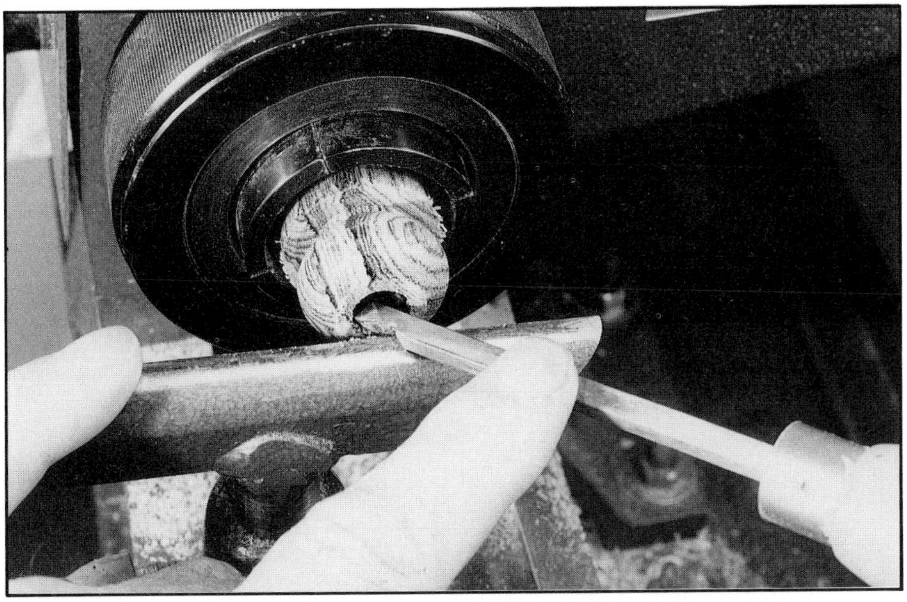

Teapot body roughed to shape – turning the inside with side cutting scraper

Teapot lid fitted, inserted and shape completed

Method

First turn down the selected timber between centres to round and to size determined by the method of holding selected. Set up the chuck and insert the prepared blank, which should be a good tight fit in the chuck and held within the collet jaws.

Using the gouges, turn the lid and knob in one piece. With the parting tool and chisel, cut a rebate to exact size. Part off with the smallest parting tool.

Bore a hole into the centre of the body using the 1/8″ gouge. With the round nosed side scraper, carefully open out the inside. A good light is essential here as it will be difficult to see the action otherwise. It will also test your nerve. An oily timber may give you trouble as the cuttings will tend to stick and obscure the cutting. Complete to inside shape and finish.

Check out the fit of the lid and adjust as necessary. Insert the lid and, moving the tool rest to the outside position, begin to shape the body to match the interior. Cut down on the point of part to enable access to finalise the underside of the body and to polish. Finally part off.

Parting off the teapot

A waste piece, bored to serve as a wood chuck. The blank for the spout and handle is being inserted

The stump remaining in the collet chuck is now used as a wood chuck. Bore it out to receive the small piece chosen in matching timber for the spout and handle. Insert the piece in the chuck and make it a good fit. Now turn the spout using the gouge and bore the hole in its centre. Be sure to leave enough timber to make the handle before completing to a finish. Part off and turn a handle on the remaining bit. Bore the centre out using the gouge once again and if necessary clean up with a tiny scraper. Finish and part off.

On the bench, carefully file a slight curve on the handle to match the curve of the body at the handle position. Shape the spout in the same way. Bore by hand a small hole into the body before gluing up with a good fast setting epoxy resin.

Turn the sugar basin in exactly the same way.

Cutting the teapot spout with the chisel, after boring

Teapot handle – boring the finger hole with the ⅛″ gouge

Parting off the teapot handle

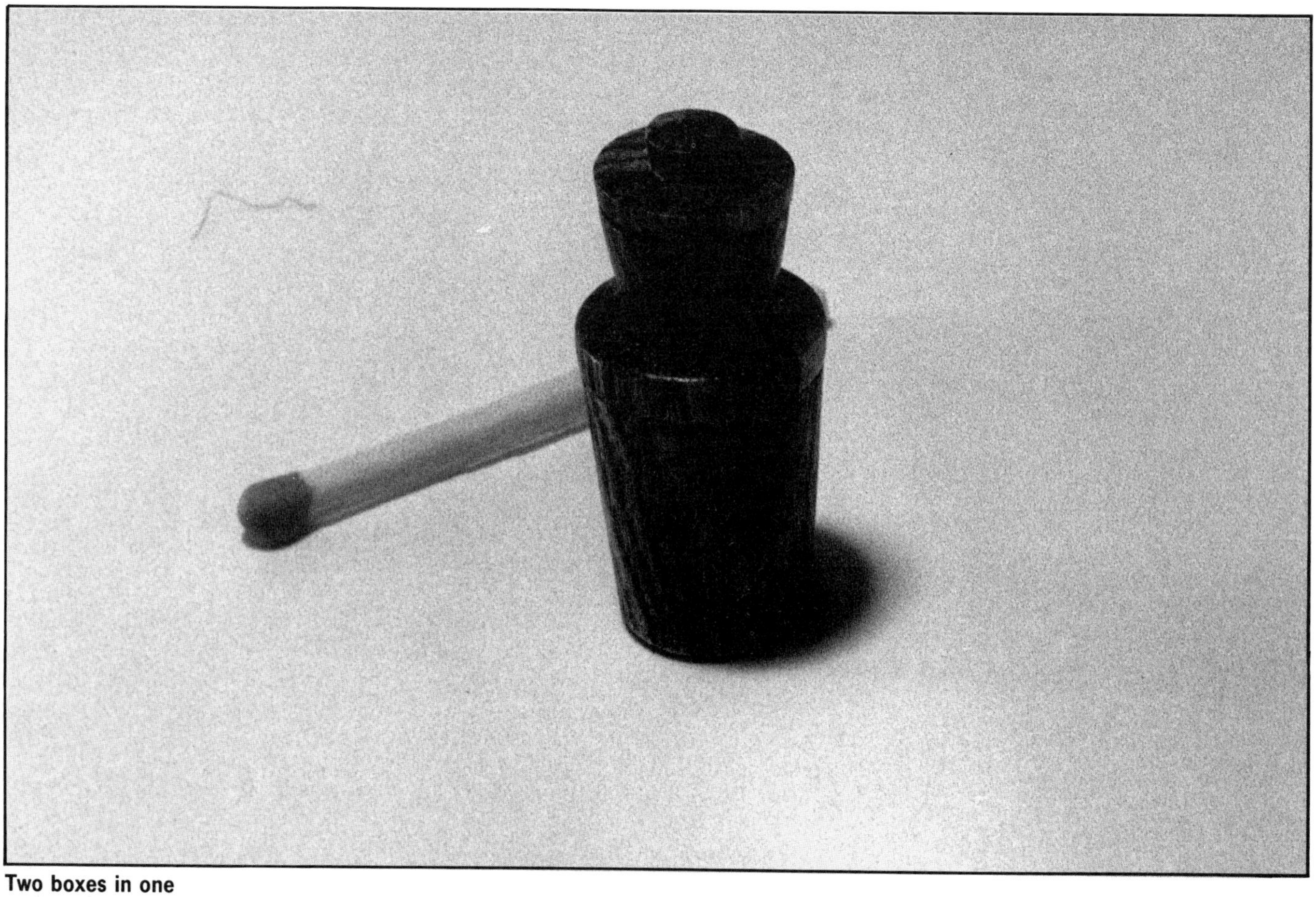

Two boxes in one

Completed parts of the 'box with a difference'

Box with a difference

This box is designed so that it will have a box within the lid.

Wood Be careful to choose one with fairly close grain and of good strength as the walls of the box will be very thin.

Method of Holding The collet mode of the precision chuck will hold this item very securely.

Lathe Speed 2000 rpm or faster.

Tools ¼″ and ⅛″ gouges and ¼″ skew chisel. Parting tool and spade scraper.

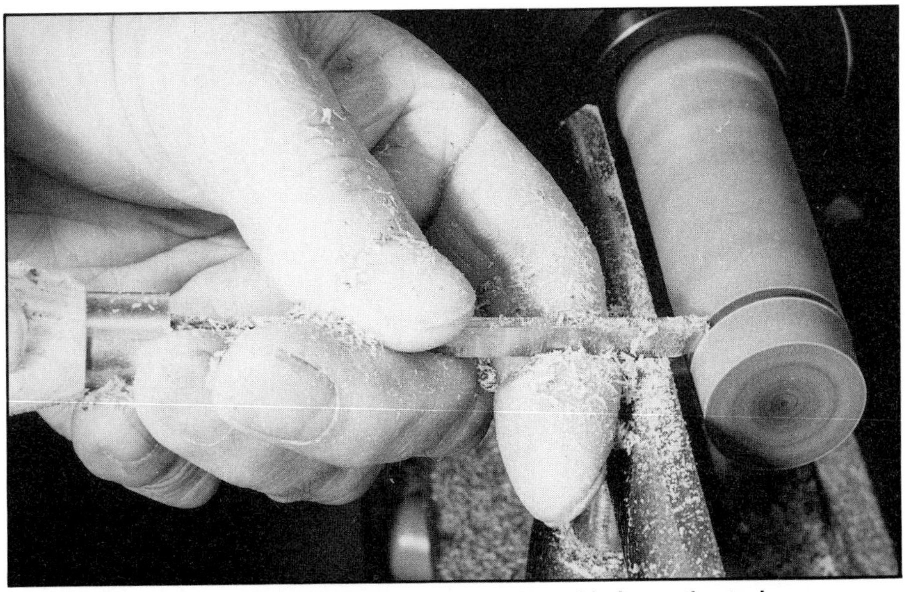

Removing the waste around the knob of the main box with the parting tool

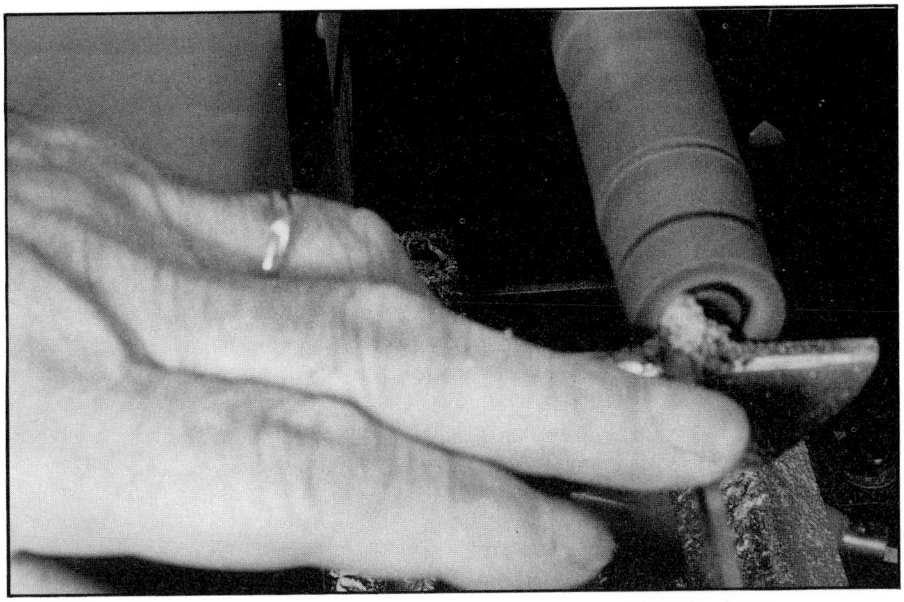

Completing removal of the waste, pushing the parting tool in from the face

Turning the first lid of the box

Method

Turn down the selected timber to round and very carefully shape up the main box knob. On the top of the knob, cut another small knob and then shape the top to make a small lid. Part off the lid and use the gouge to bore out the inside of the lid to form a small box.

Parting off the lid of the box

Squaring the face of the box within the lid

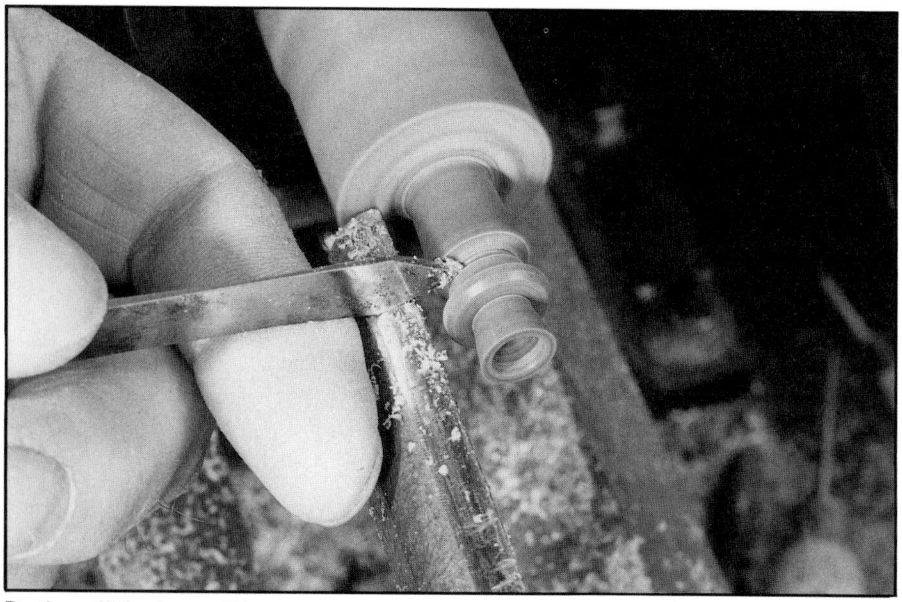
Parting off the larger lid

The inside may have to be finally cleaned up using a tiny scraper, depending on the final shape chosen. Take care to fit the small lid to a nice push fit. Put this lid on one side and begin the final shaping of the main lid. Cut an accurate rebate before parting off.

Bore out the box body with gouge and scraper to choice and carefully fit the lid. Bring the inside of the box to a polished finish. Replace the lid in the larger box and place the other lid in position in the larger knob.

It may be necessary to trim a little, but as there is very little wood, go carefully.

The body of the box turned

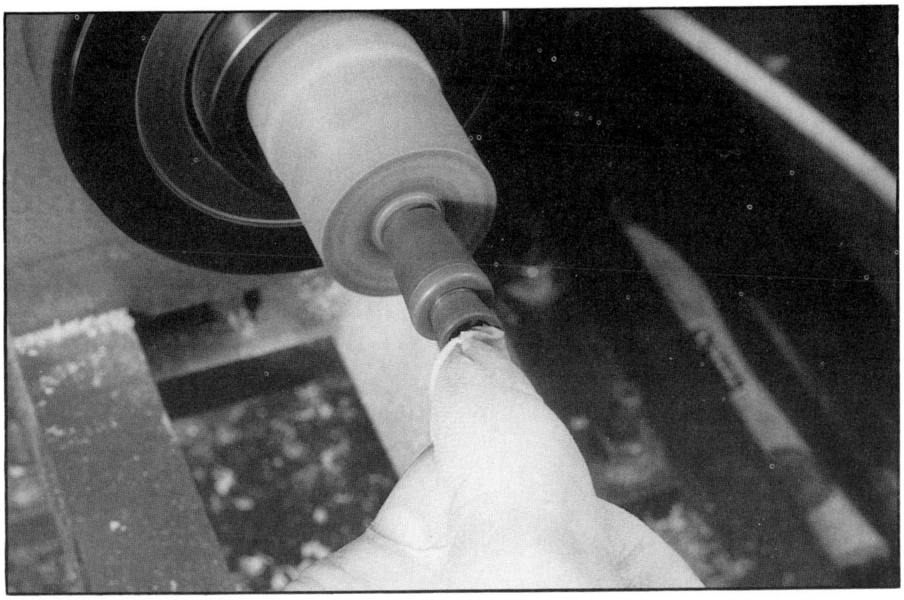

Lid inserted for final trimming

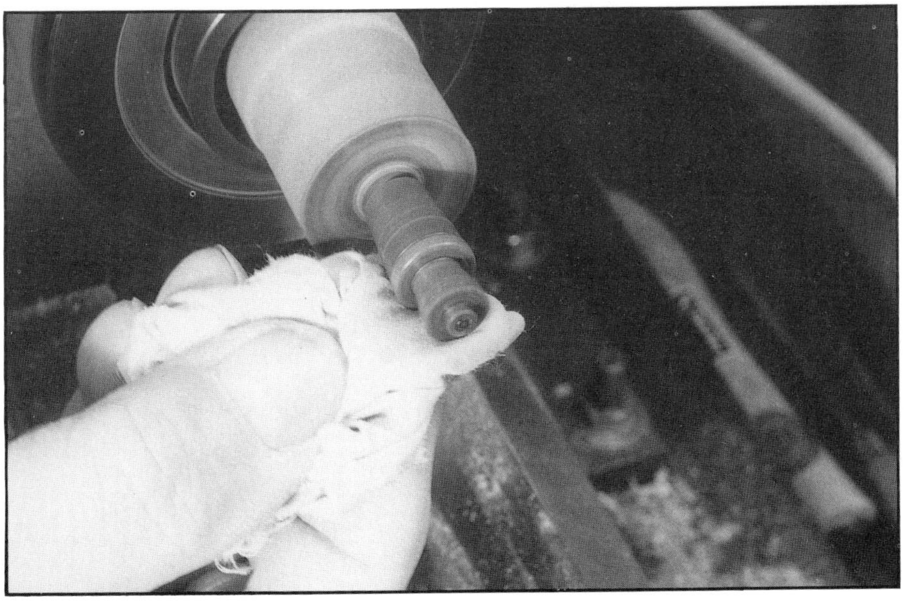

Polishing the completed box

Bowl, Teapot and Other Handles

These do seem to present a problem for some turners, but are done using the same method as turning rings in large sizes.

Wood First turn a mandrel between centres, selecting a very good piece of hardwood with long straight grain. I had a little piece of boxwood which proved ideal.

Method of Holding Mount between the small fork centre and the running centre.

Mandrel with pre-bored blank

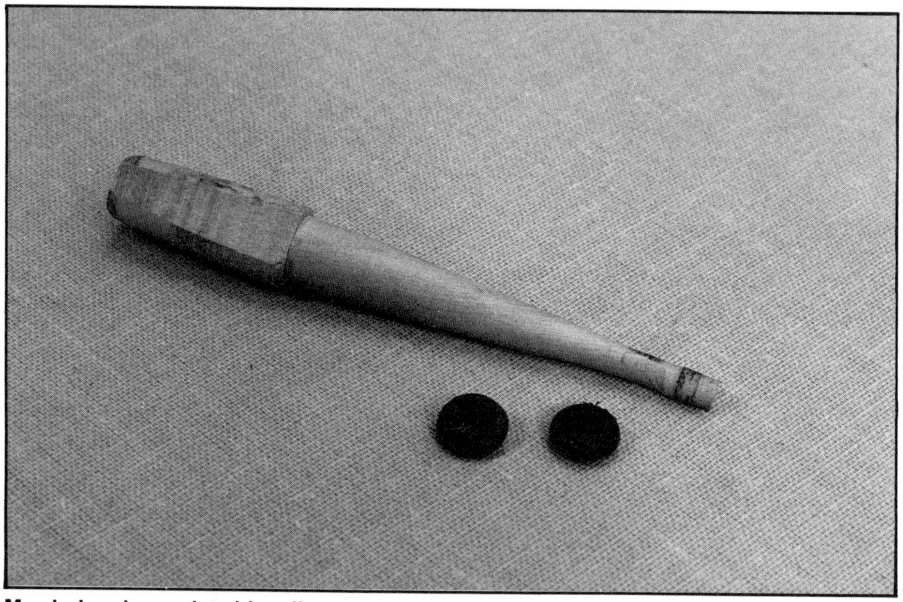

Mandrel and completed handles

Pre-bored material with boxwood mandrel

Method

Prepare the tiny pieces from which the handles are to be made by boring on the drill press. The stock could first be turned to round, but this is not really vital. The bore size will determine the diameter of the mandrel which must be turned down with a very slight taper. Thus when the little pieces are pushed on, they will be a good push fit and will not spin when cutting.

The turning is a simple matter using the chisel in the main, but turning to round with the gouge will be safer if the pieces are somewhat out of shape to start. Handles can be perfectly finished in this way if cutting is carried out properly, otherwise even the slightest push will disrupt proceedings.

A small flat or curve can be cut to correctly position each handle on the curve of the finished article.

Ready for turning – running centre essential

Parting off with the fine parting tool

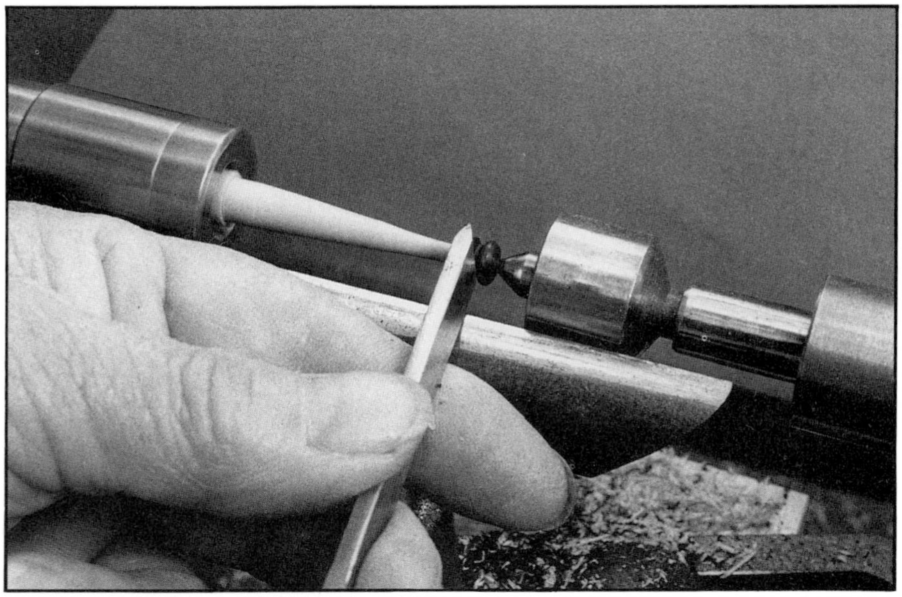
Shaping a handle with the skew chisel

Square dish completed

Squared piece mounted and centred with the dead centre

Square Dish

This makes a change, as the outside is finished with the saw and the plane, just simply turning the inside.

Wood Any piece of hardwood will do. In this case sycamore was used – it had a nice fiddleback.

Method of Holding Glue chuck.

Speed 1500 rpm.

Tools Parting tool and ¼″ round nose gouge.

Cutting the starting groove with parting tool

¼″ gouge used to shape the bowl of the dish

Facing off the square dish with the gouge

Method

Prepare the piece perfectly square and to a perfect finish. Mark on the face the centre point by drawing the diagonals in pencil. Bring up the tailstock in readiness and melt the glue on the face of the chuck. Place the block in position on the glue chuck, using the centre point to position it accurately. Remove the centre. Use the tailstock quill to face up to the block and hold it momentarily until the glue has hardened. (This glue never really gets dead hard.)

Spin the lathe by hand to check for centricity of the block and at the same time take the opportunity to mark out the final diameter of the inside with a pencil. Position the tool rest and use the parting tool to cut a groove at the pencil mark which will act as a point of start.

Use the gouge to cut the bowl, starting at the outside, bevel resting on the wood, and making cuts into the centre each time. Bring to a finish. With this particular piece of wood, abrasive paper wasn't needed. Apply polish with the machine still and polish all over. Polish the bowl with the machine running, but the square portion will need to be done at the stop position. Carefully remove as before.

Table

A three piece project with the final assembly needing a round tenon cut at each end of the pedestal.

Wood I chose mahogany since I had a small piece of delightfully figured stuff which was perfect. Save trouble by preparing the top with the plane to avoid turning it flat.

Method of Holding The glue chuck for the top and foot. The pedestal can be turned with the timber held between the driving fork and the running centre.

Lathe Speed 1500 rpm.

Tools ¼″ and ⅛″ gouges, ¼″ skew chisel and thin parting tool.

Method

Mount the piece for the top to the glue chuck. If the chuck has to be prepared specially for this job, choose a piece of soft wood which will be slightly less in finished diameter than the table top. Use the ¼″ gouge to shape the edge of the top, after first cutting down to size. Clean up, burnish and polish. If paper has to be used on the face of the top, first wrap the paper around a cork block and apply carefully. This method will ensure a perfectly flat face. When completely finished, use the thin knife and hammer to tap through the joint to remove the work. If there is any difficulty, and to avoid splitting, use a little heat from the hot air gun or a hair dryer.

Table

Turning the top of the table to round – shaping with the gouge

Polishing the table top

Place the timber for the pedestal on the glue chuck and shape using the gouge and chisel. Before polishing, bore a hole to receive the pedestal tenon. This can be done with the ⅛″ gouge, but if you have an exact size in mind, use a small drill mounted in the tailstock drill chuck. Remove the completed job as before.

Shaping the base of the table with the gouge

Shaping the table base

Squaring the base of the table for jointing

Remove the glue chuck and place the leg piece between centres, using the tiny 3/8″ driving fork. Alternatively, the bobbin drive could be used. Shaping can almost entirely be carried out using the 1/4″ skew chisel, unless deep coving is intended when the 1/4″ gouge should be used. Carefully cut the little tenon at each end using the skew or the parting tool. Complete to polished stage and part off.

The only additional work required before gluing up will be to carefully bore the hole in the underside of the table top to receive the tenon.

Shaping the leg of the table with the skew chisel

Using the heel of the skew chisel to cut a step in the leg of the table

Squaring the shoulder with the long corner of the skew chisel

Fruit Ring

This is a favourite design of mine. My wife has a large fruit ring made from Circassian Walnut which has been in use for 30 years and is much admired. In the large size it needed a wood chuck to hold it, but in the small size it is possible to make in one piece.

Wood Any attractive timber should be used, but not too open grain. I used a little piece of Bird's Eye Maple.

Method of Holding Once again I used the precision combination chuck for safety and prepared a piece between centres beforehand.

Lathe Speed 1500 rpm.

Tools ¼″ and ⅛″ gouges, small parting tool, ¼″ skew chisel.

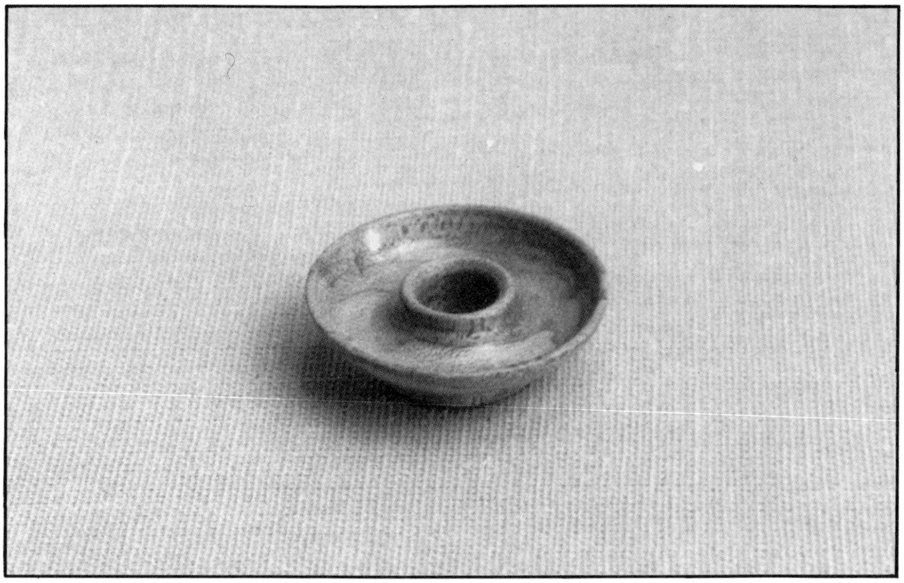

Fruit ring

Shaping the fruit ring

Shaping the fruit ring

Method

First turn down to round and check the outside diameter. Shape the underside of the ring using the gouge and skew chisel.

Boring out the centre of the fruit ring with the gouge

Finishing the fruit ring with steel wool

Parting off the fruit ring

Change the rest and place it across the face of the work. Mark out with the parting tool the ring size. Using the smallest gouge, cut and shape the ring to the final depth. Alternate cuts from the outside and inside positions to the centre of the ring. Working from a small groove once again, use the gouge to cut out the centre to a depth in excess of the actual height of the fruit ring. Bring the whole to a finish, being careful to get a finish on the inside of the centre piece.

Move the tool rest and carefully part off the ring. This cut will pass into the hole on the face, so for safety, use the parting tool in the right hand and part off the job into the left.

Slight touching up of the underside may be necessary, which can be done on an abrasive board with very fine paper.

Cutting the outer ring of the nut tray

Nut Tray

This design calls for a two part turning in order to incorporate a space for the waste shells.

Wood Any good hardwood could be used as the turning itself presents no real problems which might demand special selection.

Method of Holding Piece prepared for holding in the collet jaws of the precision combination chuck.

Lathe Speed 1500 rpm.

Tools ¼″ and ⅛″ gouges, ¼″ skew chisel and thin parting tool.

Method

The method is similar to that used when turning the fruit ring. However, the centre is turned in the same way as turning a little bowl. Remember, always work from a point of part and let the bevel look at the wood so that it rests on it and rubs it when cutting.

Burnishing the completed nut tray

Nut tray

Square Boxes

This project can make use of the short ends of square material which in many cases will already be squared up for benchwork. Many changes of lid shape will be possible.

Wood Any close grained hardwood will do, but avoid any which may be prone to splintering because the corners on this job will always tend to be accident prone.

Method of Holding The glue chuck has been used here, but many will choose to use a purpose-made square chuck which can be used repeatedly.

Lathe Speed 1500 rpm.

Tools Thin parting tool and ¼″ round nose gouge.

Square box in Ziricote

Square box – centreing on the glue chuck

Method

Prepare the square and bring to a finish ready for polishing. Place a glue chuck on the lathe. Mark the diagonals on the end of the block to determine the centre, melt the glue, place the block on the chuck and bring up the tailstock centre in order to accurately place the block in perfect centre.

Probably the trickiest part is the cutting of the division between the lid and the box itself. Any carelessness here may result in a split corner. The procedure is the same as when turning a leg to leave the pommel for the joint. First use the toe of the skew chisel to mark the point of cut and to sever the fibres at the corner, then proceed to cut with the thin parting tool. This cut will give us the position of the lid rebate which secures it in place. Shape the lid with the gouge and chisel, then part off. Leave a little of the rebated piece on the box which can then be used to act as a guide to the exact sizing of the inside of the box. Put the lid on one side.

Use the parting tool to cut a little groove, which will not only size the inside, but act as a point of start for the gouge. Use the gouge to cut a hole in the centre to the required depth of the box inside. Always with the bevel of the gouge looking at the wood and resting on it, make a series of cuts from the outside groove into the middle hole until the box is cut to depth. There should be a good polish on the job as a result of the bevel rubbing.

Square up the face of the box with the gouge moving outwards, bevel rubbing. Now carefully fit the lid, adjust as necessary to arrive at a good push fit. Again touch up to a finish.

I used Ziricote for this job, finalised by first burnishing with shavings, then with a piece of hessian. This job could be left, but a coat of sanding sealer might make an improvement to some timbers, finished with a final coat of wax.

Marking off the lid of the square box – showing thin parting tool

Shaping the lid of the square box

Wine carafe

Wine Carafe

A simple piece of design with clean lines. The only slight problem is the slanted mouth.

Wood This just has to be a piece of very close grained timber. I did start with a little piece of Pink Ivory, but it just would not stay together to give me the thin wall I needed.

Method of Holding The little bit of boxwood finally chosen was first turned between centres, then mounted into the smallest jaw of the Multistar chuck. This chuck is excellent for this type of holding.

Lathe Speed 1500 rpm.

Tools ¼″ and ⅛″ gouges, ¼″ skew chisel and thin parting tool.

Method

Turn to round. Use the parting tool to mark the height of the vessel, then shape the outside of the job with gouge and chisel. Move over the rest to the face, but before doing so, use a fine tenon saw to slant the top of the carafe.

Very carefully advance the parting tool to cut a groove which will act as a point of start near the edge. With care, insert the ⅛″ gouge into the centre to a depth equal to the final depth of the vessel. Still using the tiny gouge, start the removal of the waste and the shaping of the inside. At this point you can increase the speed of the lathe to the fastest. Careful placement of the gouge is necessary here with the bevel looking at the wood.

Bring to an acceptable finish from the tool. It may be desirable to paper the lip, with the machine still, to bring the curves together at the lip. Burnish and part off.

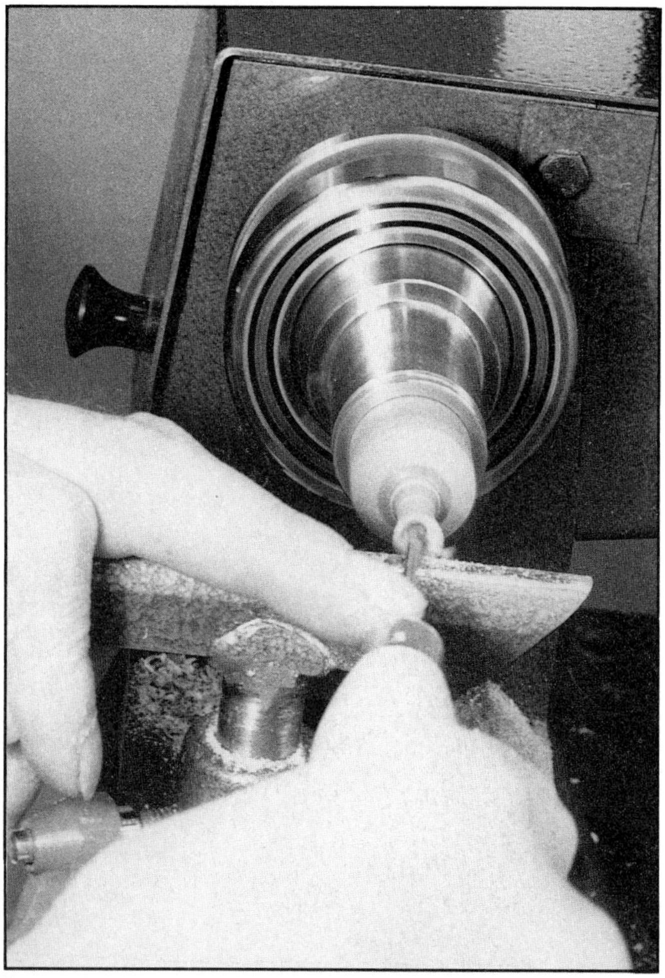
Boring the centre of the carafe for depth

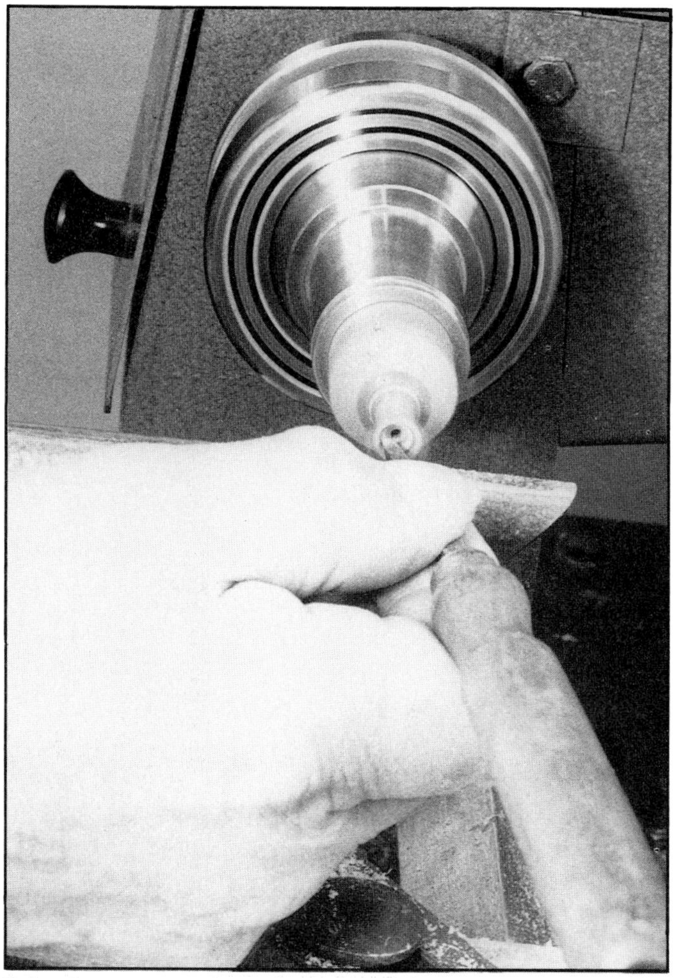
Using the gouge to shape the inside of the carafe

Beaker

This is a simple turning using the same method as for turning the cup and saucer. Care in selection of a suitable timber, combined with a simplicity of shape, will produce satisfying results. The Multistar chuck is again used.

Beaker

Parting off the beaker

Flower Vase

Held in the same way as the carafe and the beaker and made using the same method of cutting. Select a colourful timber and use a slightly more complicated approach to the shape.

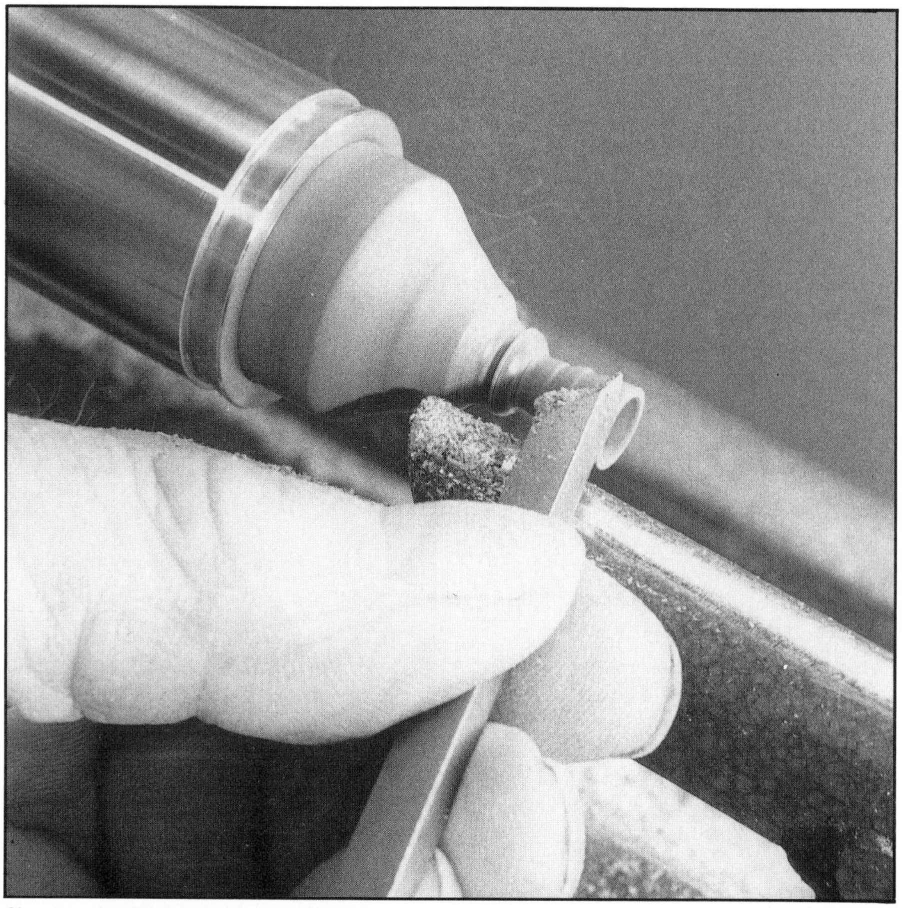

Shaping the flower vase with the skew chisel

Flower vase in Purpleheart

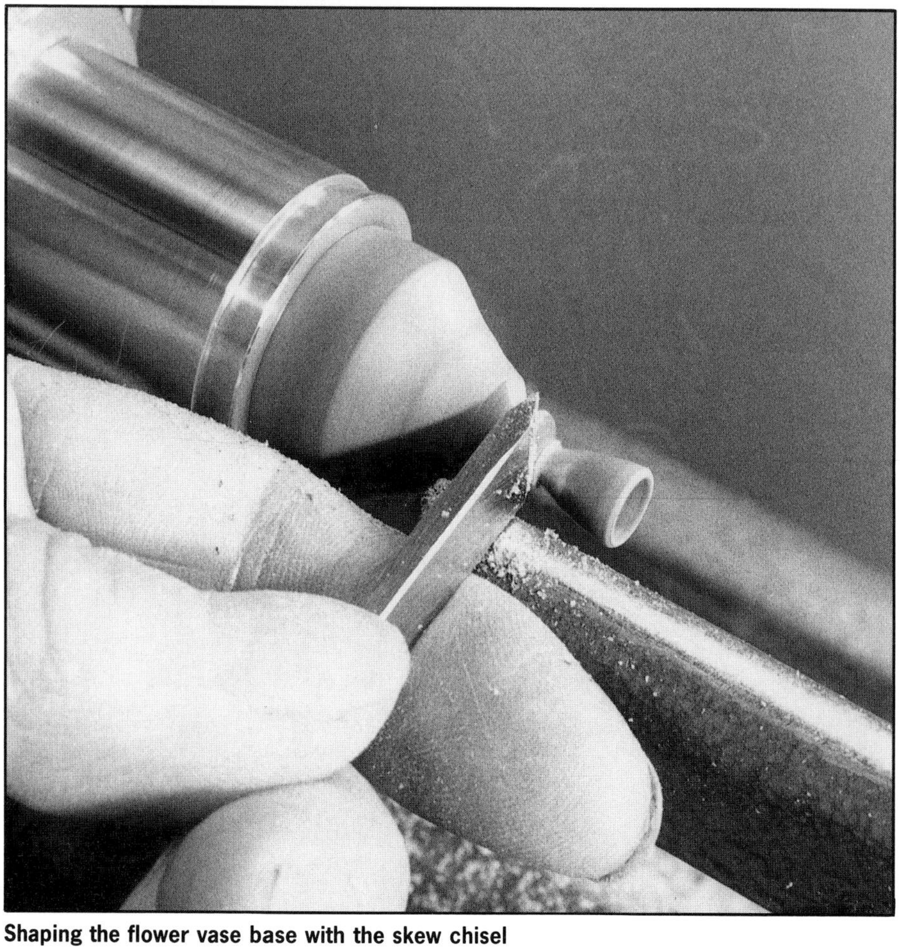

Shaping the flower vase base with the skew chisel

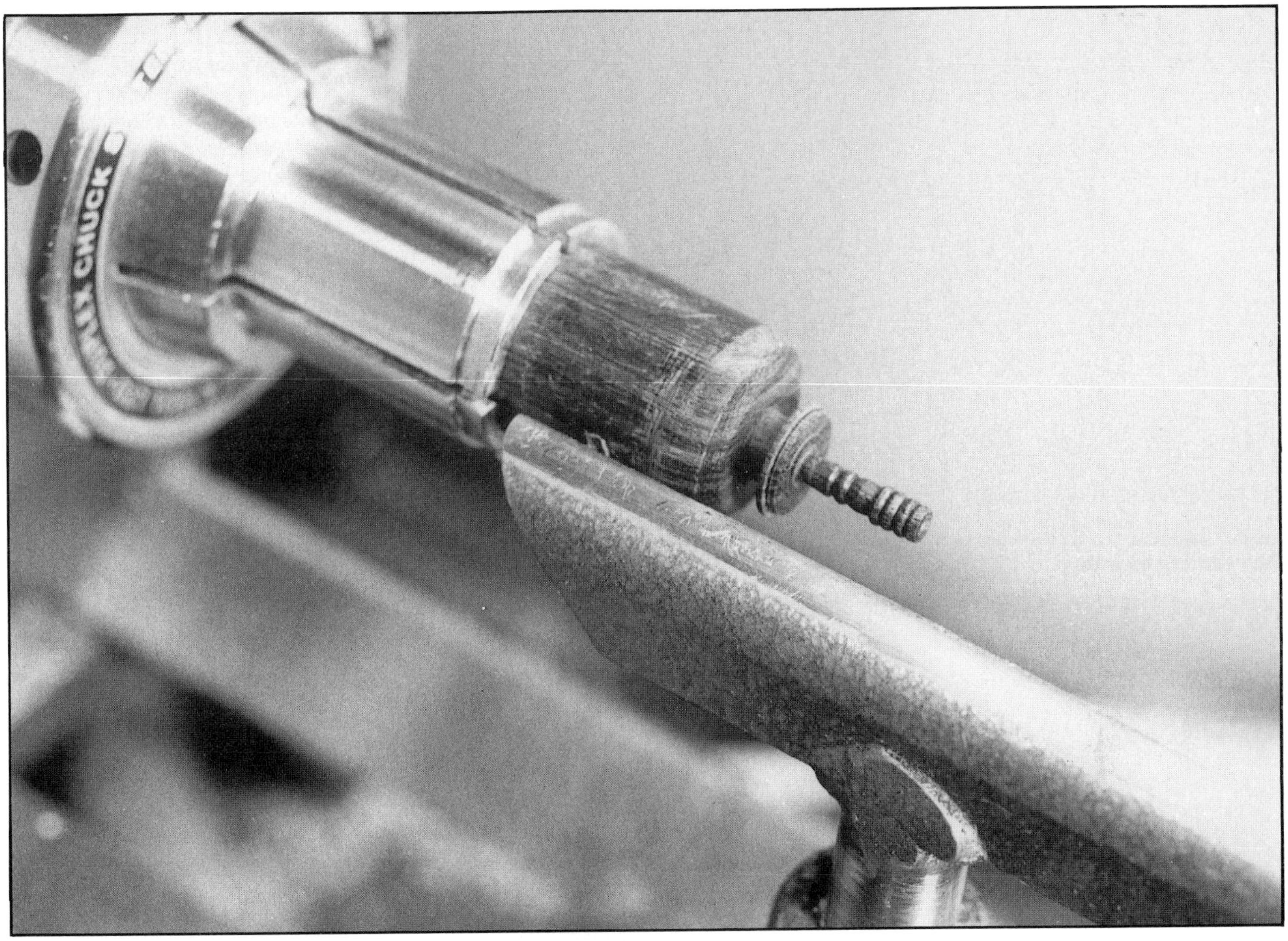

Table lamp

Table Lamp

Use an odd length of any colourful wood and hold as with the flower vase. Use the 'between centre' technique for shaping. Bore out the flex hole with a tiny drill held in the tailstock drill chuck.

Table lamp

Cup, saucer and plate

Shaping the cup

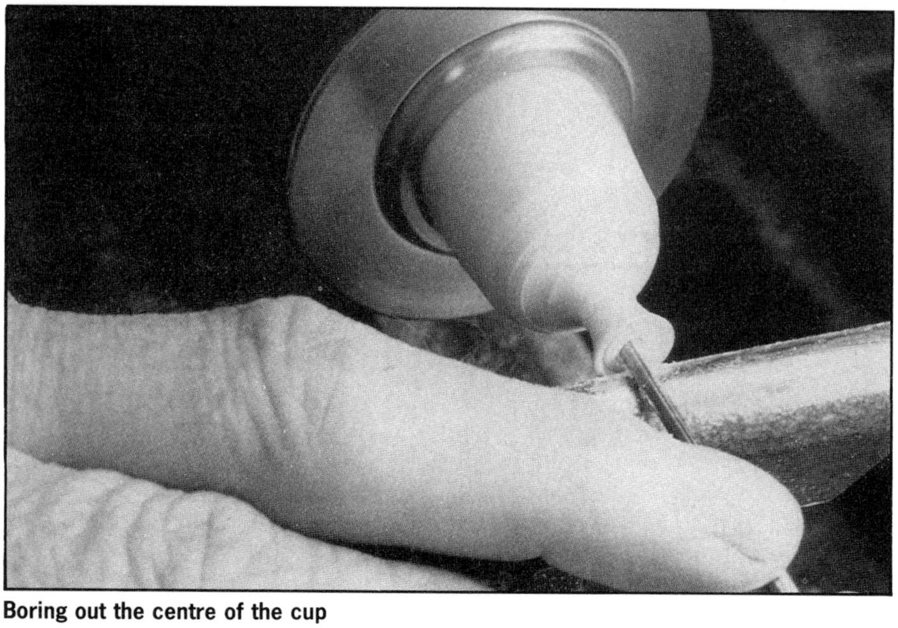

Boring out the centre of the cup

Cup, Saucer and Plate

This is a design project where great attention to detail is demanded. The three components must match, as must a complete dining set if one is made.

Keep to simple lines. The job must have an easy-to-clean finish, which should be obtained from the tools only. No applied finish is needed.

Wood For best results and to avoid trouble, choose a hard close grained timber. Luckily I had a little piece of boxwood.

Method of Holding The boxwood was first turned to round between centres, then transferred to the precision combination chuck fitted with the smallest size collet chuck.

Lathe Speed Fastest.

Tools ¼″ and ⅛″ gouges, ¼″ skew chisel and parting tool.

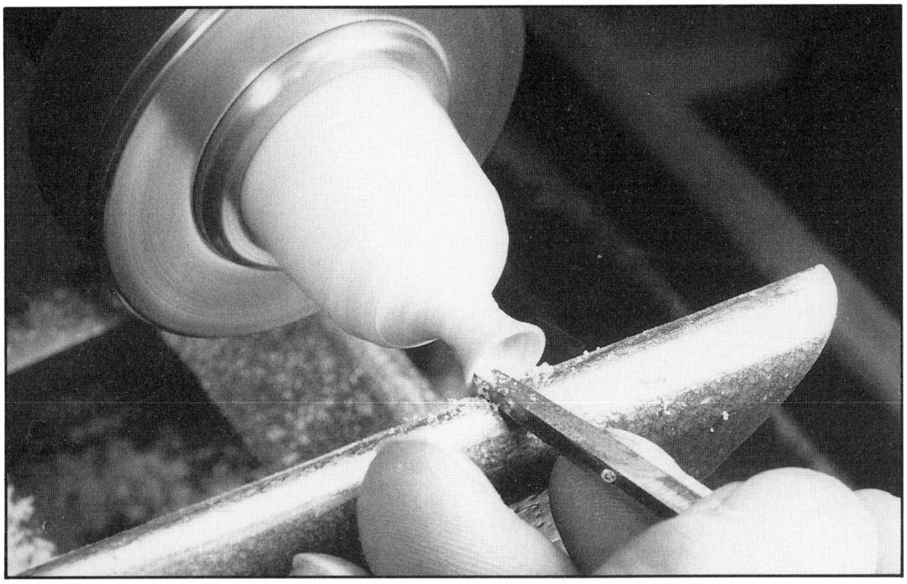
Shaping the cup

Completed cup

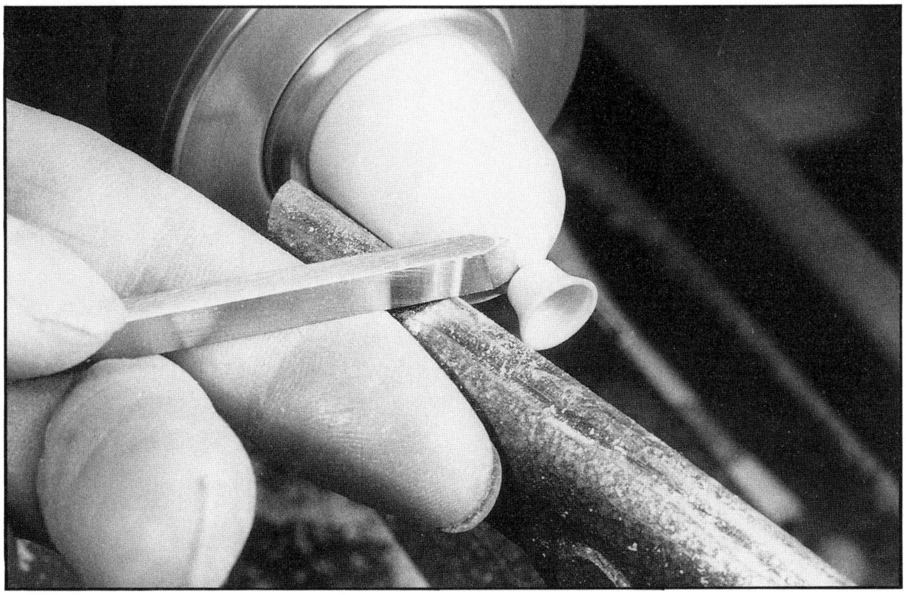
Parting off the cup

Method

Be sure to secure the timber safely in the jaws of the chuck. It's also a good idea to check periodically during turning to see this hold is maintained.

The cup is made first by turning enough of the forward piece of the timber, then using the ¼″ gouge to shape the outside to a final finish. The skew chisel can also be used here without problems. Cut the inside mark out, as always with the parting tool, to give a point of start and to indicate the diameter. Then use the ⅛″ gouge to bore a hole at the centre to finalise the depth. Carefully cut the inside shape with the ⅛″ gouge to a final finish. Burnish with shavings and part off.

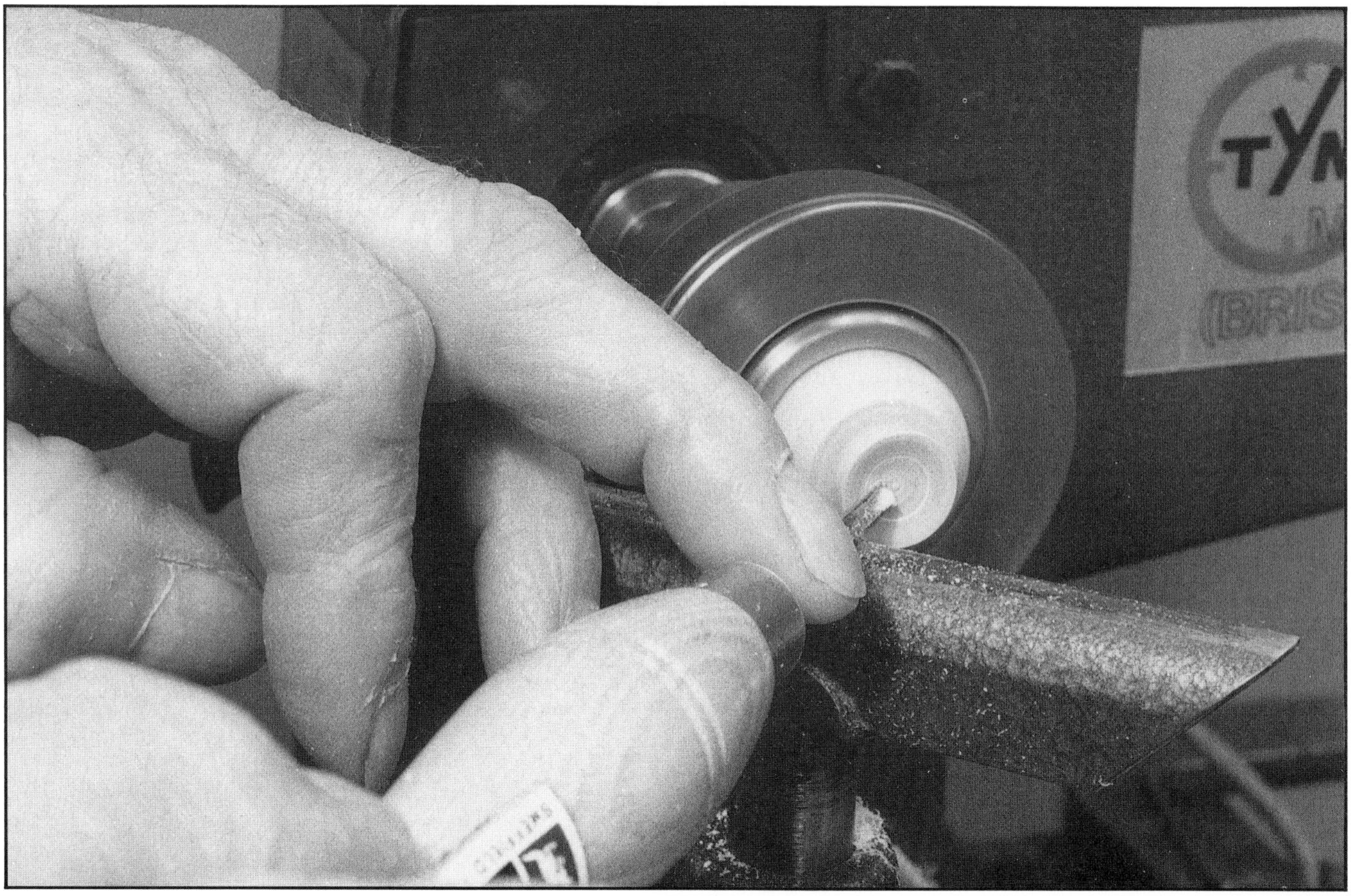

Shaping the saucer

Parting off the saucer

Face off the remaining block and mark off the size of the saucer. Again with the small gouge, shape the inside of the vessel. Cut a space at the back of the saucer of sufficient size to allow the underside of the saucer to be shaped with gouge and chisel. Finish as necessary. Part off. Cut the plate in a similar way.

Make a handle using the method described earlier. The handle may need a little extra shaping. Use an abrasive board or tiny file to produce a face of exactly the same profile as that to which it is to be attached. Glue the handle in place with rapid araldite or similar adhesive. Now have a cup of tea and a sandwich.

Shaping the plate

Shaping the underside of the plate

Rolling Pin for the Kitchen

A simple item to make. Choose Sycamore or similiar timber and mount the blank between centres using the bobbin drive if available. However, the piece used here was driven by a cone drive.

The entire job can be done with a skew chisel. Don't use the gouge, it's much more satisfying this way.

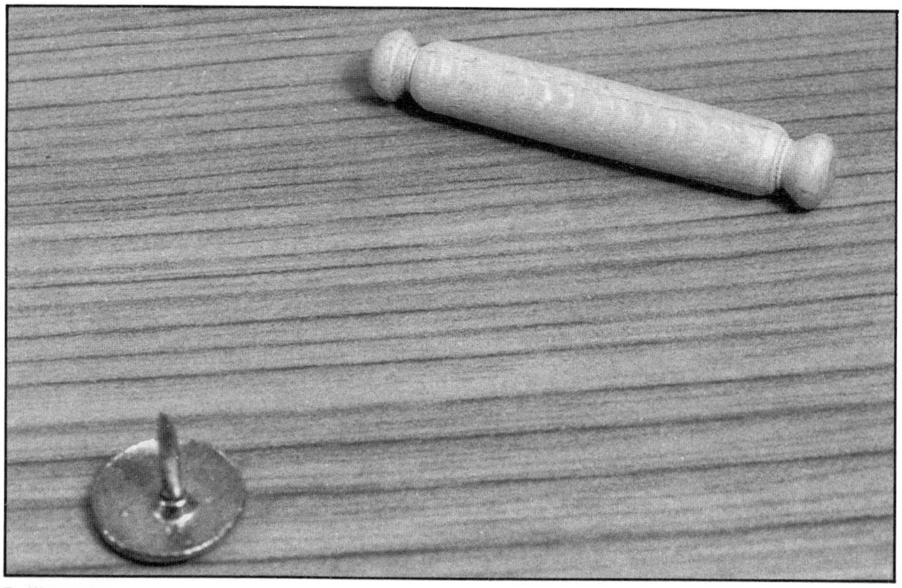

Rolling pin

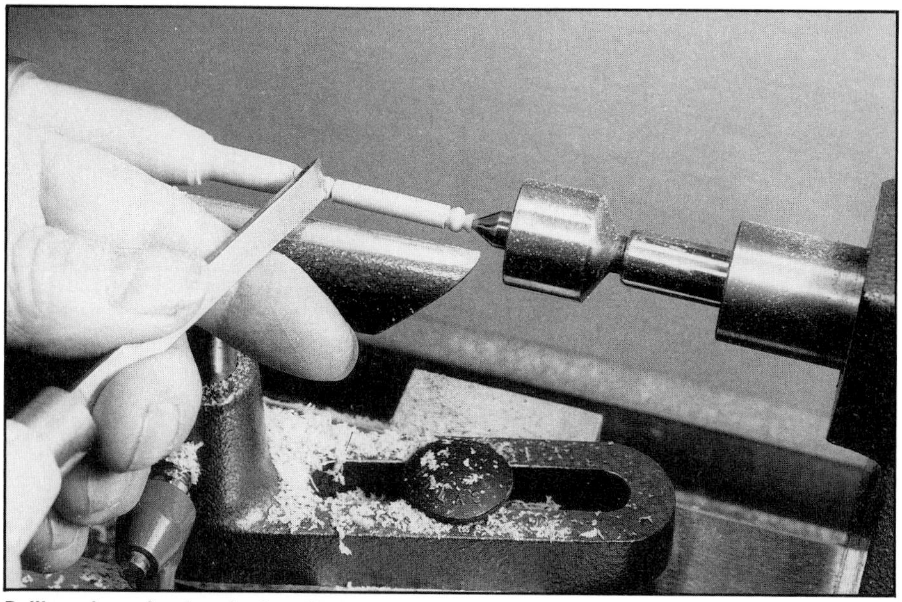

Rolling pin – shaping the handles

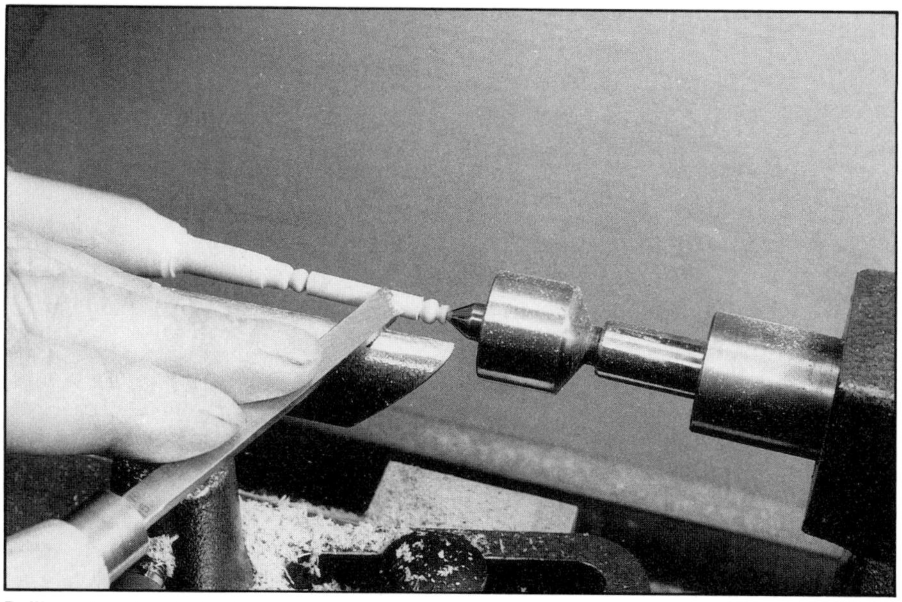

Rolling pin – final planing

Eggs

Larger eggs are most popular and some turners have made a collection of rare woods in egg shape. Any timber can be used to make these miniature eggs. As they are in the main made with the skew chisel, it becomes an exercise not only in cutting perfection but also in exploring the cutting properties of lesser-known woods. I've even used pieces from the garden for this work. The Mahonia, for example, gave the warmest yellow I have ever seen in a timber.

The timber can be mounted in the cone drive previously described. The beauty of using the cone is it will accept odd-shaped timbers and partly-turned work can be reversed into it. Part off, once again, with the long corner of the skew.

Curving with the skew chisel to make eggs

Eggs

Curving with the skew chisel

Egg mallet

Egg Mallet or Nut Mallet

A 'between centres' job using the same techniques as described before. Careful selection of long straight timber is essential.

The head of the mallet is turned at the right hand end in the example shown. Apart from the cutting of the little tenon at the end of the handle, which is done with the tiny parting tool, most of the cutting can be carried out with the skew chisel, including the parting off.

To bore the small hole in the mallet head, make a little vee block to hold it on the table of the drill press.

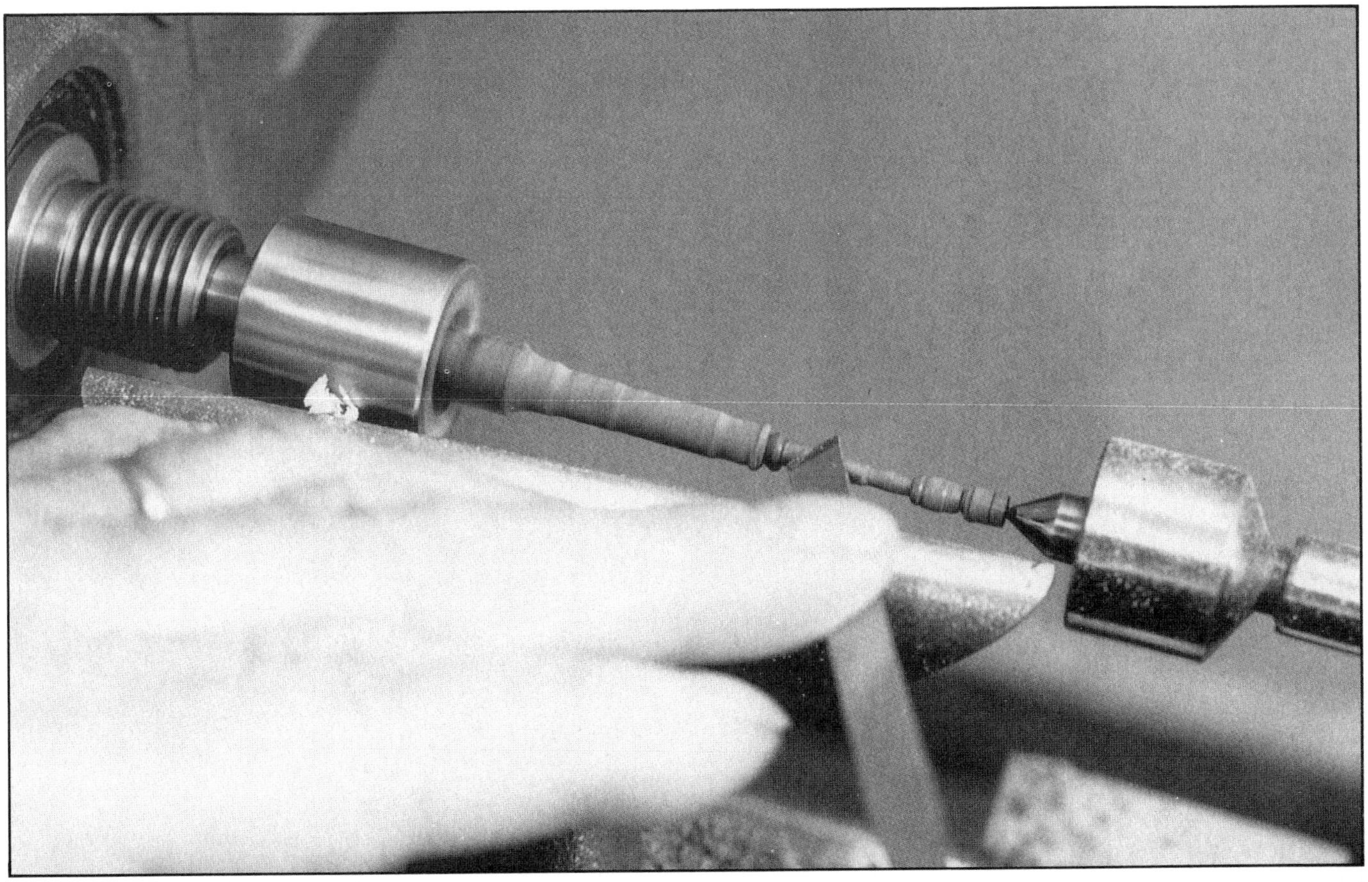

Shaping the handle of the nut mallet

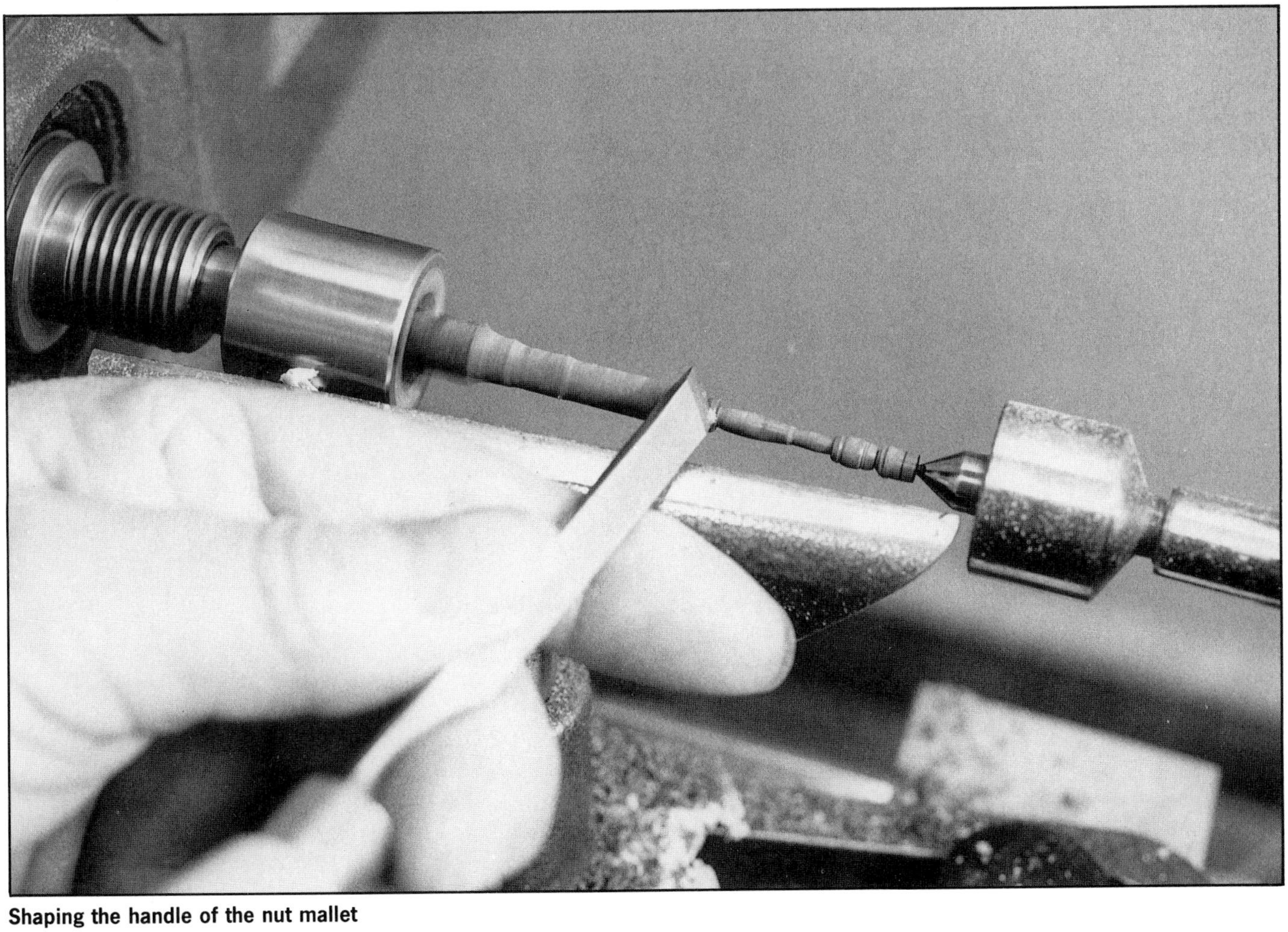

Shaping the handle of the nut mallet

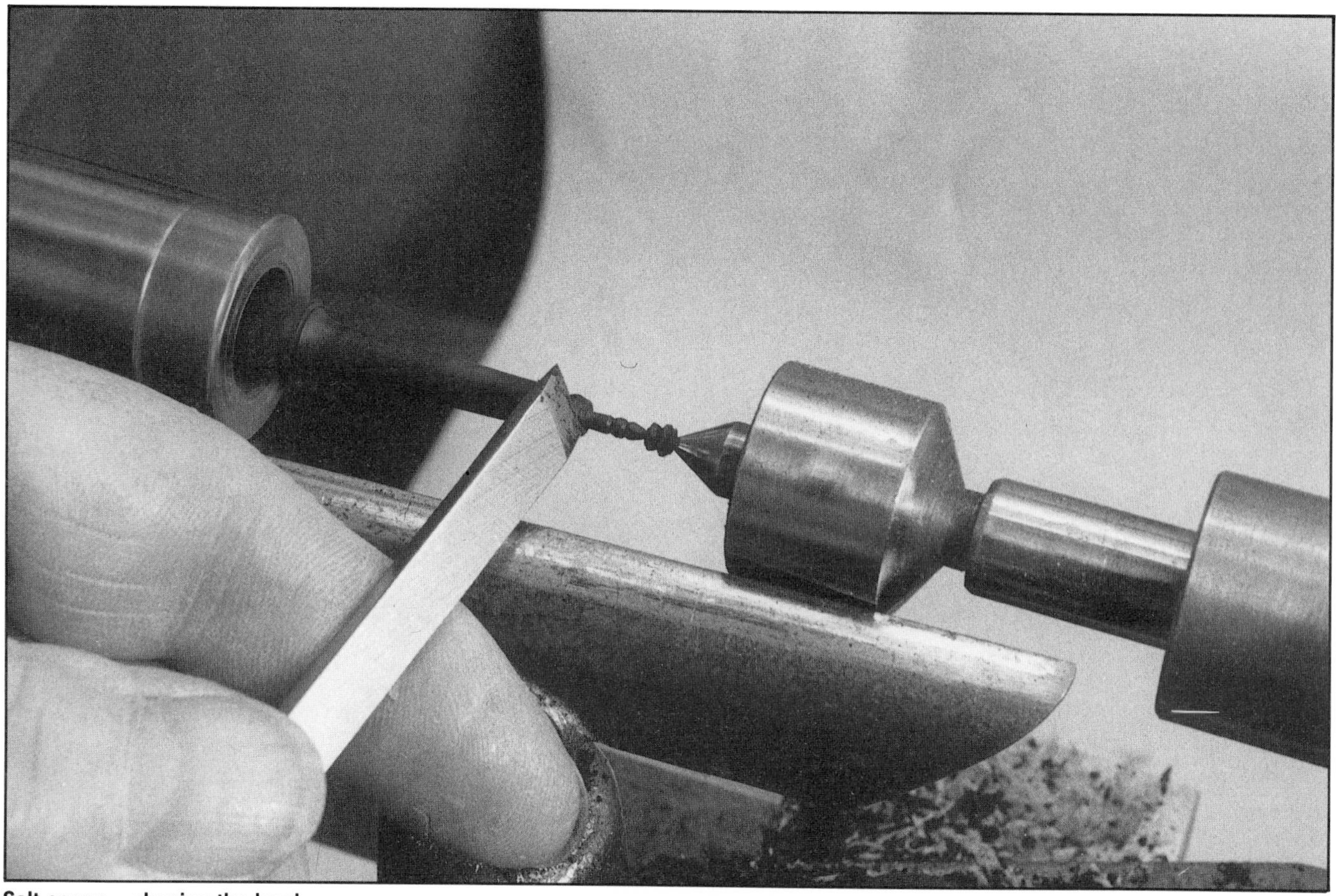
Salt spoon – shaping the bowl

Salt Spoon

A very tiny turning which presents little difficulty, except the cutting of the inside of the cup. On the bench it would be difficult to hold. The best method, therefore, is to use the electric hot melt glue gun and attach the finished turning either to a bench hook or indeed the top of the bench itself. Then use a small carving gouge to scoop out the bowl.

If the job is left on the lathe, slide the tool rest underneath to support the job and carry out the carving before parting off the finished work with the long corner of the skew.

Salt spoon – carving the bowl

Lace bobbin

Lace Bobbin

No book on small turning would be complete without the lace bobbin. There are many thousands of home craftsmen making these for their friends and relations and some earning a fair living also. Some marvellous examples are shown in the next chapter on the work of contemporary craftsmen.

Many lace bobbins are made to a size and design passed down through the years and particular to that area – East Midlands and Honiton to name just two. Lace bobbins are generally weighted with a ring of beads passing through the end, but some workers build in the weight in other ways, sometimes grooving and inserting the beads as an inlay. Wire can also be used in a similar way. Be sure to choose a timber which will give a smooth finish and is free from oil or other secretions which may harm the lace.

Making bobbins is probably one certain way in which the imagination can run riot and the turner can have endless fun.

The size is of course very important. The space for the thread should be marked out and cut very accurately. At the same time, attention must be given to the quality of finish, since rough work will present problems with the thread catching up in the wood. Care must also be exercised in the selection of finish. Oil and similar polishes cannot be used since there is a possibility of staining the finished lace.

Method of Holding In the past, this has presented a problem to many, except those who bought my first book or attended one of my courses and thus knew of a holding device I designed originally for children to use to turn small pieces. This was the little mandrel with the square pyramidic hole shown earlier. This design has now been reproduced and is shown in use here. Made by Tyme Machines, it is called the Lace Bobbin Drive.

A running centre is also needed to eliminate the need for oil or grease on the dead centre. The little one shown I made some years back and I still live in the hope that one of the leading manufacturers will produce one of these especially for the mini-turner.

Another problem arises with this particular job, for as the turnings are long and thin, even if one cuts with the

Lace bobbin – beading with the skew

Lace bobbin – planing with the skew

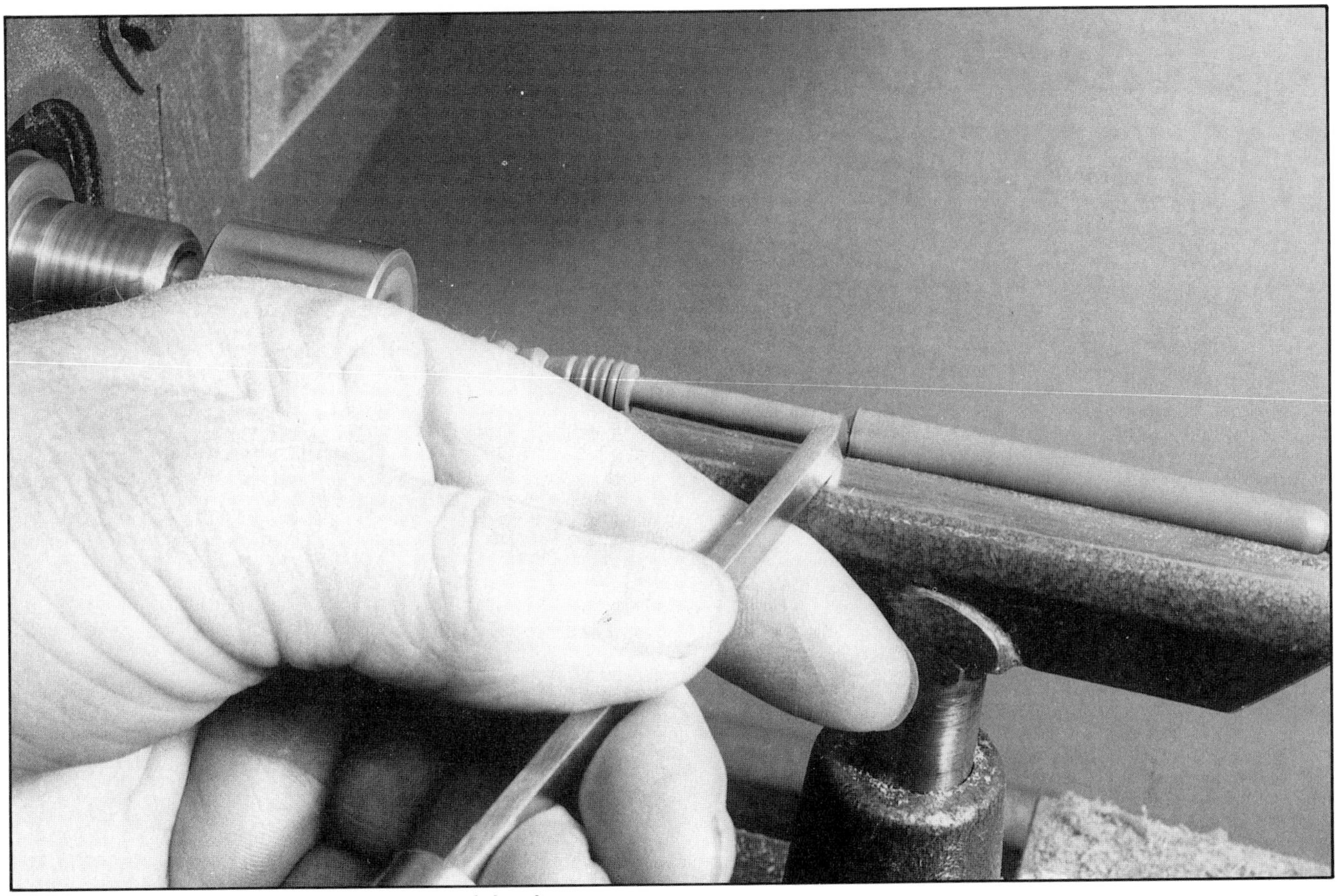

Lace bobbin – squaring with the long corner of the skew

sharpest of tools, the timber needs support in the centre. No one has yet provided the ideal answer with a perfect steady and the user must instead use his finger. I usually bring my finger over the top, but in the illustration here I have it coming up from underneath. You could burn your finger, so use an asbestos stall if you wish.

It is essential to choose timbers with long, fairly straight grain, as these are such thin pieces and short grain timber will give endless trouble with breakages. Each piece should be examined with this in mind.

If polychromatic turnings are to be made, great care in jointing together with careful selection of timber in regard to degree of hardness is vital. Strong glue will play havoc with the tool edges, but this must be used to ensure perfection.

Method

Prepare a blank of suitable length and ½″ square section. Mount between the bobbin drive and the running centre and bring into use the smallest rest. I use one made by Tyme which is ideal for the purpose.

Turn to round and mark out using a template. If a number of the same type are being cut, it may be wise to make a permanent template from thin sheet metal, but usually a cardboard one will suffice. A metalworker's awl or the fine point of a marking knife will be found useful for marking. The marking out should be done on a surface which has been planed with the skew chisel.

Use the skew chisel to make all cuts other than concave ones. I tend to use the centre of the skew, but others use the heel and also the point. Choose the method you like best and obtain a perfect, shiny surface from the tool (abrasive paper should be avoided). Shape as necessary.

Cut the thread portion with the chisel and the step by toeing and heeling. By this I mean the long corner of the skew squares and fines the end grain and the heel cuts into the corner to make a perfect square.

When cutting is complete, burnish with shavings and hessian and part off the job using the long corner of the skew. This is a safe way to part, will give a lovely shine at the part and with any luck, dependent on the strength of the timber, hold to the last fibre before freeing.

Contemporary Turners of Mini Work

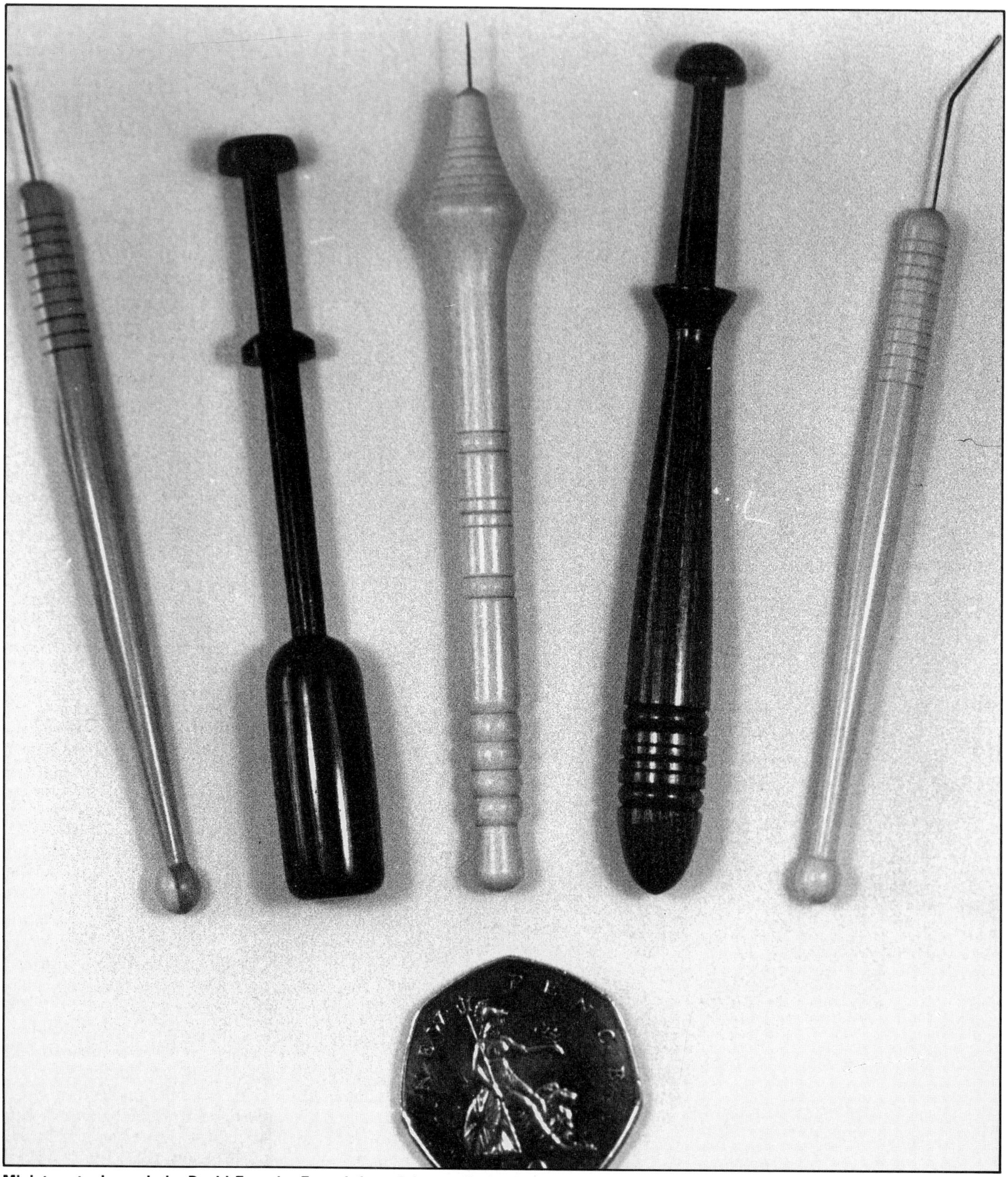

Miniature tools made by David Francis. ***From left to right:*** **needle hook, continental pricker, gimp, bent needle**

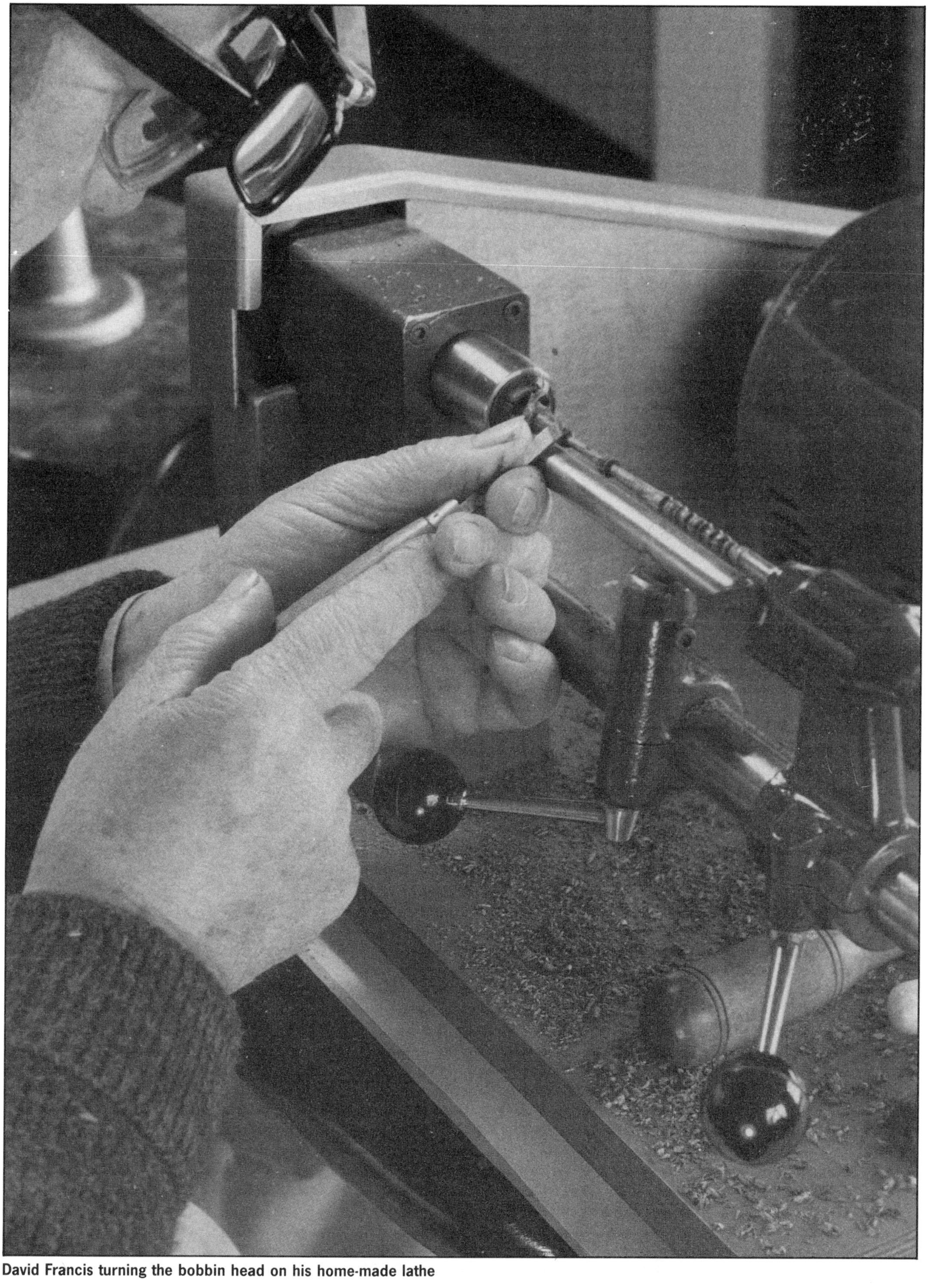

David Francis turning the bobbin head on his home-made lathe

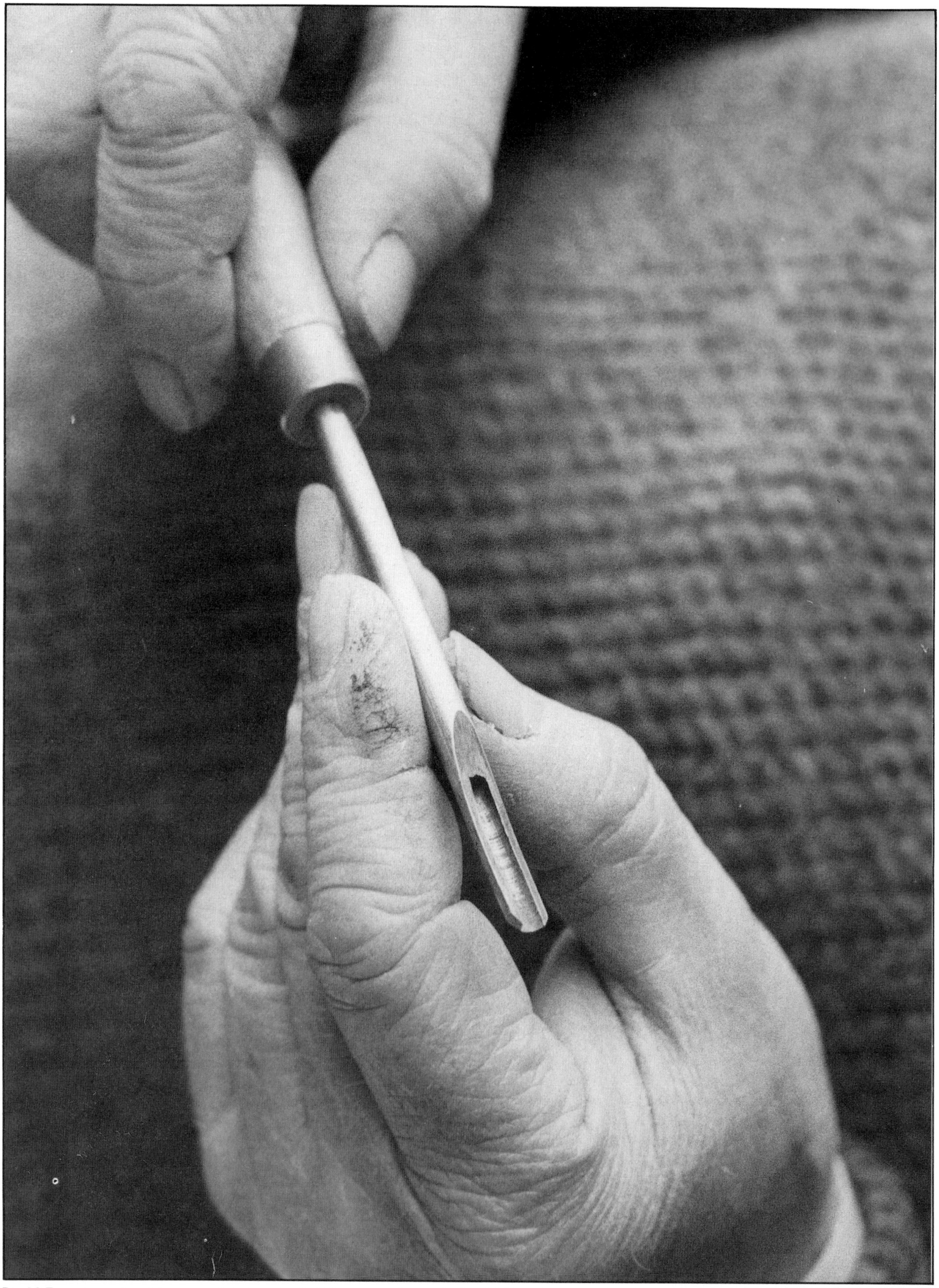

David Francis makes his own miniature tools. This gouge is made by drilling silver steel rod and grinding the side away

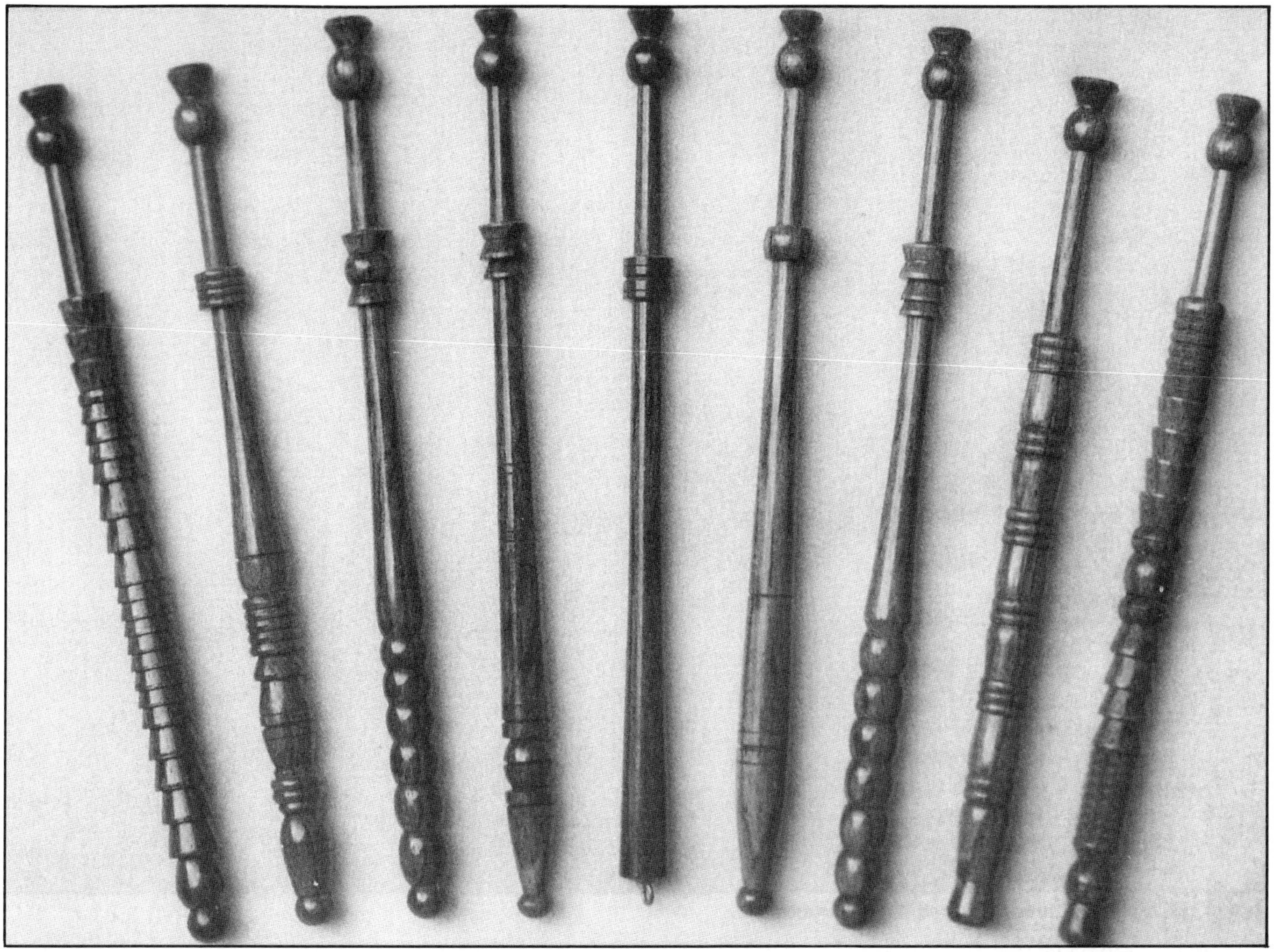

Lace bobbins turned by David Francis

DAVID FRANCIS lives in the Nottinghamshire town of Wollaton. He apprenticed in metal turning, then served throughout the war years as a marine fitter. He returned and spent many years in mapmaking. His hobby at that time was making furniture and clocks.

When his wife took up lacemaking, some dozen or so years ago, the necessity for bobbins became paramount and David set about making his own lathe. Readers will note the sturdiness of his design, but also notice it doesn't have a foot at the tailstock end and is of length and general size ideal for bobbin work. Since then he has gone from strength to strength and now turns bobbins for a living.

These bobbins are in a great variety of design and timbers and are superbly finished. He has also solved the tool problem by making his own from rods of silver steel centrally bored, then opened out by grinding. David finds himself greatly in demand to demonstrate and lecture to groups of lacemakers throughout the country.

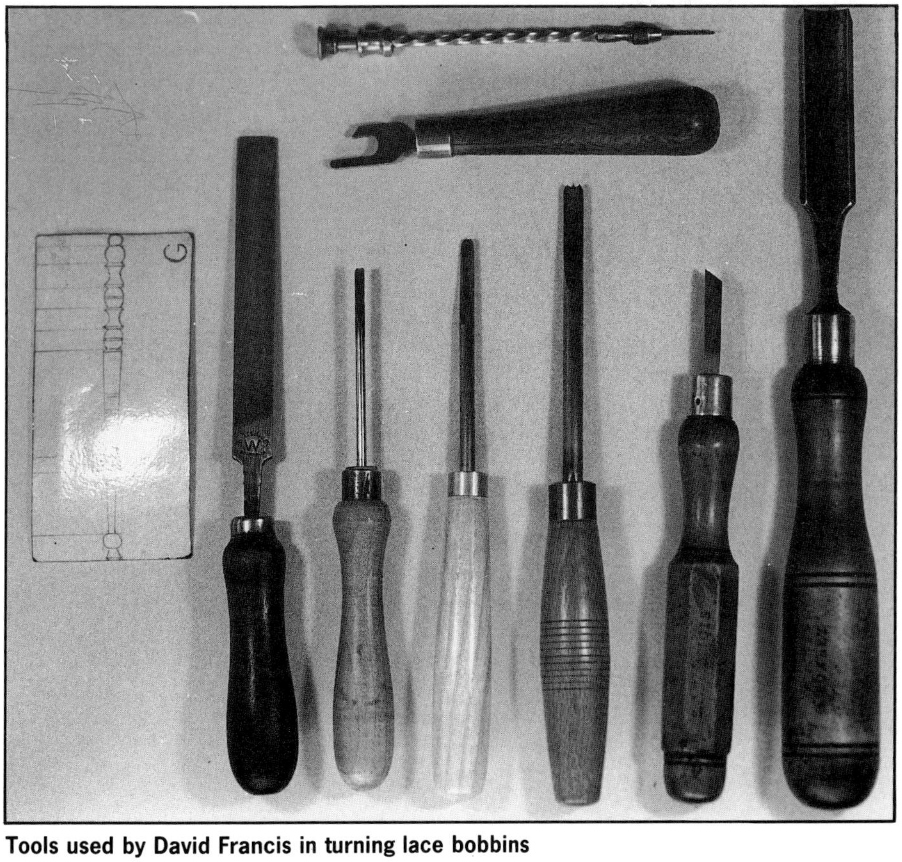

Tools used by David Francis in turning lace bobbins

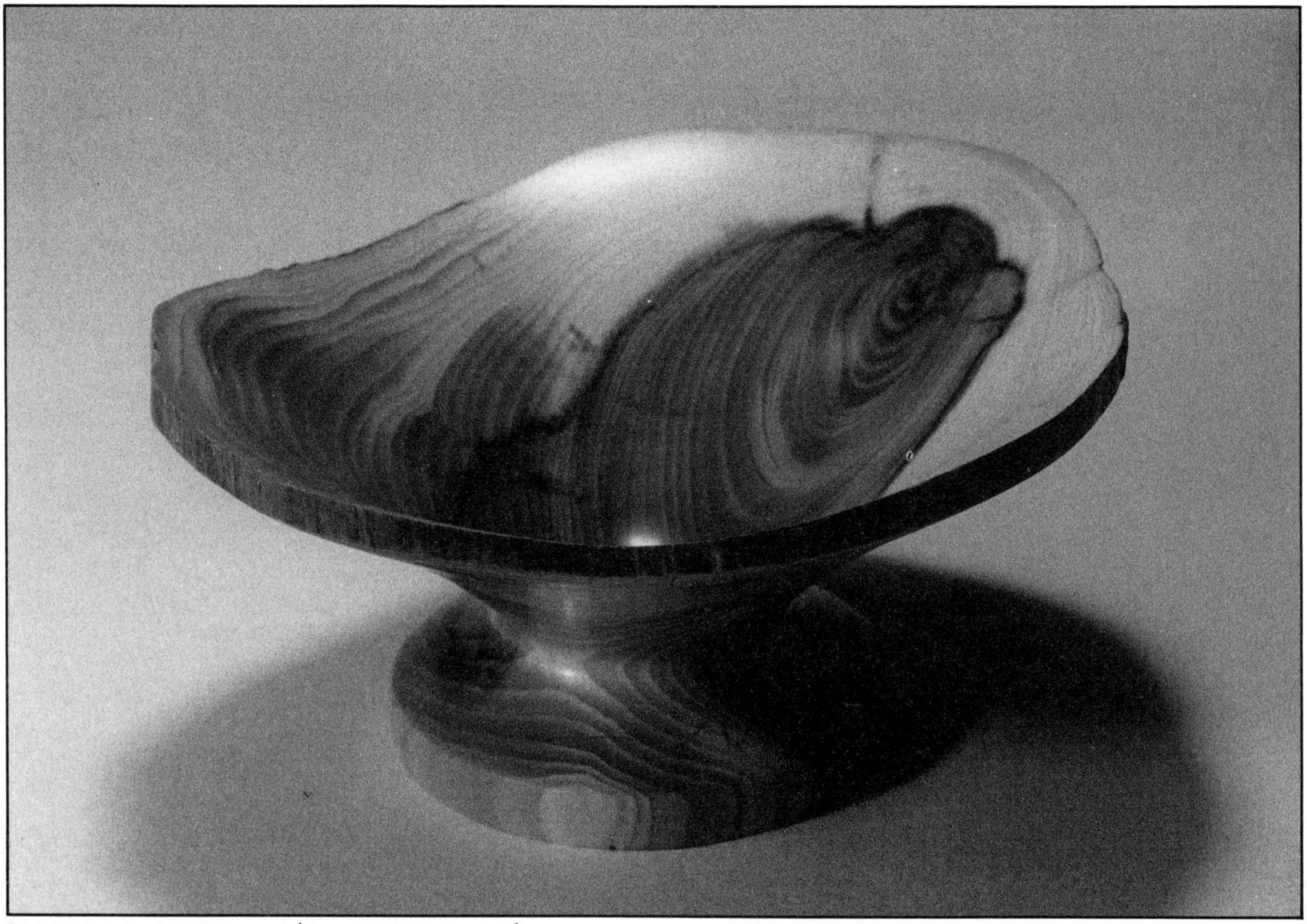

Dish in Yew by Marsh Dawes. (Turned from a branch)

MARSH DAWES lives at Thurlestone, a beautiful little village in South Devon with many thatched cottages. He works in his thatched, purpose built workshop close to his house, using a great variety of timber including many exotics. His father and mother deal in timber.

He came to me as a pupil when only thirteen and five years later he has already built up a reputation for work of a very high order. His work is beautifully thin and splendidly finished without overuse of glasspaper. He turns both large and small and we haven't yet seen the best of him.

Ivory and bone goblets from Marsh Dawes

Goblet in Cocobolo by Marsh Dawes

DAVID WADSLEY lives at Richards Castle near Ludlow and earns his living turning a wide range of miniature turnings. He makes his tools from masonry nails, ground to suit the particular job. All his work is carried out to 1/12 scale and his timbers are not only varied, but extremely colourful.

From the most delightful chess set, through boxes and bowls to handsome goblets and miniature peppermills; all are here. I fully expect to hear him answer my call through his own unbelievably turned telephone. His Jacobean table as high as a fifty pence coin and his accurately scaled spinning wheel must bring delight to everyone who is privileged to see or own such items.

Miniature turnings by David Wadsley.

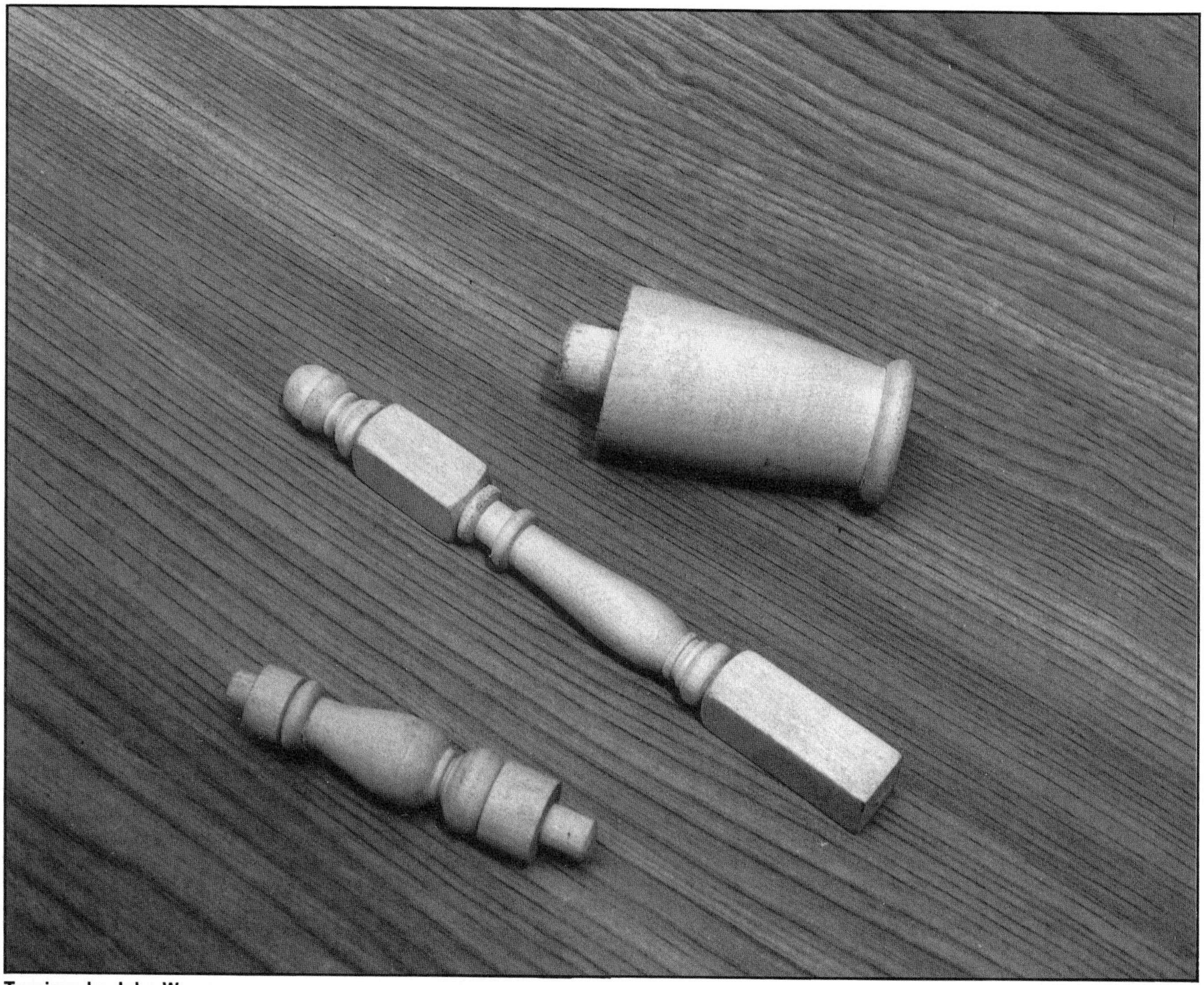

Turnings by John Warner

JOHN WARNER trades at Cutcrew Sawmills in Tideford, close by Saltash in Cornwall. John is different from others as he works mostly in Lime, unless a customer makes a specific request for a different timber.

All his work is to order and is carried out to $1/12$ scale. He's a tremendously skilful turner and dolls' house makers beat a path to his door. His work shows a marked attention to detail and glasspaper is not his favourite tool.

GRAHAM SPALDING is an architectural and industrial model maker, but also specialises in fine miniature furniture. He lives at Stanway Green in Colchester and uses a number of different materials including perspex.

His lathe is an ancient Emco Unimat which is taken apart about once a year and given a good old clean and a general service. His tools are a set of old orthopaedic surgeons' gouges, ground – wait for it – on the inside. He tells me they are made from superb steel and handle extremely thin. For very fine work he uses dentists' probes, ground down to scraper shape. Makes one wonder if he has found the back way into the local hospital! Actually he has a number of professionals amongst his friends.

His miniature furniture is as accurate as an architect would demand, with a very high degree of finish. He experiments with materials for a particular job and is certainly not tied to wood.

Chairs by Graham Spalding

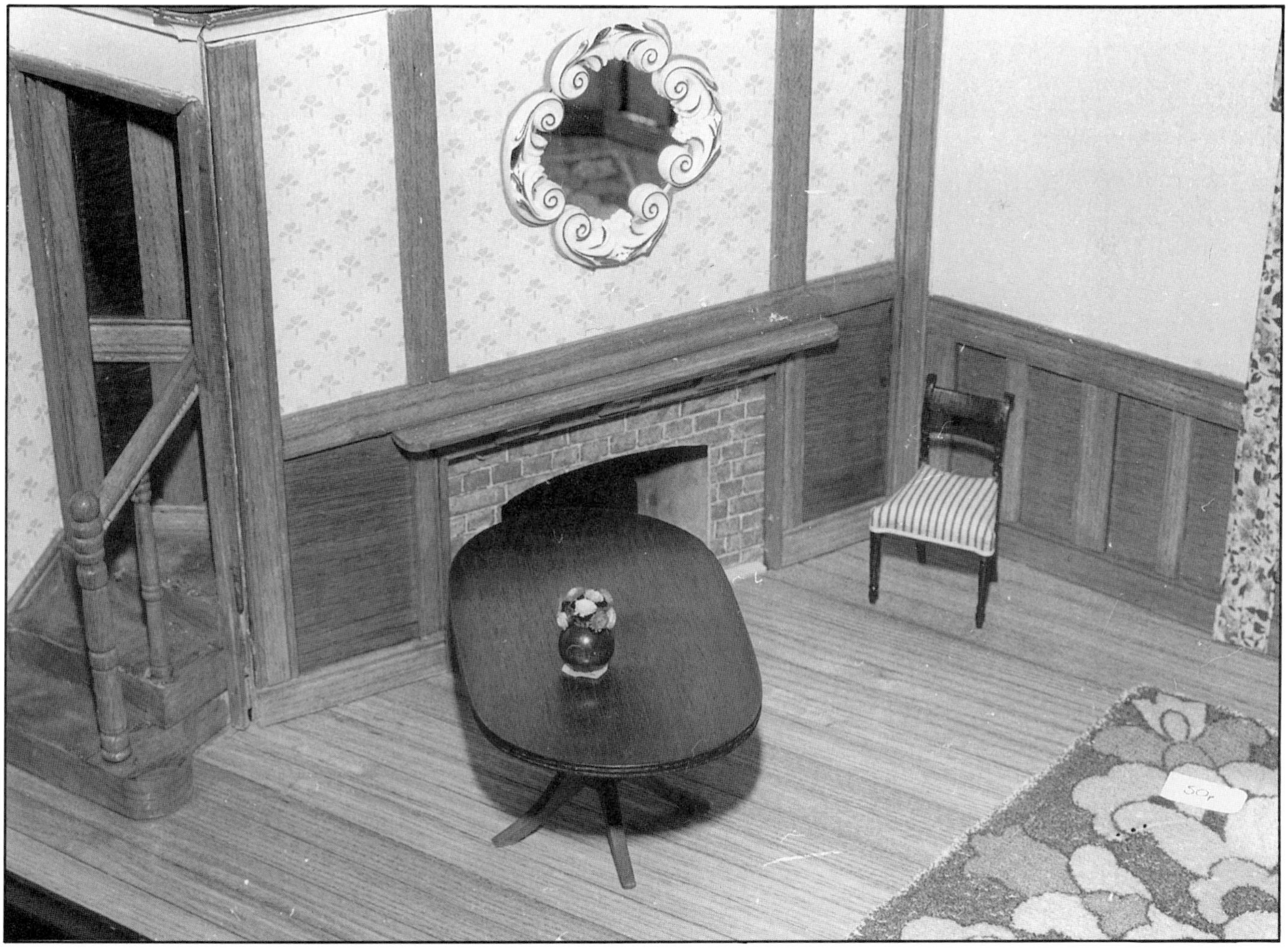

Table and chair by Graham Spalding

Table by Graham Spalding

Table and chairs by Graham Spalding

HUGH GREENLAND is a retired architect and lives for part of the year in Brixham, but when winter comes he's away to a warmer clime. Hugh hasn't any proper tools, neither does he possess a lathe. No, I'm not joking. He uses a weird contraption which centres around an electric drill, and his tools are little better than files, yet he has a full order book and seems never to have an idle moment. I've threatened to teach him to use a proper lathe, but he's reluctant.

Chair by Hugh Greenland

Chairs by Hugh Greenland

Table by Hugh Greenland

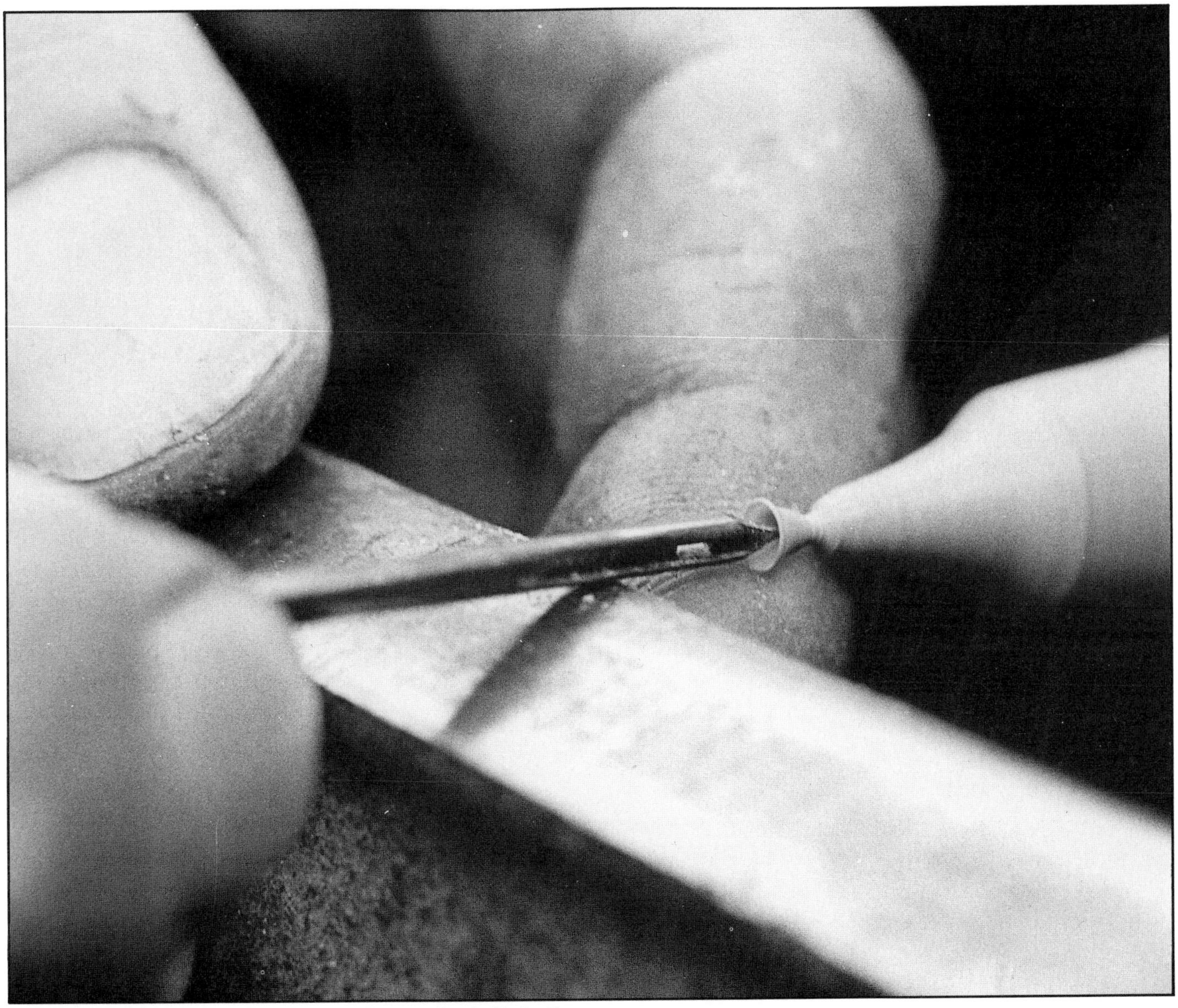

Del Stubbs turning the top of a goblet in boxwood only 5⁄32″ tall

DEL STUBBS lives in Playa del Rey in California and is well known throughout the States. He turns mostly in exotics and whether large or small, the degree of perfection in design and finished article is rarely surpassed. He is innovative and is never slow to try out new ideas.

Miniature turning by Del Stubbs really has to be seen, but in some cases you had best bring your magnifying glass. How he sees to turn such tiny pieces, I know not, but those you see in the photographs I had to handle, and only a macro lens could get close enough (even then I couldn't see them).

Del Stubbs uses a standard size lathe and for the fine work he has tiny scrapers. To see him working is a rare privilege. He lectures and demonstrates and I have yet to correspond with a more helpful person.

Goblet in ivory by Del Stubbs

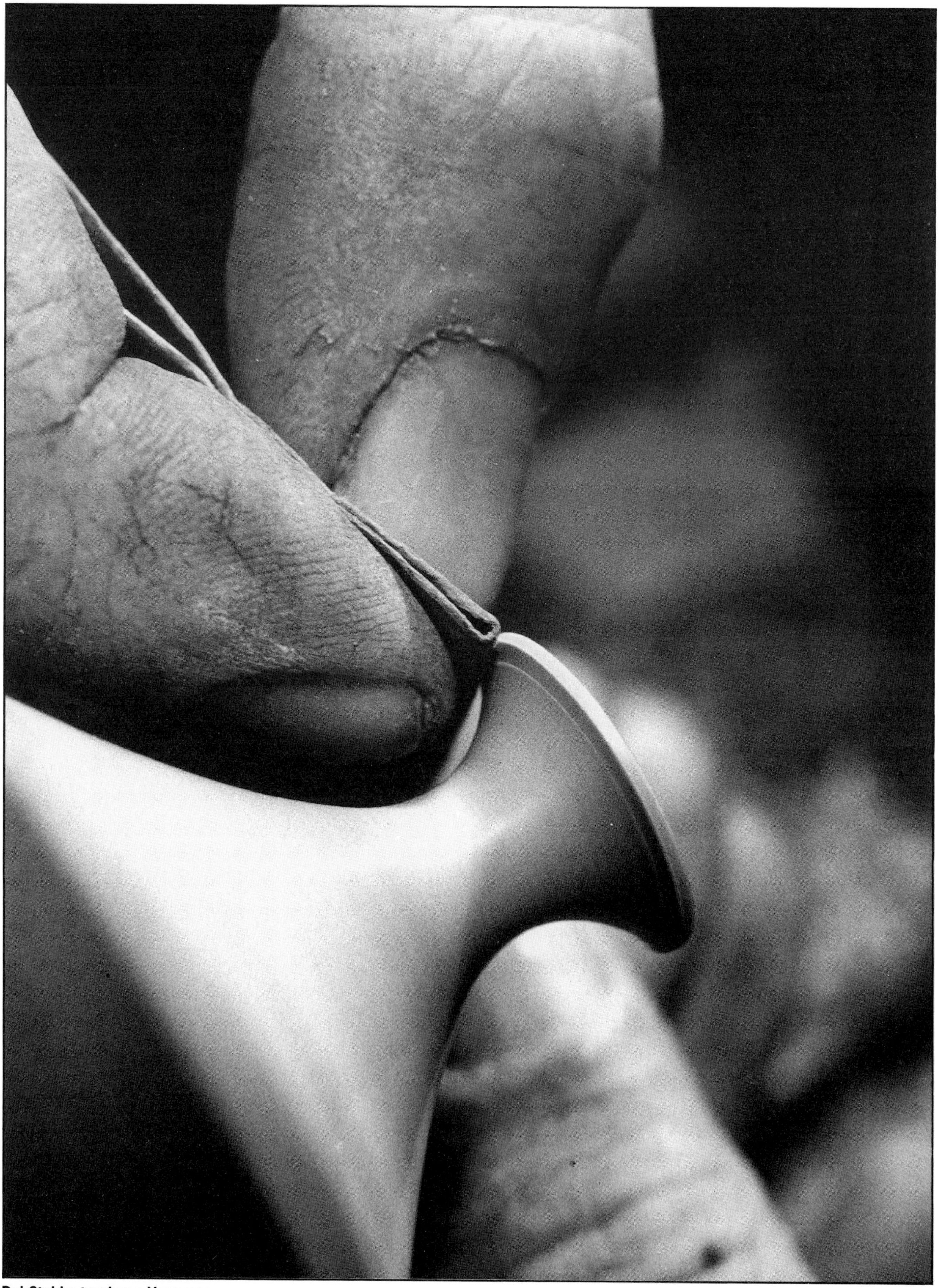

Del Stubbs turning a Yew vase

A Del Stubbs turning. The goblet fits into the small box and the small box is then housed in the larger

The boxes now shown opened up

Goblet and box by Del Stubbs. The box shown is the pedestal on which the other box illustrated sits

Miniature turnings by Mike Baker

MIKE BAKER To his friends, he's known as Scraper, yet his work belies this description. He's a Welshman who left the land of his fathers a number of years ago to find work elsewhere and here he is in Brixham. (What is it about Brixham that brings all the nuts down here?)

He has many skills in the house building business, but he turns large and small with great speed and skill. He makes his own tools from nails and can turn as good a shaving as the next man.

His sets of miniatures can be made to order, but he will tackle any job, no matter the size. He often demonstrates in public and is a joy to watch.

Turnings by Mike Baker

Ivory goblets (left) and tiny turnings from scraps by Ken Smith

KEN SMITH Ken lives at Wellingborough in Northamptonshire, not far from the castle at Fotheringhay where the ill-fated Mary, Queen of Scots was beheaded. I'm quite sure that she could not have used more beautiful bobbins in her lace work than those which Ken turns.

Although he has only been turning for the past four years since his daughter requested some, his work is not only skilled but shows an infinite degree of patience. He started off using an attachment driven by an electric drill, but soon graduated to a better machine.

Just a couple of years back he started experimenting (using exotic timber obtained from Craftwoods of Devon) and some of his patterns are made up of some 150 pieces – polychromatic wizardry plus! The pictures show but a fraction of his design ideas and the many variations on a theme of mixed timbers. Some of these will take the best part of a week to set up – it is as well he is retired. Although his work can be bought, he does it for pure enjoyment. From the small bits of timber which remain, he has fun making little goblets and other vessels.

He often lectures and gives demonstrations particularly to groups of lacemakers.

Small selection of bobbins made by Ken Smith illustrating his many design ideas and his use of mixed timbers

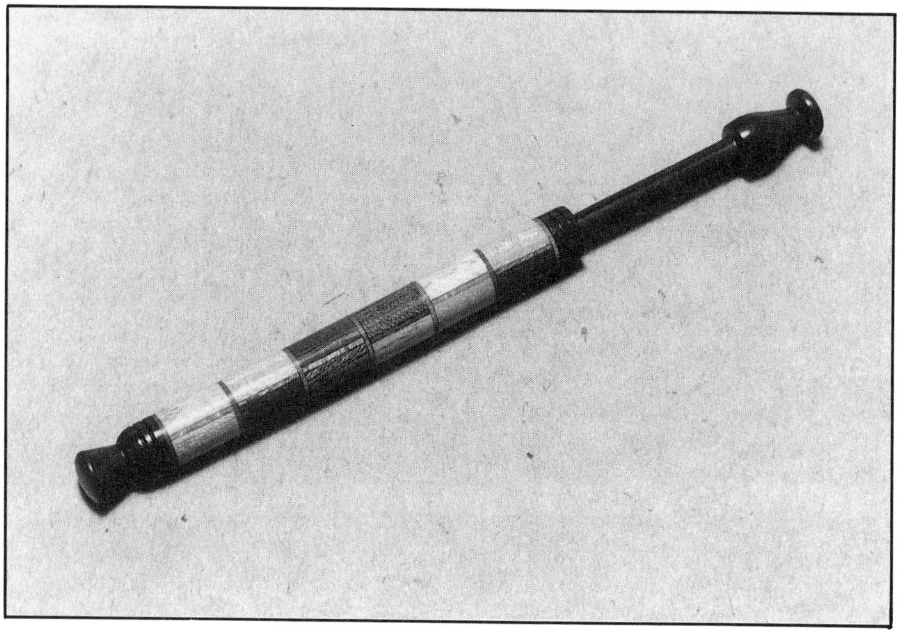

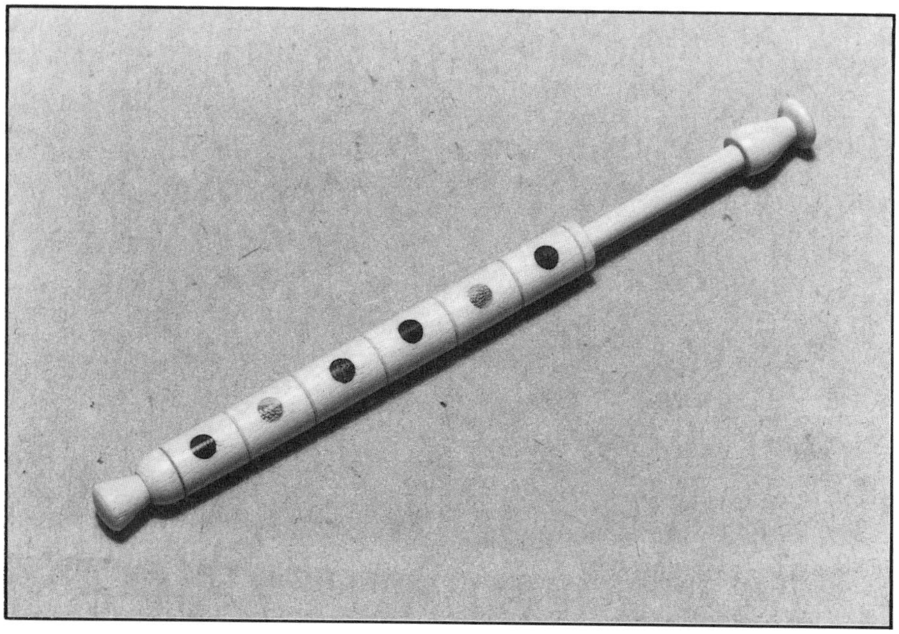

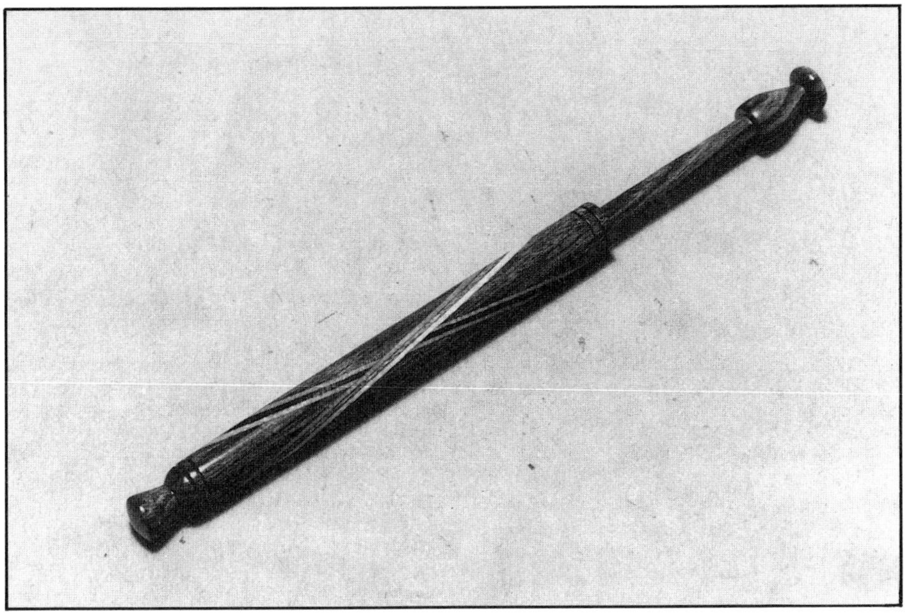

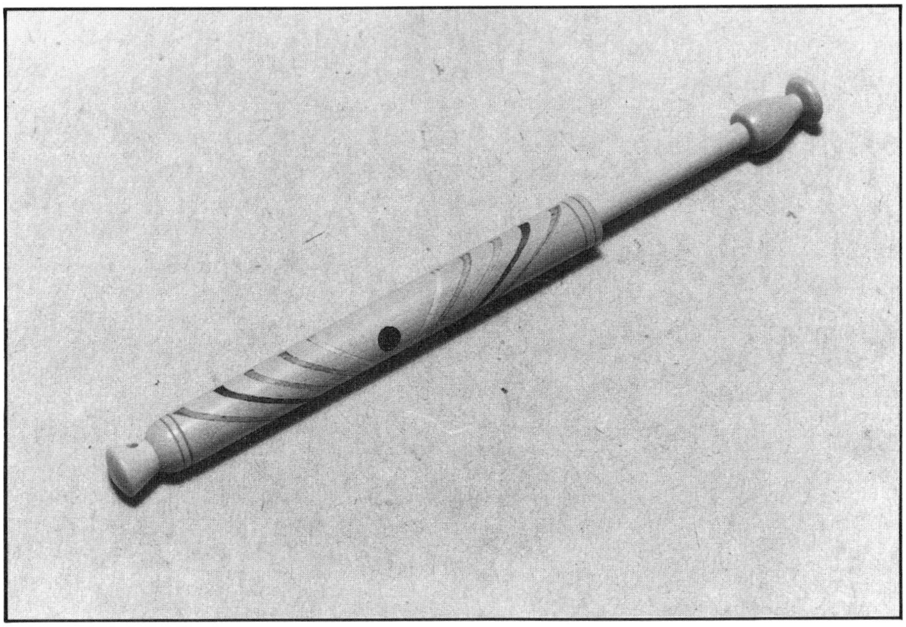

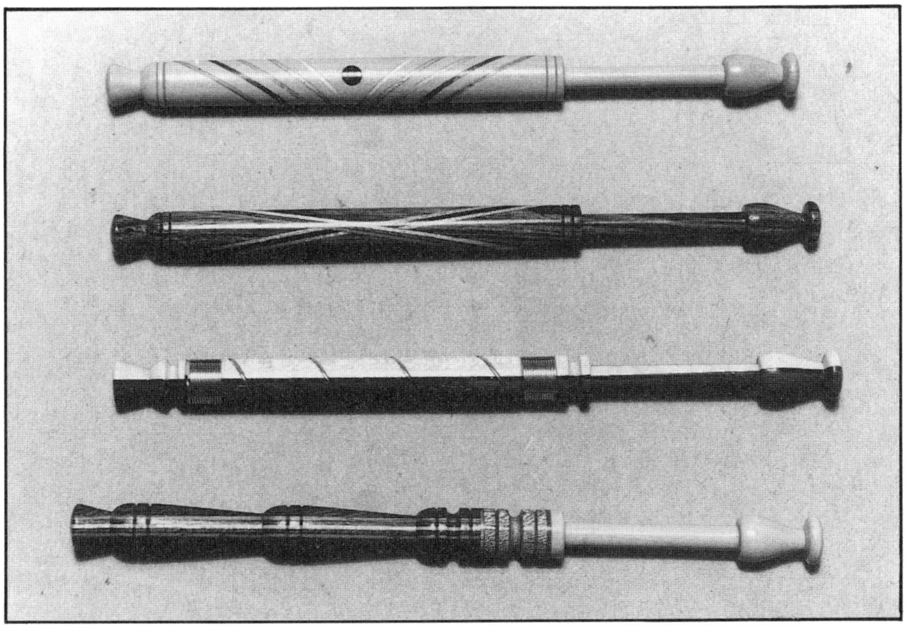

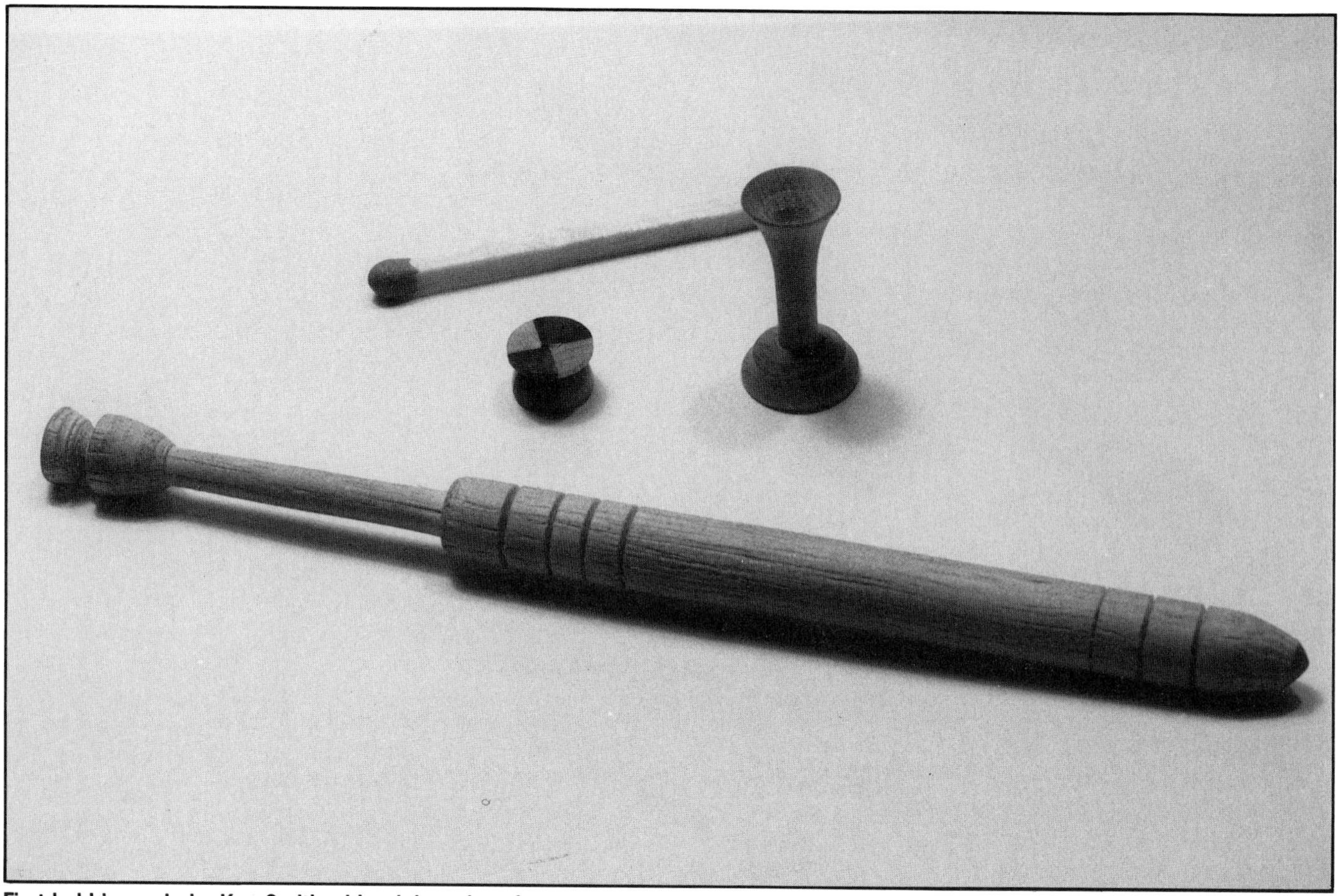

First bobbin made by Ken Smith with mini turnings from scrap

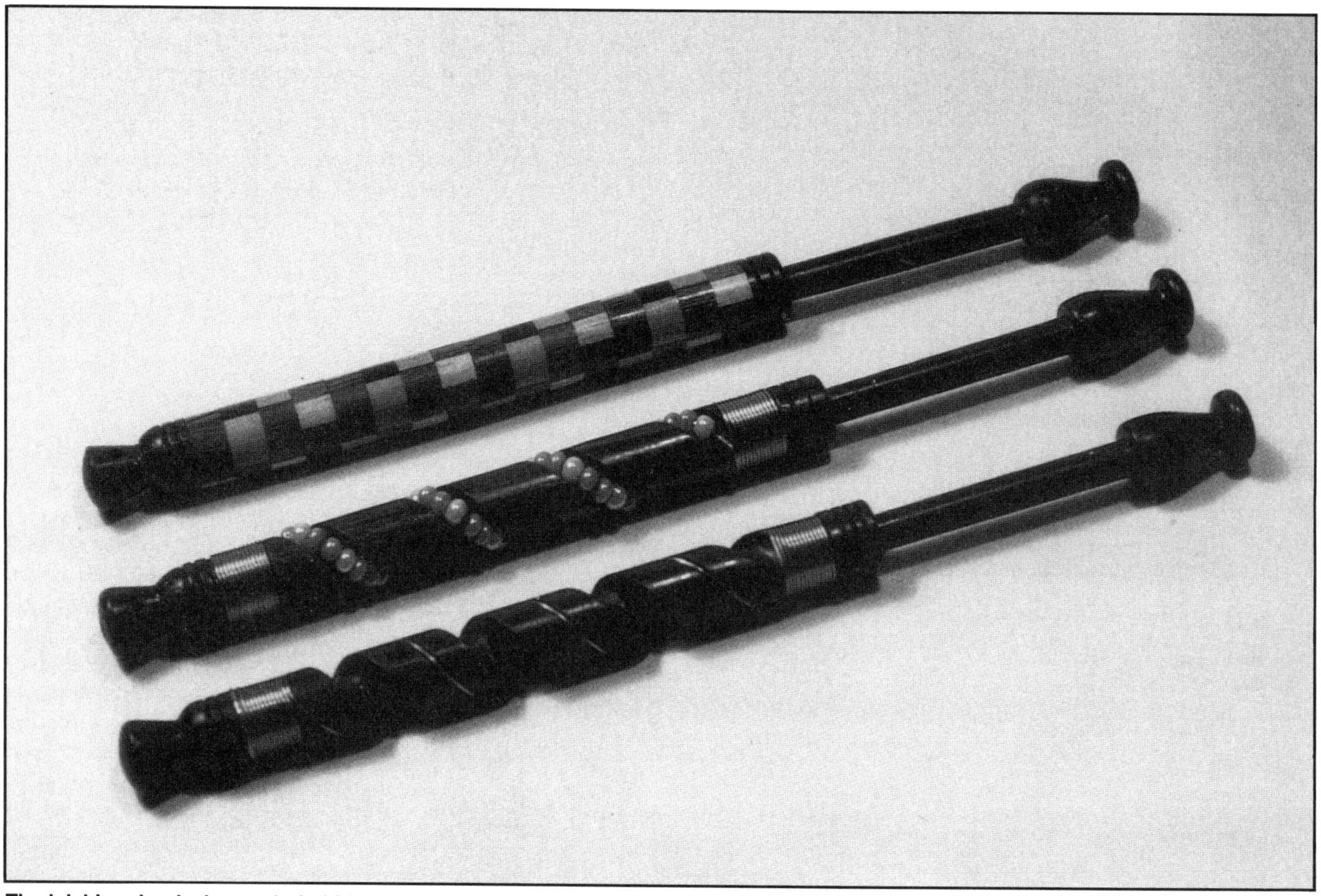

The inlaid and polychromatic bobbins of Ken Smith

Sources

Supplies of Timbers – Exotic and others; also Bobbin Blanks

John Boddy's Fine Wood & Tool Store Ltd,
Riverside Sawmills, Boroughbridge, North Yorkshire YO5 9LJ.

Charlton's Timber Centre,
Frome Road, Radstock, Bath BA3 3PT.

Craft Supplies,
The Mill, Millers Dale, Buxton, Derbyshire SK17 8SN.

Craftwoods,
Thatchways, Thurlestone, Kingsbridge, South Devon TQ7 3NJ.

Fitchett and Woollacott Ltd,
Willow Road, Lenton Lane, Nottingham NG7 2PR.

Kiln Wood,
Unit 18, Gaza Trading Estate, Hildenborough, Kent TN11 8PL.

Limehouse Timber,
5 Grenade Street, London E14 8HL.

North Heigham Sawmills Ltd,
Paddock Street, off Barker Street, Norwich NR2 4TW.

Ternex,
27 Ayot Green, Welwyn, Herts AL6 9BA.

Timberline,
Unit 7, Munday Works, 58-66 Morley Road, Tonbridge, Kent TN9 1RP.

Timber Management Ltd,
Willets Bungalow, Chiddingly, East Sussex BN8 6HR.

Treske Sawmills,
Station Works, Thirsk YO7 4NY.

Tools for the Woodturner

Clico (Sheffield) Tooling Ltd,
Unit 7, Fell Road Industrial Estate, Sheffield S9 2AL.

Alan Holtham,
The Old Stores Turnery, Wistaston Road, Willaston, Nantwich, Cheshire.

Ashley Iles,
East Kirkby, Spilsby, Lincs.

Roger's,
47 Walsworth Road, Hitchin, Herts.

Sarjents Tools,
44 Oxford Road, Reading, Oxford.

Robert Sorby Ltd,
Athol Road, Woodseats Road, Sheffield S8 0PA.

Henry Taylor (Tools) Ltd,
The Forge, Lowther Road, Sheffield S6 2DR.

Alec Tiranti Ltd,
70 High Street, Theale, Berkshire.

Toolmail (GMC) Ltd,
170 High Street, Lewes, East Sussex BN7 1YE.

Lathes and lathe accessories

Apollo Products,
100 Stone Road, Toftwood, Dereham, Norfolk NR19 1LJ.

Craft Supplies,
The Mill, Millers Dale, Buxton, Derbys.
(Suppliers of Precision Combination Chuck.)

C.Z. Scientific Instruments Ltd,
2 Elstree Way, Borehamwood, Herts WD6 1NH.
(Hobbymat Variant Lathe.)

Coronet Lathe & Tool Company Ltd,
Parkway Works, Sheffield S9 3BL.

Merlin Machine Tool Co,
17 The Vanguards, Vanguard Way, Shoeburyness, Essex SS3 9QJ.

Multistar Machine & Tool Ltd,
Ashton House, Wheatfield Road, Stanway, Colchester CO3 5YA.

Treebridge Ltd,
Mills Drive, Farndon Road, Newark, Notts NG24 4SN.

Tyme Machines (Bristol) Ltd,
Halls Road, Kingswood, Bristol BS15 2JD.

Polishes

James Briggs & Sons Ltd,
Lion Works, Old Market Street, Blackley, Manchester M9 3DU.

Fiddes and Sons,
Trade Street, Cardiff.

Henry Flack Ltd,
PO Box 78, Beckenham, Kent.

J L Products,
6 Newington Drive, Bury, Lancs BL8 2NE.

W S Jenkins,
Jeco Works, Tariff Road, Tottenham, London N17 0EN.

Liberon Waxes,
6 Park Street, Lydd, Kent TN29 9AY.

Limehouse Timber,
5 Grenade Street, London E14 8HL.

John Myland,
80 Norwood High Street, London SE27 9NW.

Rustins Ltd,
Waterloo Road, London NW2 7TX.

Weaves and Waxes,
53 Church Street, Bloxham, Banbury, Oxon OX15 4ET.

Dust Extraction

P and J Dust Extraction Ltd,
The Old Ragged School, Kings Street, Chatham, Kent.

Versator Magnifier and others

Mason and Gantlett Ltd,
29 Surrey Street, Norwich NR1 3NX.

Foot Switches

Cutler Hammer,
Elstow Road, Bedford MK42 9LH.

Bibliography

Woodturning

The Art of Freehand Turning in Miniature by Wm R. Borree (B.J. Miniatures, 1982.)
The Craft of Woodturning by John Sainsbury (Sterling, 1984.)
The Craftsman Woodturner by Peter Child (Bell & Hyman, 1971. Revised 1984.)
The Practical Woodturner by F. Pain (Bell & Hyman, 1983.)
Turning a Bobbin by David Francis (David Francis, 1985.)
The Woodturner's Companion by Ron Roszkiewicz (Sterling, 1984.)
The Woodturner's Pocket Book by Phil Reardon (John Boddy, 1984.)
Woodturning Music Boxes by James A. Jacobson (Sterling, 1983.)
Woodturning Projects for Dining by John Sainsbury (Sterling, 1981.)
Woodturning Projects with Power Tools by John Sainsbury (Sterling, 1983.)

Timber Technology

What Wood is That? by H. L. Edlin (Stobart & Son Ltd, 1984.)
Working Green Wood with PEG by Patrick Spielman (Sterling, 1980.)

Hand Tools Use and Maintenance

Garrett Wade Book of Woodworking Tools by John Sainsbury and Garry Chinn (Crowell, 1979.)
Sharpening and Care of Woodworking Tools and Equipment by John Sainsbury (GMC Publications, 1984.)

Miniature Crafts

Modelling and Miniature Crafts Magazine. Published annually by GMC Publications Ltd.

All the above books are available by mail order through:
Woodworking Books By Post,
166 High Street, Lewes, East Sussex BN7 1YE.

Appendices

Appendix A: Making Tools for Turning Miniatures

Making a 3⁄16″ bowl gouge – centreing with a slocombe drill

One manufacturer in the UK, Sorby Ltd, makes an excellent set of small turning tools ideally suited for miniature turning. However, a particular job may demand a tool shape or size quite outside the normal and a craftsman may seek to examine the problem of making his own.

I have always had in the workshop a quantity of round and square section tool steel in small sizes and generally of 13″ in length. These I use to solve problems from time to time.

Straightforward shaping of small chisels and scraping chisels is best done on the double ended grinder. With gouges however, I set up my drill in the horizontal drill stand and use tiny grinding wheels assembled in the chuck. Hold the metal underneath the wheel to shape the flute of the gouge and grind the outside shape on the grinder in the normal way. I find the use of fine wheels will produce a smooth ground surface which will be easy to sharpen later on.

Making a 3⁄16″ Bowl Gouge

Gouges can be made from any carbon steel and in the past I have used silver steel rods and squares for many of the little cutting tools I have needed. There is no doubt the gouge made from round material is the answer and since I hadn't a 3⁄16″ gouge and Sorby haven't made one yet, I decided to turn one out myself.

If the blade isn't too long, the rod can be held in the drill chuck set up in the headstock. If a three or four jaw chuck is available for the drill, this will be better and longer pieces will pass through the back of the chuck and through the headstock. Another drill chuck is needed in the tailstock to hold first of all a tiny slocombe drill for marking the centre and giving a start to the drill, then the drill selected to cut the flute of the gouge.

Do bore carefully. Use a small drop of thin oil for lubrication. A deep long bore is not needed. If the tool is too long, it may flex when in use and destroy your confidence.

After boring, remove the rod from the lathe and clean up the flute, shape the end, grind and sharpen to suit.

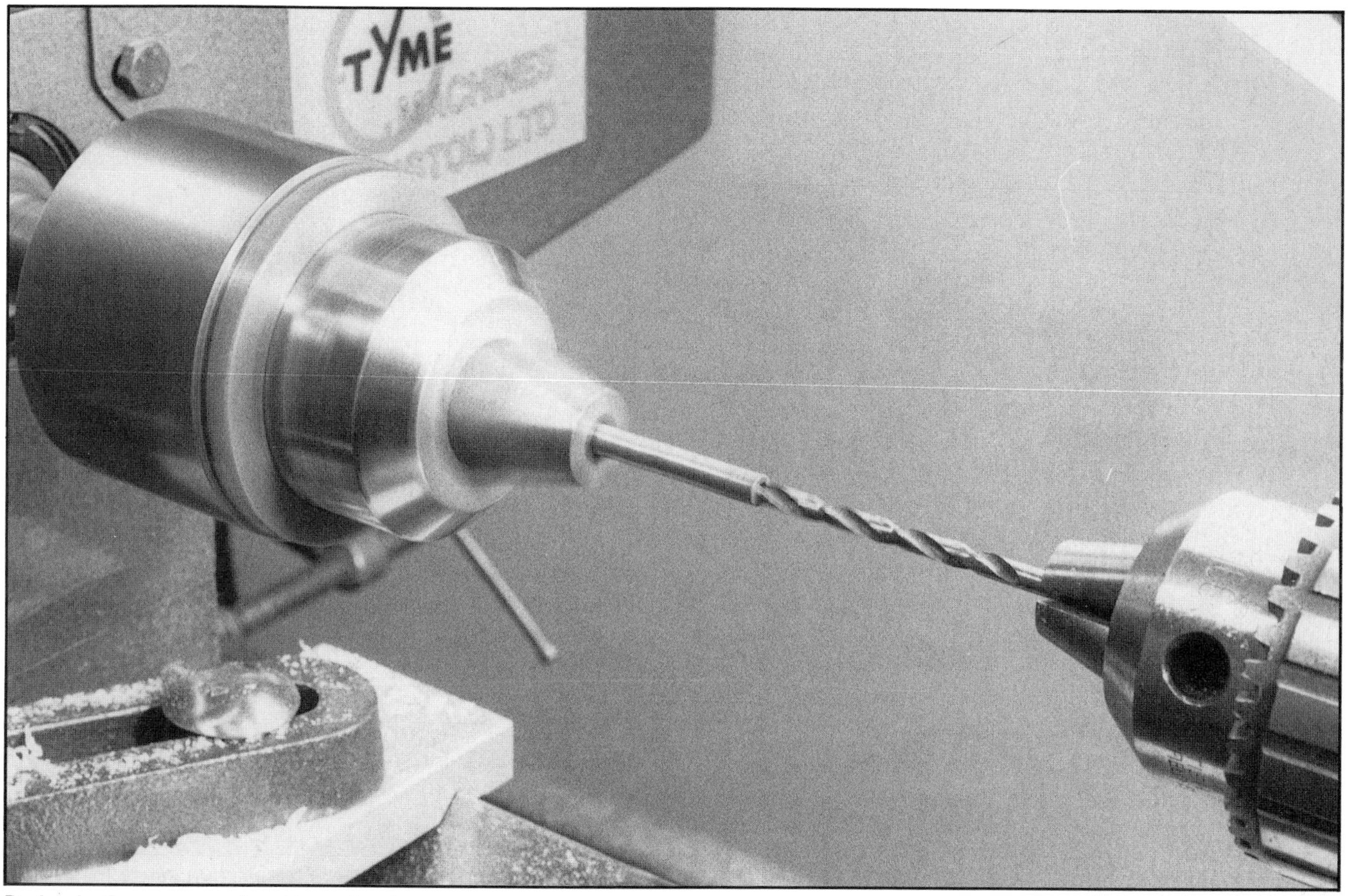

Boring in the process of making a bowl gouge

Blade of gouge roughly cut, ready for grinding and sharpening

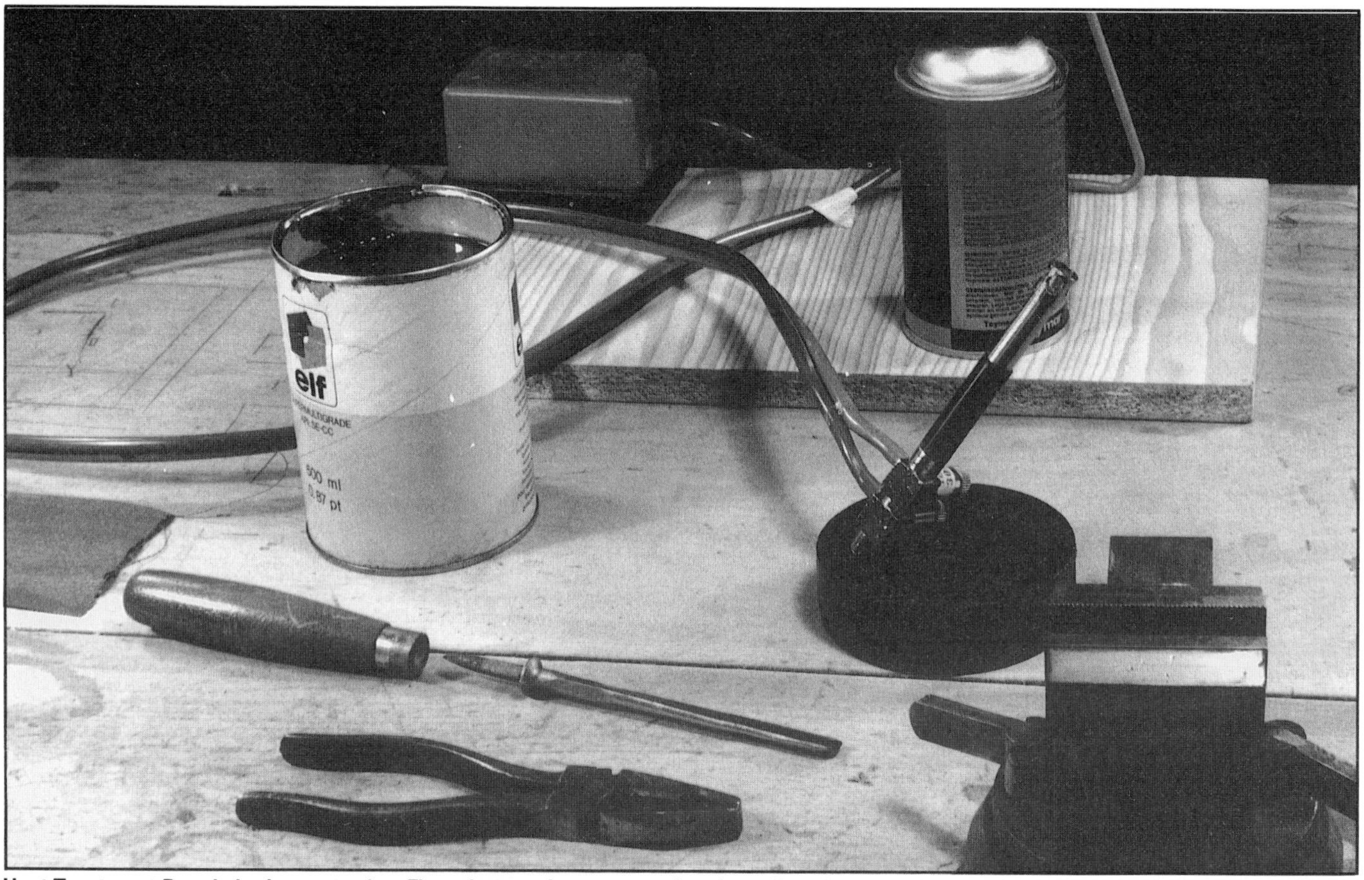

Heat Treatment Bench. In the centre is a Flamefast torch, gas control and small air blower Note blade removed from gouge handle

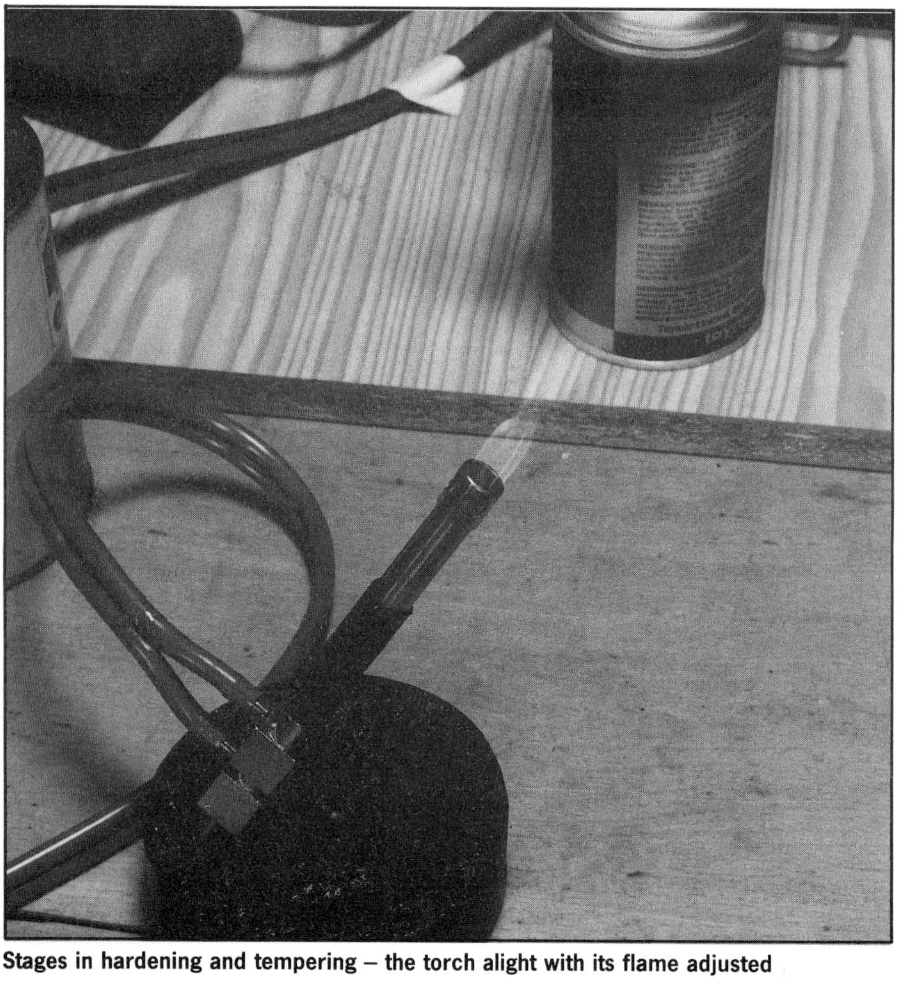

Stages in hardening and tempering – the torch alight with its flame adjusted

Grinding and Sharpening

Whatever tool has been made, after grinding the shapes, grind the bevels accurately and angle them correctly for cutting or scraping. Cut each to the correct length, which for small work will not be over long.

Tempering Explained

Completed tools will need to be correctly tempered otherwise they will not hold their edges. This is not a difficult task and only a modicum of equipment or skill is required.

Heat can be applied using a blow torch, either the paraffin or cylinder type. Alternatively, a small steel cylinder heated over a gas ring can be used for small tools. Larger tools can rest on a sheet of steel placed over the burner of a gas stove.

We shall also require oil or water contained in a small tin or drum, tongs for holding the tools and some fine emery cloth for brightening the metal.

Whenever steel is heated in the air, oxidization takes place and oxides appear on the surface of the metal. The oxides are of many hues, each depending on the temperature at that particular spot.

These colours range from very pale straw through browns and purples to

The blade of the gouge is heated to cherry red as the first stage of hardening

blue and they travel in fairly clearly defined bands moving across the metal. To see the colours clearly, the metal should be bright and it is a task best performed in daylight.

(Years ago when tools were hardened and tempered individually, if a man had badly tempered tools, it was often said that the weather must have been dull on the day they were made.)

Hardening and Tempering

All tools must first be hardened. Hold the tool in the tongs and place in the torch flame. Apply the heat about 3″ from the cutting end. When the metal reaches cherry red in colour, the temperature will be approximately 800–850° Centigrade.

Quench in the water or oil pot. Hold the metal vertically in the liquid and cool it quite rapidly. This will ensure a good hardness. A tool quenched in water will be much harder than one cooled in oil since oil cooling tends to be slower. Old motor oil can be used in the oil bath, but do use a good canful. A small quantity will tend to heat up rapidly and may well catch fire.

Do not harden the complete tool otherwise the tang end will tend to be brittle. Be careful to avoid distortion of the tool by unequal immersion.

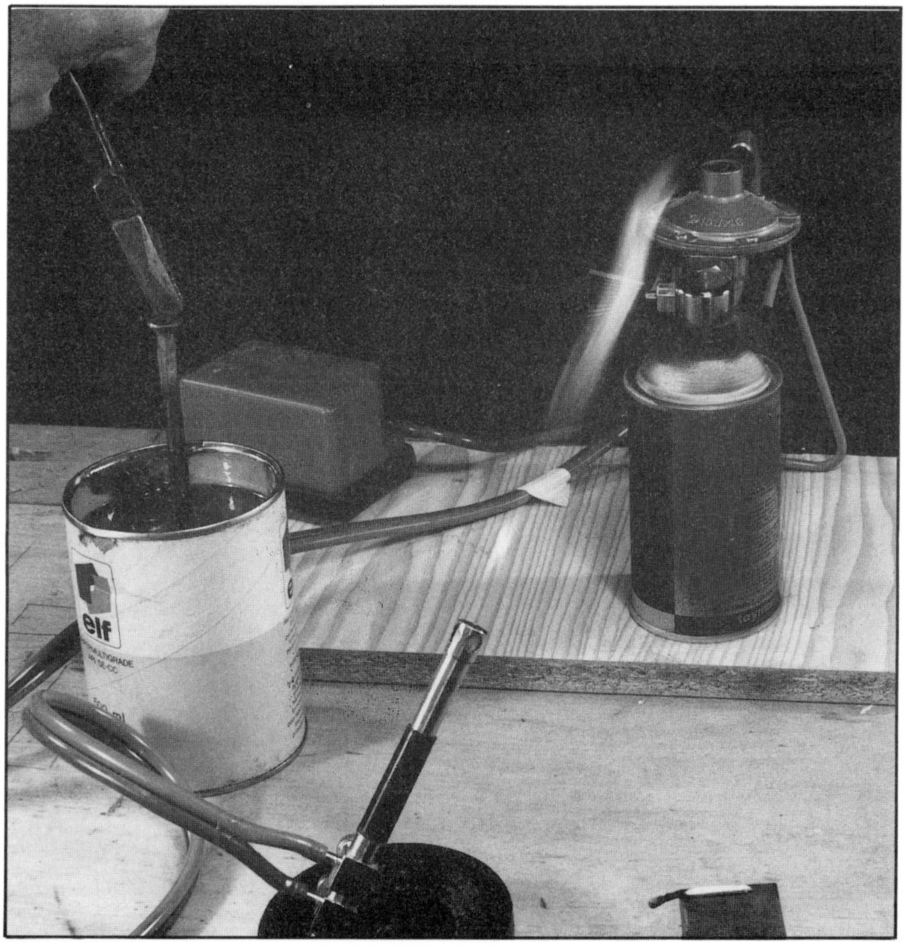

When cherry red, the blade is then immersed in oil

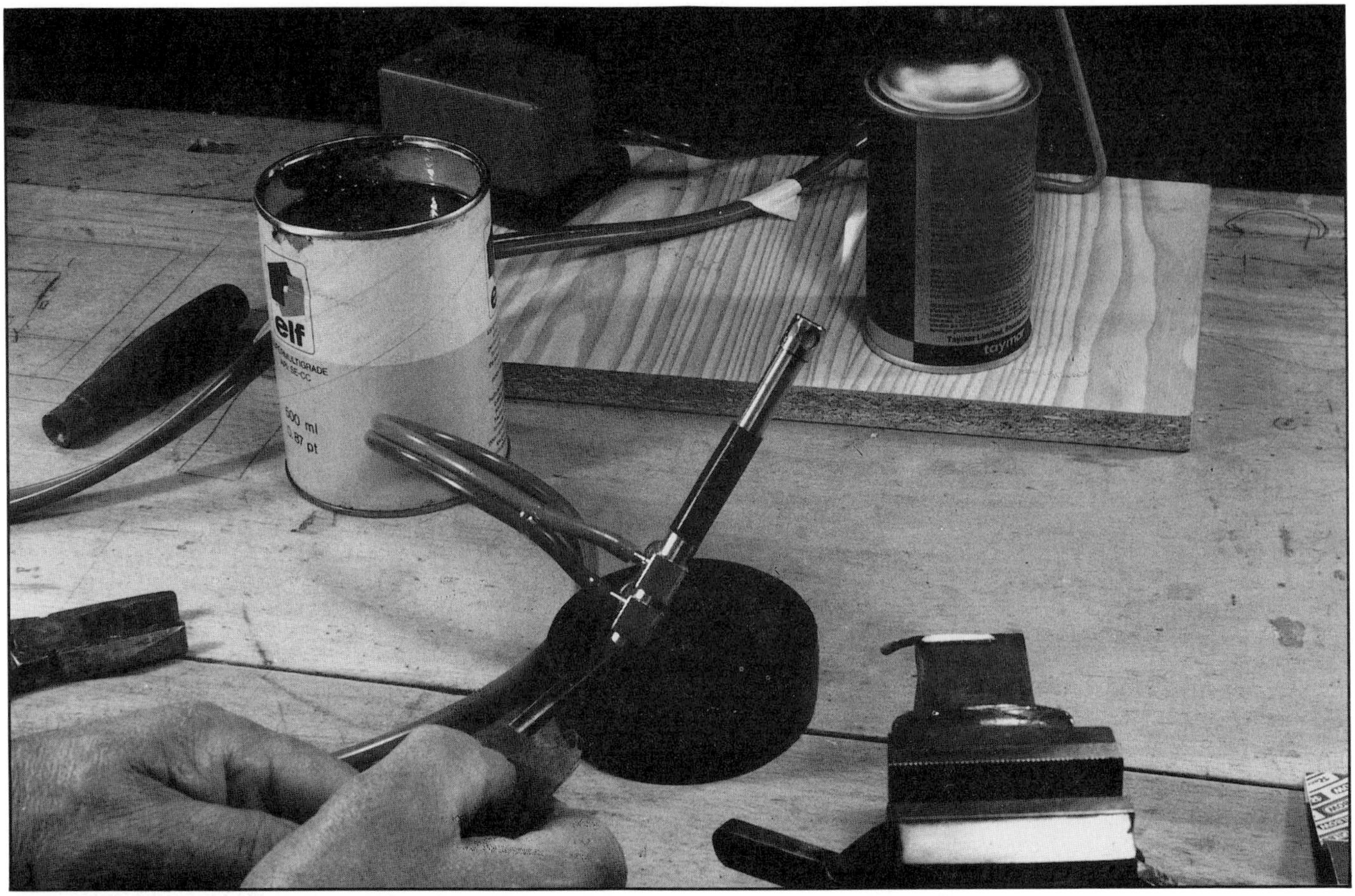

Blade wiped dry and returned to brightness with emery cloth

Heat applied for tempering and colours running

When the tool is cool, wipe it dry and use the emery cloth to polish the first inch or so. Now carefully apply the blow torch flame behind the polished area. After a very short time, a colour band will appear and move along the tool away from the torch point and toward the cutting edge. When a golden brown colour appears at the edge, very quickly quench the tool. This halts the heat and will give the correct degree of hardness at the cutting edge.

Clean up each tool with the emery cloth. Prepare handles and assemble to complete the tool.

The foregoing can be applied to any tool where the degree of hardness may be in doubt. Should a tool have its temper drawn, it can be re-tempered in this way.

Alloy steels must have careful and correct heat treatment since incorrect heat treatment may ruin the steel.

Identification of your steel
To identify a particular piece of steel, grind on a dry wheel. Whitish yellow sparks indicate plain carbon steel and the sparks will tend to keep close together. Dull red sparks will indicate high speed steel and the sparks scatter in all directions.

To ascertain hardness
Drop a spot of nitric acid on hard steel. This should produce a deep black spot. The lighter the spot, the softer the steel. The steel is not affected by the acid, but wash it off and wash your hands as well.

TEMPERING CHART for Carbon Steels Only

Yellow	Pale	428°F	For keen edges – surgeon's equipment
	Straw	446°F	
	Golden	470°F	Knives
Brown	Golden	490°F	Chisels, scissors
	Purple	510°F	Plane irons, adzes
Purple		530°F	All other woodworking tools
Blue	Bright	550°F	Saws and auger bits
	Full	560°F	
	Dark	600°F	
Red			Softer if allowed to cool in air

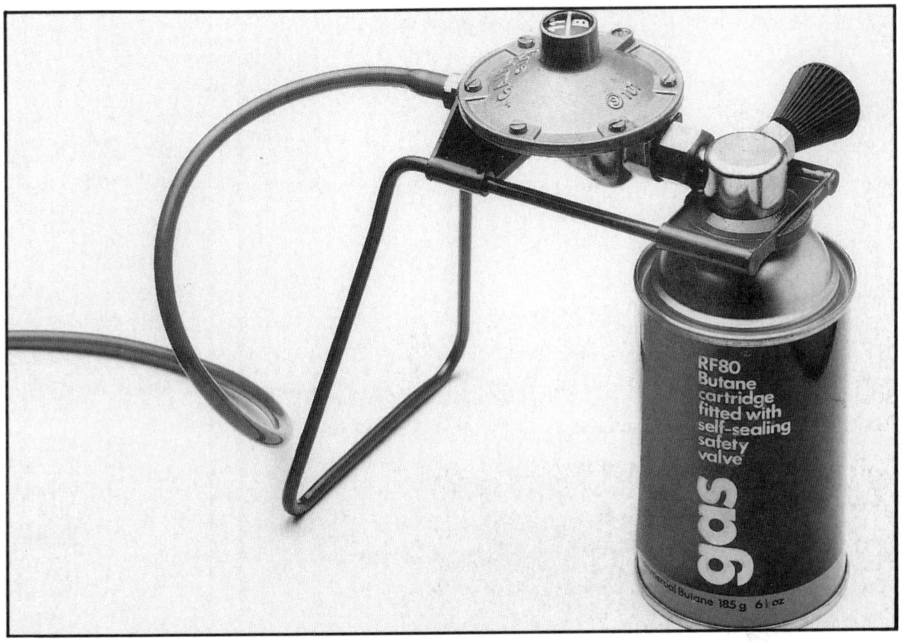

Flamefast Portaflame Portable Gas Unit (Butane)

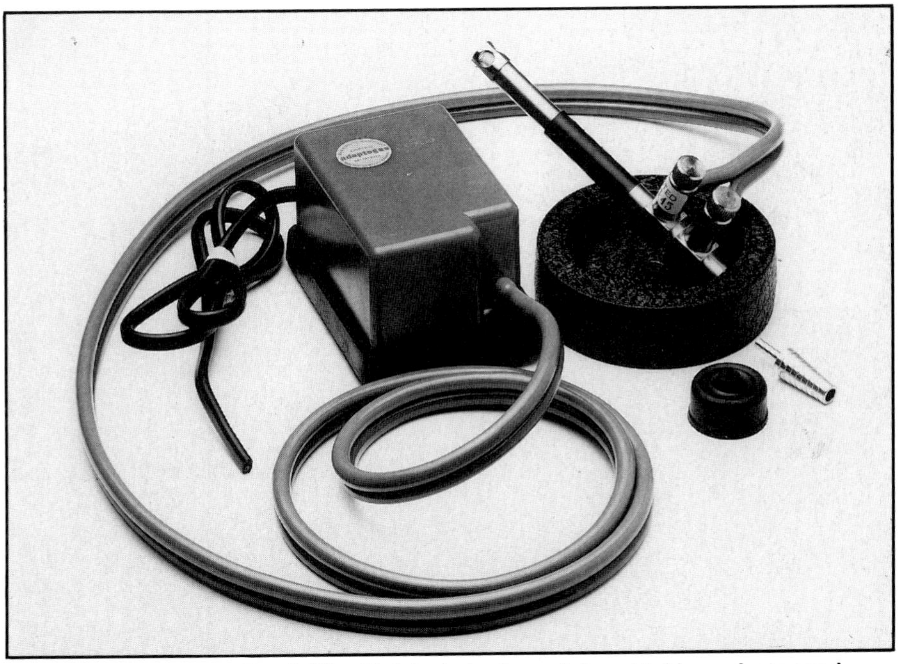
Flamefast Needleflame Torch Kit which includes base, twinned tubing, adaptor and air pump

Appendix B: Machine Speeds, Pulleys and Metric Conversion Chart

MACHINE SPEEDS

Formulae to calculate RPM on your machine:

A = RPM of Driven Pulley

B = RPM of Driver Pulley

C = Diameter of Driver Pulley

D = Diameter of Driven Pulley

$$A = \frac{C \times B}{D}$$

$$B = \frac{A \times D}{C}$$

$$C = \frac{A \times D}{B}$$

$$D = \frac{B \times C}{A}$$

FINDING THE LENGTH OF A REPLACEMENT BELT

To find the length of a belt, use the following formula where

R = radius of large pulley

r = radius of small pulley

C = distance between centres

L = total belt length

$$\pi = \frac{22}{7}$$

$$L = \pi\ (R + r) + 2\sqrt{C^2 + (R + r)^2}$$

Example

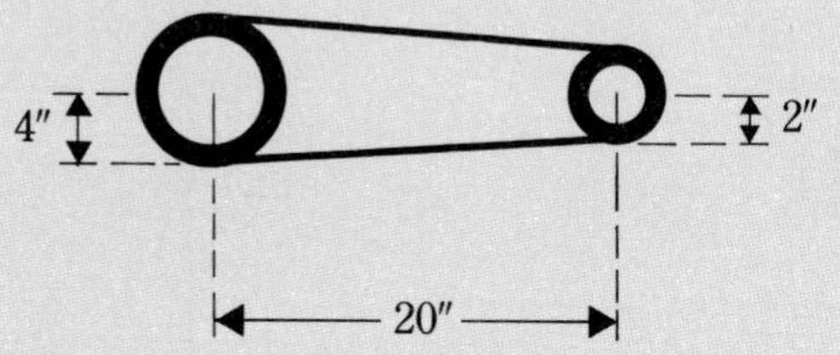

$$L = \frac{22}{7}\ X\ (6) + 2\sqrt{400 + (6)^2}$$

$$L = \frac{132}{7} + 2\ X\ \sqrt{436}$$

$$L = 18.86 + 2\ X\ 20.88$$

LENGTH OF BELT = 60.62 ins.

METRIC CONVERSION TABLE
(INCHES TO MILLIMETRES)

Inches	0	⅛	¼	⅜	½	⅝	¾	⅞
0		3	6	10	13	16	19	22
1	25	29	32	35	38	41	44	48
2	51	54	57	60	64	67	70	73
3	76	79	83	86	89	92	95	98
4	102	105	108	111	114	117	121	124
5	127	130	133	137	140	143	146	149
6	152	156	159	162	165	168	171	175
7	178	181	184	187	190	194	197	200
8	203	206	210	213	216	219	222	225
9	229	232	235	238	241	244	248	251
10	254	257	260	264	267	270	273	276
11	279	283	286	289	292	295	298	302
12	305	308	311	314	318	321	324	327
13	330	333	337	340	343	346	349	352
14	356	359	362	365	368	371	375	378
15	381	384	387	391	394	397	400	403
16	406	410	413	416	419	422	425	429
17	432	435	438	441	444	448	451	454
18	457	460	464	467	470	473	476	479
19	483	486	489	492	495	498	502	505
20	508	511	514	518	521	524	527	530
21	533	537	540	543	546	549	552	556
22	559	562	565	568	572	575	578	581
23	584	587	591	594	597	600	603	606
24	610	613	616	619	622	625	629	632
25	635	638	641	645	648	651	654	657
26	660	664	667	670	673	676	679	683
27	686	689	692	695	698	702	705	708
28	711	714	718	721	724	727	730	733
29	737	740	743	746	749	752	756	759
30	762	765	768	772	775	778	781	784
31	787	791	794	797	800	803	806	810
32	813	816	819	822	826	829	832	835
33	838	841	845	848	851	854	857	860
34	864	867	870	873	876	879	883	886
35	889	892	895	899	902	905	908	911
36	914	918	921	924	927	930	933	937
37	940	943	946	949	952	956	959	962
38	965	968	972	975	978	981	984	987
39	991	994	997	1000	1003	1006	1010	1013
40	1016	1019	1022	1026	1029	1032	1035	1038

Appendix C: Safety When Mini-Turning

Mini-woodturning can be a wholly enjoyable craft but in order that this shall be the experience of everyone, strict attention must be paid to safety. Safety can be broadly divided and contained in four areas: (1) safety to the person, (2) safety in regard to the machine itself, (3) safety to both person and machine when the machine is running, and (4) safe materials.

Attire

The turner must be properly attired; he should wear an apron or dust coat. If he is wearing a tie, it is best either to remove it or clip it to another part of his clothing so that it cannot fall freely over the lathe. Shirtsleeves or sleeves of any kind should be rolled up and long hair tied back.

Suitable goggles of the anti-misting type should be worn for protection of the eyes and these must be kept in perfect condition, or alternatively, a safety visor should be used.

Ladies should wear a net over the hair or use some other means of keeping the hair back. Should a noisy situation arise, although it is difficult to envisage such a situation, ear muffs should be available. With extremely dusty timbers, a non-toxic dust mask should be worn.

The Lathe

Press button starters should be of low voltage and overload protection type. If access to the belt or belts is through doors or panels, then these must be fitted with micro switches which break the circuit enabling adjustments to be made without any danger of the motor being switched on. The switch should be so placed on the machine, with ease of access to the hand, that the operator can reach it without bending and without the necessity of looking for it.

All parts of the lathe should be securely fixed. It is essential for the tee rest to be straight and true, that is when fixed to the tool post slide it should be parallel with the lathe bed. The chisels of the driving fork must be sharp and the centre point and the tailstock dead centre should be in good condition.

The lathe must have adequate daylight and artificial light. Where tubular lighting is in use, then this must be antistroboscopic. However, bearing in mind that this type of lighting is non-directional, it is advisable to fit the machine with tungsten lighting on an adjustable arm.

Rule of the Lathe

Before switching on the lathe, make sure that the work will rotate freely without being obstructed by the tee rest. Be sure, too, that the correct speed is being used. This will, of course, relate to the size of the timber being turned and whether the work is spindle or faceplate.

All tools must be correctly sharpened, particular attention being paid to sharpening on the ground bevel and, in the case of gouges, ensuring that they are shaped correctly. The rule of the lathe in cutting, and this is, of course, basic safety, is that the bevel of the tools should rub the wood (it should never cut when first placed on the tool rest). The tool will cut when the right hand is raised. This brings the centre of the chisel or gouge into direct contact with the wood. The tool also slopes in the direction of travel, thus a slicing cut is taken. This, again, is an added safety precaution.

If scraping tools are used, these must be sharpened correctly and unlike the cutting tools, they must rest firmly on the tee rest and be trailed, that is, they slope downwards. In this way they cut exactly like the cabinetmaker's scraper on the bench. The tool must, of course, be correctly held, lightly but firmly with the left hand across the tool and well up to the cutting edge. This will result in the shavings being moved away from the user's face. Place the tool rest as close to the work as possible, and at correct height. *Never move the tee rest with the lathe switched on.*

A revolving centre is best for the tailstock, but if this accessory is not available a small spot of grease applied to the dead centre will reduce friction and prevent burn.

Glasspapering

When glasspapering, the tee rest must be completely removed. The glasspaper should be cut to a comfortable size and preferably backed with a pad to prevent the fingers being burned should the glasspaper be applied too firmly. Hold the pad in the right hand and use the left hand to support it. This brings both hands into use and will possibly prevent accidents by careless placement of the left hand on the headstock. In spindle work, the paper should be applied underneath whereas in bowl work it should be placed inside the bowl in a clock position of between half past and a quarter to.

Polishing

Polish should generally be applied with the machine in the rest position, again using a small pad. Trailing cloths should be avoided. Burnishing of the polish should take place with the machine running and the pad applied in the same way as when glasspapering. The practice of burnishing with shavings is a sound one, so long as a ball of shavings is used and applied in the same way as the polishing cloth. Great care must be taken with all three operations to avoid excessive pressure since both wood and hands can be burned.

Timber

Careful selection of the timber for woodturning is essential, often too little attention is paid to this particular point. *One must at all times remember that the lathe is revolving at high speed and any material leaving it by accident could be lethal either to the user or to other people in the workshop. Never use timber with cracks or splits, loose knots or flaws, beetle hole or deep resin ducts.* I know this will upset quite a lot of people but there are considerable dangers in using flawed timber of this sort, many people are inclined to regard the flaws with pleasure but at the same time the possibility of flawed timber breaking from the job at high speed must be regarded as lethal.

If reclaimed timber is being used, examine it very carefully for nails, and other metallic objects. Scrutinise very carefully timber collected from the fields and hedgerows for wire, wire staples, nails, bolts or even lead shot. *If there is any doubt about any piece of timber, the golden rule is, no matter how attractive, do not use it.* If built-up blocks are being used then very great care must be taken to use only the slower speeds and to examine critically the glue joints at all times. Should there be a distinct change in sound when cutting this type of thing stop the lathe to see whether a split has occurred at a joint or elsewhere in the timber. It must be remembered that the glue is often much stronger than the material itself.

Holding the Timber

Timber can be held on the lathe, in various ways, but if blocks are to be held on the faceplate they must be screwed firmly to it with stout screws and the timber itself be flat to the faceplate to ensure complete security.

If the screw chuck is being used, a limit should be placed on the length of timber, particularly if the screw is inserted in end grain. Wherever possible, bring up the tailstock to increase the support. If a collar chuck is in use, the collar must be screwed down tightly and again it is essential for the left-hand end of the timber to be square and flat and in close abutment with the back plate of the collar chuck. If a wood chuck is being used to hold an article, the tee rest must be brought tight up to the chuck and slightly above centre so that if the article breaks loose it will revolve inside the wood chuck without it being possible for it to fly out of the chuck itself. If the Precision Combination Chuck is being used, the timber must be held firmly by using the spanners to bring up the chuck components tightly. It is an excellent idea to check periodically during turning to be sure that no part of the chuck has worked loose. If the glue method of holding is being used, the timber must be planed flat in both cases; when the paper joint is made both components must be squeezed in the vice. If the electric glue gun is being used, restrict the size of timber, again make sure the surfaces are flat, use only a thin film of glue and, once again, squeeze both components in a vice to ensure adequate contact.

Boring

When boring tools are being used it is essential for the speed of the lathe to be related to the size of the hole being bored and for the rate of feed to be as fast as the machine will allow without slowing or slipping of the belt. This will avoid scorching of the shavings and wood dust and possible drawing of the temper of the tool. Care must also be taken to ensure that the shavings will easily leave the hole. With flatbits high speed is necessary and care must be taken here not to feed too fast, since there is the possibility of the bit running with the grain and consequently off centre. In all cases of boring, the tailstock must be firmly locked to the bed; a wise precaution is to feed the bit forward with the machine stopped so that the brad point can score the centre of the work with the timber rotated by hand. All tools should, of course, be sharp so that they can feed easily and avoid excessive weight being applied.

If the lathe bed should be of untreated machine steel then it will be necessary to grease it from time to time. This should be done with care and no overloading of grease otherwise the dust and wood chips will tend to form a skin and make movement difficult. Keep the tailstock sleeve lubricated and the thread clean and lightly greased. Grease cups should be kept topped up and screwed down from time to time to keep the bearings lubricated unless the lathe is fitted with sealed bearings.

Maintenance

If the motor isn't completely enclosed vacuum clean it periodically to extract dust. Check the belt tension and replace any belt which may have become stretched or frayed. Be sure that the pulleys are locked firmly to their shafts. Keep metal tee rests straight and true by an occasional rub with a file. Wooden rests should be planed accurately with a good jack plane.

Keep the lathe centres in good condition – the dead centre should always be a perfect shape – and the chisels of the driving forks sharpened from time to time with a small tooth file. The centre itself should be slightly forward of the chisels and perfect. Never hammer the wood onto the driving forks centres as this can damage the headstock bearings. An old driving fork can be driven into the timber, using a copper headed hammer, to provide centre and chisel holds or alternatively, cut a suitable recess before centreing.

Keep all components in a clean condition; oftentimes it will be found profitable to lightly spray with a lacquer some of the more vulnerable accessories.

Examine all tool handles for security before use, a loose handle coming away from the gouge or chisel in use can create a dangerous situation. By holding the blade and striking the end of the handle, either on the bed of the lathe or on the floor, this will serve to check the security of the handle. This is particularly important.

Check the electrics, particularly the cable if it is not enclosed in conduit; be sure that there is no fraying with the risk to the lathe of becoming live in consequence. For preference, have an isolator switch on the wall close to the lathe and drop this switch when the day's work is done.

Dust

Probably one of the biggest hazards these days, with such a wide variety of timber being used, is that of dust. Some timbers can have a most irritating effect on the nostrils, can affect the skin and also the lungs. If the woodturner has any doubts about the suitability of any particular timber, it would be wise to make an enquiry of the Forest Products Research Laboratory, or one of the Government Health Departments, to be quite sure.

To avoid dust of any sort, some turners favour a mask, although this can be quite uncomfortable particularly in a warm situation. Generally speaking if timber is being cut there will be a minimum of dust, although some timbers fail to give a really nice shaving, the shaving breaking into a fine dust after leaving the tool. Excessive use of glasspaper creates a very dusty atmosphere and it may be as well to carry out a great deal of this type of work with some extraction system either fitted to the lathe or to the workshop itself. Often the industrial type vacuum cleaner can be used but unfortunately the lathe tends to send the dust in all directions and to place the extraction where most of the dust can be taken away will be found most difficult. Alternatively, there are a number of units on the market which can be used for general extraction.

Index